Praise for
How to Build a Successful Consulting Practice

"Once again Dr. Jack Phillips has written a groundbreaking book that will be a must-read around the world. Aspiring and veteran consultants will all benefit by applying his 16 Success Factors."

—Kent Barnett
CEO, KnowledgeAdvisors, Inc.

"This is the one book I will recommend to every person that asks me how to become a consultant. It will accelerate their success, blunt their risk of failure, and turn their dreams of achievement into reality."

—Calhoun Wick
CEO, Fort Hill Company, and author of
The Six Disciplines of Breakthrough Learning—How to Turn Training and Development into Business Results

"Wow! *How to Build a Successful Consulting Practice* is the most user-friendly book on consulting I've ever seen. The self-assessments, checklists, and samples are awesome resources. I only wish Jack had written this book prior to me starting my first consulting business 16 years ago."

—Donna Long
President, JukeBox Learning, Inc.

"This is an intensely practical book on consulting. If you are new to the practice, *How to Build a Successful Consulting Practice* will save you both emotional heartache and financial hardship. If you are an old pro, you will become even more effective at meeting your client's needs."

—Mette Norgaard
Author of *The Ugly Duckling Goes to Work*

"Dr. Jack Phillips' book is the definitive guide for anyone dreaming about pursuing a career as an independent consultant. As a former Vice President and Chief HR Officer for a Fortune 1000 company, I was naive to think that a great business idea, huge Rolodex, and ambition alone would guarantee success. Costly missteps could have been avoided during my transition from corporate executive to consultant. I only wish I had this comprehensive yet practical resource before taking the leap!"

—Salvatore V. Falletta, Ed.D.
President & CEO, Leadersphere, Inc.

"I learned more from this book than my actual years of practice. Although I would have treasured Mr. Phillips' guidance 8 years ago, now it is the perfect catalyst to move my business from reasonably profitable to wildly flourishing!"

—Laura Arellano
CEO, Meta Logia

To Patti, my friend, partner, and spouse—and the best consultant I know.

How to Build a Successful Consulting Practice

JACK PHILLIPS, Ph.D.
Chairman
ROI Institute, Inc.

McGraw-Hill

New York / Chicago / San Francisco / Lisbon / London / Madrid / Mexico City
Milan / New Delhi / San Juan / Seoul / Singapore / Sydney / Toronto

CONTENTS

PREFACE

General Description

This how-to book provides detailed information for anyone interested in building and sustaining a consulting practice. With checklists, forms, tactics, and strategies, the book navigates the difficult issue of building, revitalizing, or sustaining a successful consulting practice. Using examples, trends, best practices, and procedures that can help a consulting firm sustain the practice, the book is a useful guide for new and experienced consultants.

The Need for This Book, Now

Consulting continues to be a thriving and growing industry, and from all indications, it will continue to grow in the next decade. Two new trends will increase the consulting growth in the future. First, as more companies attempt to avoid the cost of maintaining employees on the payroll, executives are seeking a variety of sources of contract assistance, often employing consultants to do the same work formerly done by internal staff members. Therefore, more consultants—particularly smaller consulting firms—will be needed to fill the void when employers are unwilling to commit to permanent employees. The second trend involves the large number of baby boomers in the United States who are facing retirement age, but plan to continue to work for several years. One traditional avenue available for these retiring baby boomers is to establish a consulting practice to serve as an outlet for their expertise generated over their employment years. As more of these individuals venture into the unfamiliar territory of establishing a consulting practice, they will need assistance.

In the midst of this growth, consulting has perhaps the highest failure rate of any occupation. The critical time for success is usually within the first two years of operation. If an individual consultant or consulting firm can persevere for at least two years then it has a good chance of long-term survival. Too many mistakes are made at the onset. Improperly preparing for business, approaching the process incorrectly, failing to capitalize on the strengths, and ignoring the warning signs, all result in an excessive number of failures. Additional help is needed for consultants—showing them how to develop a basis for a legitimate consulting business, navigate through the start-up phase, wrestle with the growth and development of the business, and sustain the practice over the long term.

The Approach

This book will be very practical with a how-to format showing specifically what to do to make a consulting business successful, providing a variety of tools and templates along the way. Several important features make this book unique:

1. *Success factors:* The book presents the success factors for the consulting business today, derived from research and reviews of consulting businesses considered successful survivors.
2. *Self-assessments:* At different places in the book, assessments are provided to ensure that the right thinking, attitudes, and situations are present and are being addressed.
3. *Checklists:* A variety of checklists are included to show step-by-step how things should be accomplished and how processes should work.
4. *Building blocks:* In several areas, building blocks are presented to methodically and incrementally tackle the toughest issues.
5. *Financial records:* Examples of specific reports and documents are included.
6. *Templates:* To help the business with proposal formats and deliverable documents, a variety of models are presented.
7. *Guidelines:* For specific areas such as finance, legal, and ethical issues, guidelines are included.
8. *Results Based:* Throughout the book, there is on focus on results and accountability, capped off with a chapter on how to measure the success of consulting projects.

Target Audience

This book is designed for several audiences. Individuals considering a consulting practice will find this book to be an indispensable guide to decide if consulting is appropriate, how to start the business, and keep it going. This is a must read before starting a consulting practice. Many of the important issues that must be addressed in the early stage of the business are explored in the book.

The second audience is consultants who are already involved in the business—past the start-up phase—and are seeking ways to make their practices more effective and successful. The book will show how to strengthen the practice, improve processes, and enhance accountability.

The third audience is those consulting firms who are stable but are seeking ways to grow and expand into a more flexible and adaptive business. This book should provide help to develop and offer long-term, viable consulting practice.

Why Another Book on Consulting?

An appropriate question to ask is "why write another book on consulting?" This topic is covered in hundreds of books from almost any angle imaginable. Some of them are excellent books and are referenced here. Others offer questionable value. This book attempts to differ from others in four specific ways:

1. There is a tremendous focus on the decision to enter consulting. Although the book is appropriate for current consultants, it may have its greatest value for those considering the consulting

field as an occupation. In an attempt to avoid high failure rate, this book positions the reader to probe and analyze him or herself before making this important decision to move into consulting. Because the failure can be traumatic—financially, professionally, and emotionally, it is an important and critical decision to enter the consulting business.

2. The focus throughout the book is on results—delivering measurable, meaningful results to the client. Not many books focus on this issue. This is one of the most important reasons for consulting—to add unmistakable value that the client appreciates so to make the business successful and profitable in the future.

3. There is a focus on sustaining the business—building it incrementally and systematically to have a very successful enterprise. Few people enter this field with the notion of a short-term career. Most are looking long term, and this book will be extremely valuable in helping to build the business.

4. The book builds on the experience of many people including the author. It takes the best of many great consultants and molds it into a valuable guidance for the reader.

Experience Base

This book is based on the experience of successful consultants, and this comes from four different perspectives. First, it reflects my personal experience, as well as that of my partners. We have had the pleasure of developing a consulting business and selling that business to a New York Stock Exchange–listed company for several million dollars. The consulting business began in the attic of my home, and within five years, the business was sold. Later, we established another consulting business that is now a thriving consulting practice operating in 44 countries. There are some important lessons we have learned along the way, and there are some important strategies of building a business incrementally—all contained in this book.

The second experience base comes from those consultants that we have had the pleasure to assist in a variety ways. Several of my professional colleagues have come to me for advice in starting a consulting practice, and they continue to stay in touch. We learn from what they have done and what works and does not work for them. In addition, we have helped over 30 partners in other countries establish consulting businesses, modeling their practices after the one we developed in the United States. We have watched and learned from them what things work and what things do not work.

The third area of experience comes from many professional colleagues I have observed and admired over the years. There are many successful consultants, and we all can learn from them. I have tried to put some of their expertise and advice in this book.

Finally, the fourth area is the research of what has worked well for others. I have tried to choose the best of the best consulting books and the best of those who are successful at consulting. For example, Steve Kaplan and Seth Godin have developed very successful consulting practices, and we have learned from their approaches and their particular areas of focus.

ACKNOWLEDGMENTS

No book is the work of an author alone. This book had many individuals at the ROI Institute helping with this assignment. Much appreciation goes to Linda Dempsey, Caroline Foil, and Francine Hawkins for inputting my thoughts into words for the first draft. Don Milazzo, Margaret Marston, Kathy Porter, Crystal Bedwell, and Jaime Beard all had a hand in the editing process. I particularly appreciate Jaime's outstanding efforts to help in the final stages of the manuscript production. Jaime has been a long-time assistant, and her excellent work is certainly appreciated. Kathy has also been invaluable throughout final editing and production.

Thanks to McGraw-Hill and our editor, Melissa Bonventre. This is our third book with McGraw-Hill and we are proud to be part of the company's publishing legacy. Melissa has been very patient as we struggled to complete the book during a very hectic global consulting schedule.

I owe much to my wonderful partner, friend, and spouse Patti, who continues to support what we do in so many wonderful and helpful ways. Without her support and tolerance for a busy schedule and her helpful advice throughout this manuscript, it would not have become a reality.

CHAPTER 1

IS THIS THE RIGHT PATH?

Consulting is one of the most attractive professions in the world. Many aspiring consultants harbor visions of high levels of career satisfaction, control over pursuing and scheduling work, and a wealth of free time as an independent operator—and with all the recognition and perks that go with the job. Unfortunately, most do not achieve this level of success, failing within the first two years of launching a consulting business.

Failure often can be avoided if key issues are tackled early and appropriately. The aim of *How to Build a Successful Consulting Practice* is to assist individuals and consulting firms in this important decision-making process. The book will also help established consulting practices review these issues to determine if adjustments are needed.

In this initial chapter we will present information on how an individual or firm can function effectively within the consulting field. Following a self-assessment, we'll explore concerns about consulting and the problems created when individuals and firms are not adequately prepared for the challenges. Then we will explore the joy of consulting and detail its favorable aspects. A variety of myths will be challenged, and an up-to-date view of the consulting field will emerge.

But perhaps the most significant aspect of this chapter is the explanation it will afford on why consulting is a good choice today and how consultants are actually adding value. In discussing this, we'll outline the important paradigm shift taking place in consulting. If this is the right path, then you can find your niche based upon a realistic view of the field. For those of you who are not presently consultants, the chapter ends with suggestions about managing the transition from your current job to the field of consulting.

Self-Assessment

Let's begin the evaluation process with the 20 statements in Table 1-1. Take a few minutes and check Yes or No for each one.

No set scoring can guarantee particular levels of success, but the *Yes* response is desirable for most of the statements. In an ideal world, for an extremely successful consultant, it would be the appropriate response to all of the questions. Anything less than that foretells problems for the consultant, and

Table 1-1 Is This the Right Path? A Self-Assessment

1. Rejection does not bother me.	Yes ___	No___
2. I enjoy tackling big projects.	Yes ___	No___
3. I am okay with not being in control of my schedule.	Yes ___	No___
4. Criticism does not bother me.	Yes ___	No___
5. I am willing to work long hours to achieve success.	Yes ___	No___
6. I enjoy taking risks.	Yes ___	No___
7. I enjoy helping others solve problems.	Yes ___	No___
8. I am good at understanding the big picture.	Yes ___	No___
9. I am detail-oriented.	Yes ___	No___
10. I am an excellent communicator.	Yes ___	No___
11. I am an excellent writer.	Yes ___	No___
12. I like to sell myself and my capabilities.	Yes ___	No___
13. I can balance logic with intuition.	Yes ___	No___
14. I can balance the big picture with details.	Yes ___	No___
15. I know my limitations.	Yes ___	No___
16. I can say no easily.	Yes ___	No___
17. I am very disciplined in my work.	Yes ___	No___
18. I am comfortable speaking with people in all disciplines.	Yes ___	No___
19. I can function at all levels of an organization.	Yes ___	No___
20. I enjoy working as a team member.	Yes ___	No___

Adapted from Elaine Biech, *The Business of Consulting: The Basics and Beyond* (San Francisco: Jossey-Bass/Pfeiffer, 1999), 15.

maybe even for the client. A *Yes* for at least 15 of the 20 statements would usually be necessary for success. A number less than that may put the consultant at a disadvantage.

The need for positive responses to these statements should not be surprising, since consulting is an occupation that requires a great deal of hard work and risk-taking. A successful consultant must be able to take criticism and rejection and work with unruly and undisciplined clients. Consultants have to be team members, even though they may be responsible for a project. They must be able to interact and work with different organizations and communicate effectively in different ways, tailoring their presentation and style to the audience. Consultants have to see the big picture, but at the same time be disciplined, detailed, and a taskmaster who completes work that must be done.

Concerns About Consulting

The consulting business has enjoyed tremendous success during the past two decades, with its growth exceeding that of many professions. Most estimates predict that the consulting industry will grow in the range of 15 to 20 percent annually.

Whether restructuring, implementing systems, developing staff, changing procedures, buying new companies, or rolling out new products and services, businesses are asking consultants to assist in many ways. Companies are fervently seeking consultants for their external perspectives and expert opinions, hoping they can provide solutions that will improve business. Unfortunately, clients are often disappointed when a consultant's products and services fail to deliver anticipated results, leaving both the client and the consultant frustrated over the outcome of a project.[1]

Lack of Accountability

A major book focusing on large consulting companies delivered perhaps one of the most damaging reports about the consulting industry. *Dangerous Company*, written by James O'Shea and Charles Madigan, illustrates how consulting powerhouses are inflicting damage on many organizations. The opening paragraph best summarizes the concerns for accountability:

> *A secretive and elite army of management consultants is at work deep inside corporations everywhere, from the giants of the Fortune 500 to mid-sized and smaller companies. It is also expanding its influence all over the developing world, wherever economies are coming to life. And it has become partner to government, adviser to heads of state, and confidant to countless interests eager to exploit the promise of a growing world economy. It collects top dollar for its work, sometimes delivering all the sparkle and success it promises, and sometimes failing so remarkably that its clients seem more victim than customer. A relative newcomer to the world of business, management consulting has escaped all but the most cursory of levels of scrutiny. It has only good things to say about itself. But there is a growing sense of unease about this exploding and occasionally explosive enterprise, a feeling that it is a palace built on a foundation of shifting sand. From a distance, it glistens like alabaster. Up close, a different image emerges. It centers on a key question: "Whose interest is being served?" All too often, the answer is that it is not the best interest of the client.[2]*

It would be unfair to label all consultants and consulting firms as incapable of producing results or supplying a useful product or service. Success stories tell of firms that have enhanced organizations and even turned them around. However, in far too many cases the results are simply not there. Sometimes, the process itself causes a breakdown in accountability.

Consider, for example, the following consulting project for a regional financial institution. A well-known and respected consulting firm was engaged to analyze areas where efficiency could be developed to add immediate bottom-line value to the organization. The consultants pored over financial records, analyzed operating reports, and interviewed dozens of managers and specialists. In the end, they seized the ideas and suggestions of the organization's operating managers, presenting projects that were already under way or in the planning stages as recommendations to improve operating efficiencies. When the senior staff of the firm objected to the consultants' report, the CEO, who had hired the consultants, praised their work and suggested that their recommendations be adopted. The staff resisted and ultimately did not act upon what had originally been planned. In short, the consultants' recommendations were never implemented. In a reference check by another organization seeking consulting advice, the CEO praised the report and gave the consulting firm very high marks for its efforts. Privately, he said, "Although we did not implement all the recommendations, and some were already in planning, it was a good exercise for the organization."

From most perspectives, this scenario represents a failure in the consulting assignment. Although the project was completed, recommendations were made, and the primary client—the CEO—was satisfied, the result fell short of what should have been accomplished and, more important, what *could* have been accomplished. The problem involved a breakdown in the processes that led to the consulting intervention and its ultimate result.

Many consultants would agree with this negative assessment. According to Robert Schaffer, in his book *High Impact Consulting*:

> *Most management consultants subscribe to a model of consulting that is inherently loaded against success. This consulting paradigm, followed throughout the world by external and staff consultants alike, is unnecessarily labor-intensive, long in cycle time, and low in return on investment. It locks both clients and consultants into a fundamentally ineffective mode of operation. In this, the conventional consulting model, there is a clear divide between the parties: The experts are accountable for creating the best possible solutions and tools, and the clients are accountable for exploiting those solutions and tools to improve organization results. In too many cases, however, clients do not or cannot implement the consultant-developed solutions in ways that yield significant improvement.[3]*

Beyond the flawed issues surrounding implementation and support are the problems of a lack of clear definition up front, a lack of focus on specific objectives, and a lack of emphasis on obtaining results throughout the process. While many consulting projects do yield results, they often fall short of the significant results they might have achieved, and in far too many cases they produce no results at all.

In this book we will discuss the tools and processes needed to measure the success of consulting projects and ensure that consulting projects are properly initiated (with the end in mind) and that they place the necessary emphasis on results, including various feedback mechanisms to keep a project clearly on track. When implemented, this process will ensure that a consulting project not only produces results but also that the results are significant and in alignment with what should reasonably be expected from major interventions.

Tarnished Image

Closely related to a lack of accountability in the consulting industry is a problem with the tarnished image. Elaine Biech, in her book *The Business of Consulting*, lists as one of her myths that "consulting is a respected profession." Biech explains that she thought she had chosen a respected profession and was shocked the first time she was called a "Beltway bandit"—a term assigned to consulting firms in and around the Washington, D.C., Beltway. Since her initial encounter, she has been called a "pest" and a "con person."[4]

Indeed, the consulting profession has come under fire, particularly from the employees who have to work with consultants and deal with the outcomes of a consulting assignment. This is visibly underscored in the depiction of consultants in the popular Dilbert comic strip. In fact, nearly 10 percent of the book *The Dilbert Principle*, which was number one on the *New York Times* best-seller list, is devoted to consultants and consulting. The cartoons depict the petty and stupid requests and activities of consultants and consulting projects that litter cubicles throughout the corporate world.[5]

Some of Scott Adams's observations of consultants include:

- A consultant is a person who takes your money and annoys your employees while tirelessly searching for the best way to extend the consulting contract.
- Consultants will hold a seemingly endless series of meetings to test various hypotheses and assumptions. These exercises are a vital step toward tricking managers into revealing the recommendation that is most likely to generate repeat consulting business.
- After the correct recommendation is discovered, it must be justified by a lengthy analysis. Analysis is designed to be as confusing as possible, thus discouraging any second-guessing by staff members who are afraid of appearing dense.
- Consultants use a standard set of decision tools that involve creating alternative scenarios based on different assumptions. Any pesky assumption that does not fit the predetermined recommendation is quickly discounted as being uneconomical by the consultants.
- Consultants will often recommend that you do whatever you are not doing now.
- Consultants do not need much experience in industry in order to be experts; they learn quickly.

The author continues with his list of advantages that consultants bring to a company:

- Consultants eventually leave, which makes them excellent scapegoats for major management blunders.
- Consultants can schedule time on your boss's calendar because they do not have your reputation as a troublemaker who constantly brings up unsolvable issues.
- Consultants often are more trusted than your regular employees.
- Consultants will return phone calls because it is all billable time to them.
- Consultants work preposterously long hours, thus making the regular staff feel worthless for only working 60 hours a week.

While this is a humorous attack on the consulting field, it unfortunately rings true for many consultants, bringing confirmation on at least some of the points.

An Unlikely Top 10 List
The attack on consultants appears in all types of communications, even on the Internet. In ascending order (in which the last is least likely) here's the "Top 10 List of Things You Will Never Hear a Consultant Say":

10. You're right; we're billing you way too much for this.
 9. Bet you I can go a week without saying "synergy" or "value-added."
 8. How about paying us based on the success of the project?
 7. This whole strategy is based on a Harvard business case I read.
 6. Actually, the only difference is that we charge more than they do.
 5. I don't know enough to speak intelligently about that.
 4. Implementation?

3. I can't take the credit. It was Linda in your marketing department.
2. The problem is, you have too much work for too few people.
1. Everything looks okay to me.

Certainly, some of the criticism toward consulting is unjustified. Employees who are often the subject of job loss, job redesign, transfer, or relocation as a result of a consulting initiative will undoubtedly view that process as unfair and distasteful. But the hostility and negative attacks go beyond the outcome of the consulting process. They illuminate the fact that many consulting interventions are not a value-added process: Given the time and resources allocated, they do not provide a payoff for the organization. A well-designed and properly focused project that brings value would not be the subject of the ridicule and negative comments consulting interventions often draw.

Excessive Costs

The cost of consulting is increasing significantly. The story of the employee who was fired and rehired as a consultant at twice the salary is becoming commonplace, except these days it is three or four times the salary.

While most employees understand that an hourly rate for a consultant must be more than a corresponding hourly rate for an employee, the differential is staggering. An MBA fresh out of school may command $200 an hour for a big consulting firm working hand in hand with employees who know far more about the process than he or she does. In essence, the consultant is learning on the job with a resulting increase in salary.

Middle-level or senior consultants in a large consulting firm may command $250 to $350 an hour, while a senior partner will charge more than $500 an hour. These are not short-term assignments, but often continue for as much as a year. The notion of a higher hourly rate was built on the idea that there are only a certain number of billable days, usually 60 percent of all possible workdays. Today, that number has increased, and in some firms junior consultants bill as much as 80 or 90 percent of their time—sometimes on a requirement or expectations. These costs, when spread over a large organization, add up quickly. AT&T, for example, was spending roughly $100 million a year in the mid-1990s on outside consultants until a CEO put a clamp on the spending. Other firms are beginning to put a stop to such spending until there is some sense of control and more evidence of additional value.

The underpinning of these three issues—accountability, image, and costs—is the lack of a focus on results; it is the absence of a process that defines, emphasizes, and delivers results throughout the project. In this book we will create a consulting practice that focuses on results.

High Failure Rate

Consultants themselves report frustration and anxiety in terms of their reputations and the work they're doing. Clients do not always meet their expectations, and projects are constantly changing. Some clients are unwilling to pay in full, even when terms are agreed upon in advance. Further, consultants who are resented in organizations have difficulty getting the necessary information from individuals, and there are frustrations associated with the measures of success, which are often not appreciated by those who initiated the project in the first place. Add to this the fact that many consulting engagements are made for the wrong reasons—to achieve political motives and hidden agendas, or to stroke the egos of those who hired the consultants. These problems concerning their work, their progress, and their image, prompt many consultants to leave the field.

Consulting and Life Balance

Successful consulting requires a tremendous number of hours of demanding work, particularly in a firm's early stages. The work is overwhelming for some, at times requiring an unbelievable numbers of hours when projects are new. Social and family lives deteriorate to levels far below those the individual enjoyed prior to joining the ranks of consultants. Despite the anticipation that considerable effort and time will be necessary in the early stages, the required time and effort can far exceed expectations for family and friends, as well as the consultant him- or herself. Consultants report that they lose touch with friends and family, and a good number experience divorce, caused in part by the long work hours and the extended travel demanded by some consulting assignments. Consequently, once again, many of them leave the field.

These issues and others also bring about a high failure rate among consultants. In fact, of all occupations that include a significant number of people, the consulting industry suffers the highest failure rate. Some estimate it at over 50 percent within the first two years of beginning a consulting practice. In addition, there are a tremendous number of failures that are not reported. Surviving consulting practices experience great disappointments because they are not living up to expectations. Consulting is a high-risk process. We will go into the reasons for success and failure more fully in the next chapter.

The Joy of Consulting

Now that we've painted a dismal picture of consulting, it should be said that for most individuals in the profession, the joys of consulting outweigh the concerns surrounding consulting. This is why they are consultants. Even so, many admit that they did not study and take enough time to understand the issues of consulting; otherwise, their decision might have been different. Understanding both the negative and the positive sides of the issues is crucial to making an informed choice and ultimately to achieving greater satisfaction.

Measurable and Immeasurable Rewards

Perhaps there is no more exciting profession than that of a consultant when projects are completed successfully, clients are satisfied, and value is added by the consultant. Not only are the rewards evident in financial terms, which can be very lucrative, but consultants are also rewarded through the intangibles of self-satisfaction and the feeling of accomplishment when those who hired them see the value in what they've done. Seeing satisfied clients describe the extent to which a problem has been solved, a new project has been implemented, costs have been reduced, customers have been added, cycle time has been reduced, or some other important milestone that has been reached can be gratifying. Together with the measurable results, it can build excitement and make consultants strive to do even better.

Utilizing Expertise

The consulting profession provides tremendous opportunities for the consultant to display expertise and a noteworthy experience base. Most consultants bring to the assignment a wealth of experience, which is sometimes the actual basis of the engagement. In addition, consultants bring expertise that enables them to convert their experience into a value-added process for the client. Individuals in organizations rarely have the opportunity to see their work in such a completely isolated way as in a consulting project. In these situations, the efforts of the consultant—or the consulting team—are clearly evident.

Using Creativity

The heart of the consulting process is the ability to work with the problem or project in a creative way. The consultant can consider all the elements or issues and transform the situation into a productive project and a desired outcome that is viewed by his or her clients as successful. Consultants tackle and solve some of the most difficult problems. Success stories filling the pages of books, newspapers, and magazines describe how a consultant, or a team of consultants, has worked on a particular issue.

Myths About Consulting

Probably nothing gets in the way of successful consulting more than the myths that surround this field and this industry. These myths are often perpetuated because of a lack of understanding and a failure of insight regarding the facts about the consulting itself. Here are 12 of the most common myths.

Myth 1: Consulting Is Easy

From an observer's position, consulting does appear to be easy since consultants breeze in and out of organizations, meet with key people, including managers, take the ideas of other people, present a report, and receive a great financial reward. However, as this chapter and other chapters will show, consulting is a very challenging and difficult process.

Myth 2: Individual Consultants Do Not Have a Boss

Many individuals are tempted to flee organizations and, particularly, their bosses. Consulting seems an attractive—even compelling—alternative. Individuals see themselves working in an organization structure but without a boss. "To be my own boss" is the response of many when asked the reason for choosing the consulting profession.

In reality, consultants may have many more bosses than a person inside an organization. The number one boss is the client, who passes judgment on the work and ultimately determines if the consultant is rewarded financially or is engaged for further consulting work. Therefore, the consultant must please the boss, and that is the client. Other "bosses" may be just as critical; partners and team members must be convinced that the project is adding value, and prospective clients must be convinced up front that the consultant has expertise and is credible in his or her work. So the boss does not go away. That position is simply diverted to other individuals—most of it with the client.

Myth 3: Consultants Make Lots of Money

This is certainly a myth, and a seductive one. While it's true that some top consultants do receive tremendous compensation for their work, those are rare exceptions rather than the rule. Many consultants cannot charge rates at those high levels.

Average consulting rates may be in the neighborhood of $1,000 per day, which still seems like a great deal of money. Consider, though, that consultants spend only a limited number of days on actual consulting. They spend a substantial amount of time developing, promoting, managing, and sustaining the business. When compensated time and uncompensated time are averaged, the money earned monthly or annually is not equivalent to that of a professional employee in a typical organization.

Myth 4: Consultants Have a Lot of Free Time

Some believe that consultants have expanses of free time because they appear to work only a few days out of the year. What observers do not see is the behind-the-scenes work, including business development and other time-consuming activities required in managing the business. In truth, most consultants have a lot less free time than their typical organizational counterparts.

Myth 5: It's Easy to Start a Consulting Practice

Some individuals see consulting as an easy business startup. With some business cards, letterhead, a telephone, a Web site, and an e-mail address, you're in business! That's what some people think. The reality is that it is a difficult business to start, as we will detail later in the book.

Myth 6: Consultants Are Respected

Consultants are often highlighted in magazines and books in a favorable way—for achieving dramatic turnarounds for struggling corporations, for instance. It seems, then, a respected profession. At the same time, however, consultants as a group—sometimes even the previously revered consultants—are berated in the press or ridiculed in the comics, as we have already noted. Consultants are often resented in organizations and just as often have a less than desirable image.

Myth 7: Consulting Success Is Measured with Soft Data

Some individuals think that consulting success rests with intangibles and the relationship with the client only. They believe that perhaps even the chemistry between the consultant and the client is the best measure of success. Unfortunately, this is not true in most cases. Many projects must be justified on the basis of hard data, which we will go into later in the book.

Myth 8: Being a Consultant Means Having Expertise

Some people think that having the label of consultant means you have instantaneous expertise. After all, the fundamental prerequisite to consulting is to be an expert in something. However, far too many people enter the profession with little or no expertise, leading to many of the problems that are detailed in this chapter and the next.

Myth 9: Consultants Do Not Add Value

This is an extreme view from those who are cynical about consultants because they've seen so much waste and deficiency, including the dysfunctional habits we described earlier. However, contrary to this opinion, most consulting projects do add value in many different ways, which we'll go into later in this section.

Myth 10: Consultants Are Only Appropriate for Large Organizations

Because there are so many consultants in large organizations—based on the absolute numbers—many conclude that large organizations become the predominant field of consultants. Although there are more consultants working for large organizations, many opportunities still exist for consultants in smaller organizations. In fact, smaller organizations sometimes need consultants more than larger ones because they often lack the expertise or the trained staff to complete projects or solve problems.

Myth 11: It's Not Possible to Isolate the Effects of Consulting

This issue often surfaces when a consultant takes credit for a particular solution or improvement measure. Other factors of course contribute to the results, and some assume that it's impossible to isolate the effects of the consulting engagement. This is not the case, and as we will see in a later chapter, one of the fundamental analytical steps is to isolate the effects of the consulting from other influences.

Myth 12: There Must Be Standards for Consultants

Because there are so many consultants in so many different fields, some take for granted that there must be standards for the profession and standards within which consultants actually complete their consulting processes and engagements. However, consulting presently has neither agreed to standards for professional engagements nor to practices or credentials and requirements for entering the profession. Surely, change will come with increased efforts to bring accountability to consulting.

The Consulting Field

The consulting field has grown significantly in recent years, and the complexity in a variety of approaches to consulting has changed.

What Is Consulting?

According to *The Ultimate Business Dictionary*, a consultant is:

> *… an expert in a specialized field brought in to provide independent professional advice to an organization on some aspect of its activities. A consultant may advise on the overall management of an organization or on a specific project such as the introduction of a new computer system. Consultants are usually retained*

by a client for a set period of time during which they will report, detailing their recommendations. Consultants may set up in business independently or be employed by a large consulting firm. Specific types of consultants include management consultants and internal consultants.[6]

Whatever the definition, consulting involves very simple processes. A consultant will:

1. Investigate a problem or situation.
2. Listen to, or observe, stakeholders directly involved in the situation.
3. Analyze the facts and data to reach conclusions.
4. Provide a recommendation for action.
5. Facilitate an implementation of the recommendation, if appropriate.

In a later chapter we'll go into more detail, describing a recommended process and steps where the focus is on securing results from the project.

Everyone Is a Consultant

One reason consulting is so attractive is that there is a consulting element in almost every professional—and sometimes nonprofessional—job. Individuals are required to analyze situations, listen to others, investigate issues, and make recommendations. Thus, in a sense, many individuals have been consulting for years, although the process has not been formal or structured, and it certainly has not constituted the majority of their efforts. However, this experience does help ease the transition to full-time consulting.

Trends Related to Consulting

Consulting clearly is a growing occupation, at least among small consulting businesses. The following trends underscore its tremendous growth:

- Organizations are attempting to reduce staffing levels to keep their total employee count very low. This is driven by the desire to be efficient, and the employees on the payroll represent a fixed cost that can be very significant. Reduced staffing leads to opportunities for consultants to provide specialized assistance.
- Organizations and the work accomplished within are becoming more complex. This means that managers need help with a variety of work-related issues and processes.
- The continuing growth of globalization requires specialized assistance with rules, regulations, culture, and change issues, creating opportunities for consultants.
- In the United States, baby boomers are moving into their early retirement years. Many of them are seeking new challenges away from the bureaucratic structure of traditional organizations. Wanting to use their expertise and experience in a profitable way, they see consulting as a rewarding and natural next career.
- Shareholders of organizations increasingly demand more efficiency, profitability, and growth from organizations. This trend requires management to examine processes and work flow to

ensure that organizations are the best that they can be. This, in turn, creates opportunities for consultants who can assist in this important goal.

- Demanding customers are changing the dynamics of customer service. Organizations are constantly under pressure to provide the fastest, most reliable, and friendliest customer service. Consultants provide assistance in this vital area.
- Executives often require external validation of particular processes, products, performance areas, and outputs. External validation leads to the need for external consultants.
- Globally, there are many opportunities for consultancies as emerging nations eagerly seek to become more modern, up-to-date, and efficient in their processes.
- Demographic shifts in all countries are creating changes in market demands, creating opportunities for those who understand these issues and can help organizations meet these particular needs.
- The constant flow of fads in and out of organizations creates opportunities for consultants to help organizations address these fads and attempt to make them work in their organization. Some executives constantly seek the newest fad and employ consultants to help implement it.
- Executives sometimes prefer to use outsiders rather than rely on the input and advice of their own staff. They feel that the independence of the external viewpoint is important.
- In an attempt to become streamlined and efficient, some organizations outsource major parts of their work, creating opportunities for consultants. Often, these consultants come from the ranks of their previous employees.
- Executives and managers often have unpleasant tasks, processes, and issues to address. They prefer to use external consultants who are viewed as dispensable and can be quickly removed after the dirty work has been done.
- Finally, organizations, desperate to survive, seek all types of assistance and support to improve their situations. This creates many opportunities for consultants.

These trends and others create growth for the consulting industry. Depending on whose estimates are used, the figures range from a growth of 15 to 25 percent per year for this profession. At the same time, the actual growth of large consulting practices is not as strong.

Based on these trends, it becomes abundantly clear that consulting is a good choice as an occupational option for those considering an outlet and a use for their expertise and experience. For those who want to have their rewards tied directly to their contributions, it is a logical choice. When considering the dynamics of workplace displacement from early retirement, mergers and acquisitions, outsourcing of major components, and converting employees to contract consultants, the opportunities are plentiful, making consulting a great option.

Consulting Activities

Although there are many different types of consulting activities or projects, the most common include:

- Management consulting, perhaps one of the largest categories, involves providing assistance and support, solving problems, and resolving issues for managers at all levels of an organization.
- Process improvement consulting emphasizes improving a variety of processes in an organization with an attempt to reinvent the engine or reconfigure the work flow or processes.

- Human resources consulting provides advice on a variety of issues, from recruiting, employment, and retention to compensation and workforce relations.
- Legal and compliance consulting provides expert advice and input on legal issues and matters related to compliance with governmental regulations and standards for a particular industry.
- Information technology consulting employs a large number of consultants who provide assistance with technology and the implementation and integration of technology, covering hardware, software, and systems.
- Sales and marketing consulting provides input on all aspects of sales, promotions, marketing events, and marketing strategy to help organizations improve their customer focus.
- Financial consulting addresses matters surrounding finance, accounting, regulatory, and compliance issues.
- Subject-matter expert consulting provides expert input in a particular area of specialty. In almost any field, there are experts who understand the processes better than most other individuals and can provide advice to help organizations.

This list could be longer, but it does cover the major categories of consulting projects.

Consulting Involvement

Another important issue when examining the consulting process is to consider the extent to which the consultant actually provides work versus advice. Figure 1-1 shows the degree of involvement of the consultant and represents a continuum from the consultant who solely provides advice to the consultant who performs most of the work, essentially almost becoming a contract employee. Many degrees in between show the various levels of activity that can be shared by the client organization and the consultant. When planning and designing the consulting firm, the consultant must answer this question: "At what point on the continuum will the typical approach for this consulting firm be?"

Figure 1-1 The Degree of Consultant Involvement

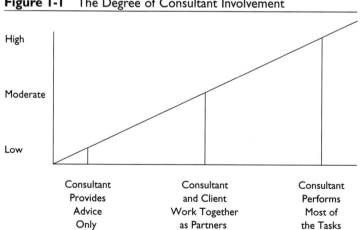

Transfer of Knowledge

Another important issue is the extent to which consultants are willing to transfer what they know to the organization. Many consultants prefer to keep their knowledge and expertise to themselves, attempting to protect their job security and help ensure that they will be called again. Others prefer to teach the client knowledge and skills so the client does not have to call a consultant constantly to perform a task or do the work. This avoids the narcotic effect of always calling a consultant.

The issue presents a dilemma because some feel that if the knowledge and expertise are transferred to the client, there will be no basis for repeat business—ultimately putting the consultant out of business. However, many client organizations prefer to work with consultants who will teach what they know to the extent that the client wants to learn. These consultants are more likely to work with the client organization not only for the initial engagement, but also for follow-up work as the client becomes more effective with the processes.

This is best shown in the grid in Figure 1-2.[7] This grid shows the range of potential consultant interventions as defined by particular client need. On the left side is the resolution of the issue, which

Figure 1-2 Range of Potential Consultant Interventions as Defined by Client Need

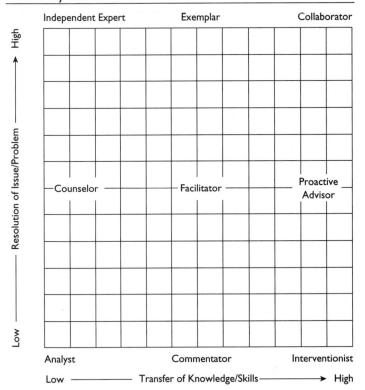

Adapted with permission of Alan Weiss, *Million Dollar Consulting: The Professional's Guide to Growing a Practice* (New York: McGraw-Hill, Inc., 1992), 15.

obviously is a top priority for many clients, and at the bottom, the transfer of knowledge and skills for the job, the second issue.

The challenge for consultants is to decide the appropriate place—the right place—on the grid for them. Some prefer to operate as independent experts where they solve problems and, routinely, get called back; yet they make no effort to teach the organization what they know or do. Others may serve as facilitators, helping the organization resolve the problem while transferring a moderate amount of skill and knowledge to the organization. Still others prefer to be interventionists who know very little about the problem or issue but have excellent skills to reach the resolution using the resources at hand. These consultants are very interested in teaching the client what they know—and what they do not.

In many situations the desired position is the collaborator. In a collaborative role, the problems or issues are resolved and every effort is made to transfer the necessary knowledge and skills to the client organization. In our experience at the ROI Institute, consultants gain much by taking this approach. Clients appreciate the willingness to share information and often follow up with repeat business to help them with more difficult issues, to provide an independent view to the work they are doing, and to address politically sensitive issues.

Typical Clients

Clients for consulting can vary significantly from large to small organizations and can be in all types of settings. Sometimes the client is actually an individual or small business owner who needs some specialized help or is an individual within an organization who needs assistance with a particular project.

The range of organizations seeking consulting services varies considerably, from nonprofits, nongovernment organizations (NGOS), a full spectrum of public sector groups such as cities, counties, states, and the federal government to educational institutions and, of course, the private sector. The private sector covers a vast array of organizations, including all industries and all sizes within those industries.

All these possibilities challenge the consultant whether to specialize in a particular area, such as government, or on a particular industry, such as automotive, or even to consider size, such as consulting for small organizations. Sometimes part of the process of becoming a niche consultant is to leverage expertise in a particular industry or sector and build on that experience. Some consultants prefer to work exclusively with types of institutions, such as pension funds managers. Still others prefer to specialize in a particular field, such as engineering, accounting, or software design. Choosing the type of clients is an important part of the business plan discussed in Chapter 3.

How Consultants Add Value

Despite negative perceptions and a tarnished image, consultants do add value. It is helpful to review this from three perspectives.

What Consultants Bring to the Client

Figure 1-3 illustrates what the consultant typically offers the client. The consulting assignment often begins with a current situation that prompts the need for consulting advice. Consultants bring a wealth of

Figure 1-3   What the Consultant Brings to the Consulting Engagement

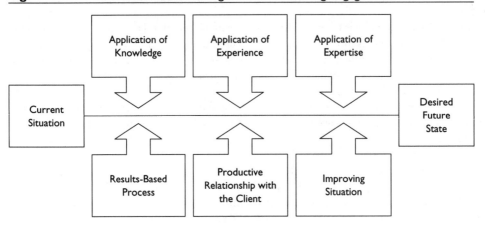

experience based on previous work in that situation or industry or setting. They also bring a knowledge base obtained from constantly working with the issue, problem, or situation. They know which processes are effective and which ones are not. Finally, the consultant brings expertise, being able to combine knowledge and experience to ferret out the correct solution or resolution for the problem.

Along the way, the consultant brings a results-based process where the focus is on improving the organization, the business, the department, or the function. Also, they operate in a productive relationship with clients so the process flows smoothly and efficiently. Most of all, consultants bring integrity and ethical behavior that establishes the appropriate trust with the client. Through this proper ethical behavior, consultants build the credibility needed to convince the client that things will work as planned and described. Each of these factors adds value to the organization because all of these areas focus on value-adding elements.

Why Clients Need Consultants

For many logical and rational reasons, clients need consultants. Sometimes problems need to be solved that simply cannot be solved with the current staff. Other times there are projects that cannot be accomplished with the current staff. In other situations, expertise is needed that is not present in the client organization. Table 1-2 shows a list of the reasons why consultants are needed.

The rationale for using consultants is based not only on what they do, but also upon the viewpoint they bring. They offer objectivity and, because of their independence from the organizational structure, are not afraid of saying what they think or what they actually believe about a situation. Because of their cumulative experience, knowledge, and expertise, consultants can frequently see things that those in the organization cannot. Having been through similar situations before enables them to see where things are in a given process, as well as how things are evolving and developing. They recognize the impediments, barriers, and inhibitors, along with the enhancements, enablers, and supporters. Consultants can sometimes gain certain access that perhaps the client has difficulty finding.[8]

Table 1-2 Why Consultants Are Needed

Compliance	Efficiency Problems
Production Bottleneck	New ideas
Staffing Flexibility	Lack of experience
Lack of expertise	Lack of knowledge
Lack of time	Lack of resources

Documented Results

Fortunately for consultants, hundreds of published case studies document how they have made a difference—how they have added value and helped organizations achieve new milestones. The popular press, financial journals, and industry publications regularly present these stories. Top executives, plotting their memoirs and boastful biographies, often credit consultants who made a difference in their particular decisions. These documented case studies, many of them actually showing a return on investment (ROI) in consulting, add to the credible evidence that consultants add value to the organizations—not just on intangibles and subjective values but also on hard results, including the ROI.[9]

Paradigm Shift in Consulting

Fortunately, things are changing for the consulting field—an established profession is getting even better. During the past decade there has been a paradigm shift in consulting. Table 1-3 shows the traditional view of consulting compared to the emerging view. As this table reveals, the traditional view of consulting is activity, an undirected and almost unnecessary process. An emerging view is based on value, is measured, and is productive.

Consulting is more than just having projects, activities, and relationships with clients. It involves determining needs and very precise measures that translate into objectives. Objectives are not just about project activities but include business measures as well. The team and other stakeholders are involved in the project and understand their roles in order to make the project work. Efforts are often undertaken to ensure that the project is successfully implemented, and the results are reported using a variety of measures, including the calculation of the ROI. This emerging view is encouraging because it positions consulting as a credible and legitimate process that is perceived as a source of value.

Finding Your Niche

It is assumed that an individual entering the consulting business will have expertise. The fundamental premise is that the individual is able to offer a combination of knowledge, experience, and expertise to deliver value to the client. By design, the expertise should be in a particular niche—a discrete area

Table 1-3 Paradigm Shift in Consulting

Traditional View	Emerging View
The business need of consulting is not established.	Consulting is linked to specific business needs before implementation.
No assessment of performance issues is made prior to implementation.	Assessment of performance issues is made before implementation.
Specific measurable objectives for implementation and business impact are not developed.	Specific objectives are developed for implementation and business impact.
Stakeholders/participants are not prepared to achieve results.	Results/expectations are communicated to stakeholders/participants.
Work environment is not prepared to support implementation.	Environment is prepared to support implementation.
No measurement or analysis of results is pursued	Measurement and analysis of results is pursued.
Planning and reporting on consulting are input-focused.	Planning and reporting on consulting are output-focused.
Consulting expenses are considered costs.	Consulting expenditures are viewed as a source of value.
Consultants are perceived as a support staff.	Consultants are perceived as strategic partners.
Each department is involved in setting the consulting budget.	Top executives are increasingly involved in allocating the consulting budget.
Consulting metrics focus on cost and activities.	Consulting metrics focus on results.
Consulting metrics are created and maintained by consultants alone.	Clients are involved in the design and use of metrics.
There is little effort to understand the return on investment in consulting.	The use of ROI has become an important tool to understand the cause-and-effect relationships.
Consulting success focuses on the data at hand.	Consulting focuses on the data needed.
The use of consultants is based on what GE and IBM are doing.	The use of consultants is based on what is needed in the organization.

that this particular consultant understands and can manage better than anyone else. If the industry, organization, process, discipline, or function is known and understood by the consultant, then he or she can deliver ideas and support in unique ways, representing either a direct service or an improved delivery method.

Perhaps the most critical challenge when establishing a consulting practice or when revising or reviewing the effectiveness of a consulting practice is to examine the forte. Finding a niche has many different dimensions, and Table 1-4 shows some possibilities.[10]

Although it's almost impossible to achieve, the ideal consulting environment yields 5s on all factors. The higher the number, the better the situation. Any given item can raise concerns if it is not in the most favorable category. The level of competition, the product life cycle, the reputation of the consultant, and the markets are very important issues. In considering the product life cycle, very long life cycles are desired—a product that rarely changes. It would be nice if there was no competition and the consultant had high levels of expertise. Business development should be easily and inexpensively accomplished, and the financial rewards should be high. Nevertheless, short of the ideal, the

Table 1-4 Finding Your Niche

	1	2	3	4	5
Expertise	Very little expertise	Some expertise	Moderate amount	High level	Very high level
Competition	Overwhelming competition	Highly competitive	Competitive	Negligible competition	Almost no competition
Change Rate for Service Area	Supersonic change	Rapid change	Fast change	Moderate change	Little or no change
Product Life Cycle	Very short	Short	Moderate	Long	Very long
Complexity/ Predictability	Low complexity; predictable	Moderate complexity	Complex but predictable	Somewhat complex; unpredictable	Highly unpredictable and complex
Your Reputation	Not known	Some reputation	Moderate amount	Well known	Very well known
Business Development Required	Very little business development	Some business development	Moderate amount of business development	High level of business development	Very high level of business development
Target Market	Limited/Very specific	Somewhat limited	Moderate range of application	Broad range of application	Very broad range of application
Financial Rewards	Very little reward	Some reward	Moderate amount of reward	High level of reward	Very high level of reward
Diversification	No ability to diversify	Limited amount of diversification	Moderate diversification	High diversification	Very high ability to diversify

Adapted from Jim Underwood, *What's Your Corporate IQ?: How the Smartest Companies Learn, Transform, Lead* (Chicago: Dearborn Trade Publishing, 2004).

consultant or consulting firm should review these issues periodically, examining strengths and weaknesses to find areas that might need to be reviewed or reconsidered.

Realistic Preview

Before jumping in, it may be helpful for first-time consultants to get a realistic picture by examining all sides of the issues, from the very negative concerns to the positive aspects and rewards. With this in mind, you may want to interview successful consultants and ask the 12 questions shown in Table 1-5.

Asking consultants in the same field or similar fields may yield enlightening responses—candid comments and realistic assessments. When consulting competition for your niche or in your geographical area is intense, talking with consultants in your area may be awkward. If so, try reaching consultants in another field or in another geographical area. An experienced consultant who does not consider you as future competition might be more frank.

It's also helpful to try consulting on a part-time basis before launching a business as a first-time consultant. Part-time consulting may reveal some insights that could either be reinforcing or inhibiting to the decision to move into consulting full-time.

Table 1-5 12 Consultant Interview Questions

1. How long have you been a consultant?

2. How did you get started?

3. Why did you decide to become a consultant?

4. How did you develop your niche?

5. Describe your consulting practice.

6. How have you structured your business?

7. How do you find clients?

8. Describe a typical project.

9. Describe a typical day.

10. How do you market your services?

11. What's your greatest challenge as a consultant?

12. What would you miss most if you quit consulting?

Most important, size up the competition to see who is in the business and how strong they will be. If there is competition, first-time consultants must understand the strengths and weaknesses of competing organizations to determine if the competition can be challenged successfully and to understand how their approaches might change in the future. Although this is only one of the issues in finding your niche, it must be considered before launching into the profession.

Managing the Transition

After the decision has been made to move into consulting, the transition must be organized, planned, and managed appropriately to help the new consultant avoid the mistakes, miscues, frustrations, and anxieties described in this chapter. If the transition is not properly planned, surprises and disappointments can cause an early, and perhaps unnecessary, departure from the field.

An important part of managing the transition is to ensure that appropriate levels of experience, expertise, and knowledge are there. This is more crucial than assessing the competition. A beginning consultant must have confidence that what he or she has to offer is better than what the competition offers. Assess any deficiencies and take action to improve them; ensure that knowledge, experience, expertise, and confidence are in place before the business is launched.

Credibility is also a critical factor. It's one thing to have the appropriate expertise and another to have it perceived as credible. Credibility increases through making presentations, writing articles, submitting case studies, authoring books, and completing successful projects. Credibility and quality of work go hand in hand. When these matters are addressed, the transition can be organized and managed in a way that helps ensure success.

This slow migration to consulting builds a foundation to achieve certain milestones—including the financial resources needed to be successful. All of these issues should be documented in a written transition plan prepared for the consulting launch or the move to a full-time effort. This preparation is a precursor to the actual business plan covered in Chapter 3.

Final Thoughts

In this chapter we explored the key issues surrounding the consulting field and addressed the question, "Is it the right path for me (or for us) to choose?" We discussed the concerns about consulting, as well as the joys, along with the dramatic shifts taking place in the consulting business. The good news is that the trends are favorable for continued growth in consulting, even greater than has been experienced previously. But though this is an excellent opportunity for many, a new consultant must select the right niche, develop a transition plan, and become fully prepared for the adventure.

In the next chapter we'll discuss what makes consultants and consulting firms successful.

Notes

[1] David Craig, *Rip-Off!: The Scandalous Inside Story of the Management Consulting Money Machine* (London: The Original Book Company, 2005).

[2] James O'Shea and Charles Madigan, *Dangerous Company: The Consulting Powerhouses and the Businesses They Save and Ruin* (New York: Times Business/Random House, 1997).

[3] Robert Schaffer, *High-Impact Consulting: How Clients and Consultants Can Leverage Rapid Results into Long-Term Gains* (San Francisco: Jossey-Bass, 1997).

[4] Elaine Biech, *The Business of Consulting: The Basics and Beyond* (San Francisco: Jossey-Bass/Pfeiffer, 1999), 15.

[5] Scott Adams, *The Dilbert Principle: A Cubicle's-Eye View of Bosses, Meetings, Management Fads & Other Workplace Afflictions* (New York: Harper Business, 1996).

[6] *The Ultimate Business Dictionary: Defining the World of Work* (Perseus Publishing, 2003), 72.

[7] Alan Weiss, *Million Dollar Consulting: The Professional's Guide to Growing a Practice* (New York: McGraw-Hill, Inc., 1992), 15. Adapted with permission of the author.

[8] Alex Dembitz and James Essinger, *Breakthrough Consulting: So You Want to Be a Consultant? Turn Your Expertise into a Successful Consulting Business* (London: Financial Times/Prentice Hall, 2000).

[9] Jack Phillips, *The Consultant's Scorecard: Tracking Results and Bottom-Line Impact of Consulting Projects* (New York: McGraw-Hill, 2000).

[10] Jim Underwood, *What's Your Corporate IQ?: How the Smartest Companies Learn, Transform, Lead* (Chicago: Dearborn Trade Publishing, 2004).

CHAPTER 2

SUCCESS FACTORS
FOR CONSULTING

In this chapter we will explore the critical success factors for developing a consulting practice. For those considering the leap to consulting, these are the issues that will determine success. These factors are crucial to success regardless of how success is measured. For those already involved in consulting—perhaps in a larger consulting firm—they will serve as benchmarks for assessment and indicate areas that need to be adjusted.

The success factors in this chapter were derived from a variety of personal resources, studies, and experiences and accumulated as case studies of successful consulting practices.[1] We have indicated what the various studies considered the most significant factors, which are consistent with the research in this area and the practice of many consultants.

Prepare for the Leap

Making the leap to consulting is one of the most critical factors to address. The process begins with establishing the credentials necessary to build a high-quality consulting service, and preparation is essential. Documenting your experience with speeches, case studies, articles, and books ensures that you have genuine expertise and that it's known to others. Related to this, of course, is that the consulting service you offer should not be readily available from other sources. Filling a niche that others are not serving helps ensure that there is a demand for your services. Why offer a service that is already available in the market, especially if it is oversupplied?

Preparing for a consulting practice from a financial perspective is another essential step. Sufficient start-up funds and cash flow are needed to keep the business afloat during its first few months, perhaps years. The initial financial structure must be in place, including cost control, reporting records, budgets, and tax matters.

Exceptional management and organizational skills are decisive during the early stages of the practice. New consultants must be able to manage projects *and* manage the business. This includes managing time and having the discipline to stay on track consistently. Managing the financial, strategic, operational, administrative, and even legal contexts all are all vital issues as well. Weaknesses should be addressed early so that they do not create problems later.

The support of friends and family is important when starting any new business. Supportive relationships are necessary because of the stress connected with a new venture, and the long, hard hours that are inherently required in consulting. A completely different lifestyle usually will emerge. The business will consume the individual, not only with the commitments, but also with the constant attention required to keep the new business on track and moving in the proper direction.

Triggering events sometimes motivate an individual to launch a consulting business. A layoff, early retirement, unexpected job loss, or reaching a specific financial milestone are all factors that can spur the beginning of this transition. Preparation for such an event is critical to ensure business survival for the first two years.

Adjust to a Different Work Life

Moving to a consulting practice often means tremendous adjustments. For many individuals, the transition is from a safe, secure larger organization where there is a routine, support, and often, great security. The shift to consulting is a dramatic shift in the work life of an individual. As Table 2-1 shows, the difference can be dramatic, particularly in the areas of culture, work life, and support. For some, this is good news. For job security, there is almost complete control. Branding and positioning often are more exciting. Things such as business plans and sales pitches are much simpler. The shifts should be studied carefully, since some individuals have a difficult time adjusting to this new environment.

Develop a Strategy and Business Plan

Every organization must have a strategy with strategic objectives. Developing a business plan is often perceived as a tool only for large organizations. However, small and new businesses need a business plan.

Strategic objectives are crucial to developing the success of a consulting business. One objective, for example, may be to define the region of operation, whether local, national, or global. Another strategic objective could focus on the type of consulting and related services one would offer. Still another objective would be on the type of organizations targeted for the practice.

Developing a business plan should begin with a mission, vision, and values. The mission defines the purpose of the consulting firm; the vision describes the ultimate outcome desired; and the values are the important principles and beliefs necessary to achieve success. One example of a mission statement for a team-building consulting firm is to provide a variety of consulting services and to develop teams and team-based models within client organizations so that the organizations will achieve the desired success.

Your business plan should identify what will make your consulting business successful. Typical areas addressed in the plan are:

1. Background information thoroughly documenting why the business exists and what has transpired to date. This would include statements of expertise and a description of the niche opportunity that exists.

Table 2-1 The Work Life Shift to Consulting

Areas and Issues	Large Organization	Small Consulting Firm
1. Work Life	Routine schedule, usually 9 a.m–5 p.m.	Hectic, frantic schedule; long hours
2. Business Plan	200 pages with historical data and extrapolation	20 pages of dreams and wishful thinking
3. Positioning	Being all things to all people	Finding a niche and dominating it
4. Culture	Developed and refined over the years	Based on the philosophy and value systems of lead consultant
5. Sales Pitch	75 slides and two hours	12 slides and 20 minutes
6. Job Security	Very little	Complete control
7. Branding	Advertising on network TV	Networking, evangelizing in the trenches
8. Staff Support	Ample, but decreasing	Little or no support
9. Recruiting/Training	Structured recruiting from *Fortune* 500 firms; formal training and transition process	Recruits high-risk takers, no formal training or transition
10. Expense Control	Staying at the Marriott instead of the Ritz-Carlton	Staying with a friend instead of Motel 6
11. Partnering	Developing win-lose deals that sound good to the press	Developing partnerships and alliances to increase sales

Adapted from Guy Kawasaki, *The Art of The Start: The Time-Tested, Battle-Hardened Guide for Anyone Starting Anything* (New York: Portfolio, 2004).

2. Strategic objectives detailing what needs to be achieved in the long term to make the business successful.
3. Tactical objectives relating to short-term implementation steps as the business grows.
4. Resource requirements for sustaining and growing the business. These include marketing support, new locations, additional funding, and expertise.
5. Progress and performance since the last review of the business plan.
6. Outlook showing the realistic prospects of the business and what can be accomplished in the future under different scenarios.

The business plan is a living, workable document. It must be reviewed and updated periodically. "Plan, do, and adjust" is the philosophy. While the plan becomes a working document for the consulting staff, it also is an important document for others, such as bankers, alliance partners, key clients, prospective staff members, and potential owners. The next chapter is devoted to developing the plan.

Attract and Retain New Clients

An obvious and essential ingredient for success in a new business is attracting and retaining the right clients. Along with selling personal services, a consulting practice must focus on marketing processes and concepts. This involves several key elements:

1. A marketing plan, which details the types of marketing, the appropriate mix, and the implementation strategy, including timing, costs, and other issues.
2. The image of the principal owner, which is created through presentations and documentations and which addresses the philosophy, mission, approach, expertise, and niche process the consulting firm can offer.
3. Marketing materials, which present the consulting practice on business cards, letterhead, brochures, handouts, and the firm's Web site. Documentation also may include testimonials, articles, and books.
4. The use of the Web and the Internet, which are among the best marketing tools for presenting the image and approach and for capturing success.
5. Proposals and contracts, which detail the terms of how the consultant focuses on clients.
6. Building client relationships, which strengthen existing business relationships and expand into new opportunities.

Create the Right Structure

The structure of a consulting firm involves several issues that must be addressed early in the process. Among these issues is the basic type of legal entity planned, whether it is a sole proprietorship, corporation, or partnership. The extent to which other associates or employees will be involved is another issue, as is the decision to have formal office space or to conduct business in a home office. The desired scope of operation in terms of local, national, or international reach is another consideration. If a global strategy is the aim, then appropriate representation must be secured in other countries.

The organizational structure, reporting relationships, lines of authority, and working relationships must be designed. Will they be rigid, loose, or somewhere in between? An example of a loosely structured organization is Indigo Partners, a Silicon Valley consulting firm with six consultants specializing in marketing for high-tech firms. Indigo has no office, no secretarial pool, no overhead, and no assets to manage. A partner can take off as much time as he or she wants.

The use of subcontractors is still another issue. Some consulting firms choose to subcontract some of their work, while others do not. Collectively, these and other structural issues determine the basic organizational form of your consulting practice.

Address the Financial Issues

No topic is more important than the finances of a consulting practice. The initial funding often is the first step in developing the business. The type of ownership (i.e., who owns the business) and what type of stock is issued also are important considerations. The need for adequate capital to keep the business going should be part of the original plan, and having the appropriate budgeting process to take the organization through its early startup is critical. Appropriate, fair, and equitable fees and pricing structures must be established, and financial reporting must be in place so the operational results will be known and cash flow can be followed. Later, several issues may surface, such as increasing fees to cover rising prices, the collection of revenue, and addressing bad debt situations should they arise.

Most consultants typically do not have financial and accounting expertise. If this is the case for you, it will be necessary to arrange for that expertise, employing an accountant or CPA, at least part-time. Financial issues are vital and must be addressed often and thoroughly to ensure that the business remains fiscally sound. We will explore financial issues in a later chapter.

Manage the Business Effectively

For some consultants, the most unpleasant and distasteful aspect of consulting is managing the business itself. Because most entrepreneurs are not good managers, one classic reason for failure is that they neglect this important issue. Even a one-person practice involves some management issues.

As the practice grows, you may need to employ a business manager, operations manager, or administrative manager. One of the key issues here is not only finding the appropriate person, but also being willing to let go of operational control of the organization. A common fact that must be dealt with is that many consultants/owners—particularly sole proprietors—are unwilling to let others manage the business.

An effective business manager can maintain the operations, implement appropriate controls, and build the team. The consultant/owner is often absent due to working in the field with clients. With increased success come increased absences from the office. The support staff needs direction and someone available to make day-to-day decisions. A business manager may be the answer for most small consulting businesses. We will go into this in a later chapter.

Develop a Unique Approach

Every consultant uses a process that clearly defines the practice—usually an expertise developed over several years. The process may include accepted principles with defined and articulated techniques, models, and methods. That process usually determines the niche opportunity and enhances the uniqueness of the practice.

The consulting practice may be connected to an existing, well-known model or methodology. In this case, the consulting process must be standardized with procedures and practices that are documented and spelled out, ensuring that the expressed method is available, adhered to, and consistent from one project to another. As other consultants use that process, the same standards and procedures must apply. The documentation of the process may include an underlying philosophy as well.

Develop Products and Support Tools

Some consultants find an advantage in developing other products and tools. Without them, the only source of revenue for the practice is the consultant's time, and when the consultant does not work—whether due to vacation, illness, or other factors—no revenue is generated.

Additional products and services complement the consulting process not only in terms of income production, but also as excellent tools for clients and patrons to understand and use the processes. Products and tools often enhance the credibility of both the process and the consultant and should complement the consulting process and not be perceived as add-ons to justify charging more or larger fees. The client should be provided with useful tools that can make the consulting assignment more successful, while the products and tools offered generate other sources of revenue for the consulting business.

Create Effective Proposals and Reports

A well-written proposal can make the difference between attracting and losing a new client. Some consultants prefer to document as little as possible in a proposal, attempting to describe the project in conversations and to bind the consultation commitment with a handshake. This informal approach inevitably creates problems later. Written proposals avert misunderstandings and miscommunications. More important, a well-crafted document represents an opportunity to showcase the organization and sell the consulting firm.

A winning proposal begins with clearly defined objectives. The elements of a proposal can vary considerably, but should include the following:

1. *Background and situation.* This is a detailed understanding of the problem and the current situation. It is presented so that the client and consultant agree on the current situation and the statement of the problem that will be addressed.
2. *Objectives of the project.* These objectives define what will be accomplished and the ultimate outcome of the project.
3. *Assumptions.* Various assumptions important to the project are developed and listed.
4. *Methodology.* The consulting process is outlined and includes steps, techniques, models, and approaches that are clearly established. This is the heart of the consulting practice and provides the beat by which the consulting project will move forward.
5. *Deliverables.* Include a list of exactly what will be delivered at the end of the project.
6. *Specific steps.* In addition to the methodology, the specific steps that will be needed as the deliverables are developed and presented are detailed.
7. *Project costs.* A detailed listing of costs is presented. Sometimes there is concern about detailing too many costs; however, it's better to show the client the detailed costs in advance than to have

added costs at the end of the project. This approach builds credibility and respect for the consultant and the practice.

8. *Satisfaction guarantee.* A statement of a guarantee is essential.

Once it has been accepted, the proposal provides a reference point throughout the project, spelling out exactly what is to be delivered, when, how, and at what cost. It should be reviewed often—and not allowed to collect dust until the end of the project. Because of the importance of the proposal process, we will devote an entire chapter to it.

Use a Results-Based Process

A pivotal concern for the consultant is focusing on the results that are attuned to client expectations. Without the proper focus on results, consulting assignments can easily go astray. The client ends up being dissatisfied, and this may result in not only lost business, but also in litigation. A well-defined philosophy of delivering results forestalls this eventuality. The ultimate outcomes (expressed as deliverables) are clearly delineated, as is the process for meeting client expectations throughout the project.

A results-based approach to consulting consists of several elements:

1. Consulting projects are designed with precise measures and are initiated, planned, developed, and implemented with the end in mind.
2. A measurement and evaluation system is in place for each consulting project.
3. Several approaches are used to measure consulting success, representing a balanced profile of data.
4. Return on investment evaluations are developed for a few selected consulting projects.
5. Stakeholders understand their responsibilities in making the consultation engagement successful.
6. Support groups (i.e., management, supervisors, and coworkers) help to achieve results from consulting.
7. Consulting results are routinely reported to a variety of target audiences.

An important element of the results-based approach is to guarantee satisfaction. This concept, presented in Christopher Hart's book *Extraordinary Guarantees,* shows how service providers can gain a competitive advantage by guaranteeing their work.[2] The following is the author's own consulting firm's guarantee:

> *Our work is guaranteed to the complete satisfaction of the client. If the client is not completely satisfied with our services, we will, at the client's option, either waive professional fees or accept a portion of those fees that reflect the client's level of satisfaction.*

At first this might seem outrageous—a professional firm guaranteeing work! How can you make a guarantee like that when consulting services are subject to so many influences? It's important to point out that what is guaranteed is *satisfaction.* It's not a guarantee that a specific *result* will be achieved, but rather, a guarantee of the client's complete satisfaction, which most firms say they are dedicated to anyway. It is certainly a concept worth pursuing, particularly early in the proposal process.

Operate in an Ethical Way

Operating ethical standards, defined as the value system of the owner/consultant, typically are developed as the consulting firm is structured. These standards often are a reflection of personal convictions and define how the consultant will operate in given situations.

Ethical issues surface in many ways. In the professional arena, the consultant may be asked to deliver results completely different from those that were planned. In the personal sphere, the client may require that the work be completed on an unrealistic, perhaps impossible schedule. In an interpersonal situation, the relationship with a client may be difficult and demanding. There could be organizational issues where the culture and dysfunctional practice of the organization interfere with the completion of the project.

Whatever the ethical issues, when they arise, they must be addressed quickly. Ethical issues materialize from the perspective of both the consultant and the client. The consultant must establish appropriate ethical standards and communicate them clearly, so that the consultant her- or himself does not become the ethical issue.

Measure Success and Communicate Routinely

The success of individual consulting projects is directly linked to the overall success of the firm. But, of course, success is measured in different ways.

Positive financial results are usually the first definition of success: profits or the reduction of losses extending over an initial time period. It may also include other financial goals, such as the profit per assignment, office expense, revenue per consultant, and so forth. Without financial success, at least in the long term, the consulting firm will not survive.

But in reality, client success must come before the consultant's financial success. After all, if clients are dissatisfied, the consulting business probably will fail ultimately. Not only will there not be repeat business with that client, but there likely will be a loss of engagements with other clients as well. Routine client satisfaction data must be collected to keep tabs on this critical dynamic.

And then there is the personal success one experiences in delivering consulting services. Consulting is a rewarding process when it operates correctly—when the consultant provides counsel that assists the client in measurable ways. Personal success is a powerful motivator in maintaining the discipline and determination necessary to make the practice work.

When measuring the success of a given consulting project, seven types of measures are necessary: satisfaction, learning, implementation, impact, costs, ROI, and intangibles. This approach reflects a balanced set of measures by which data are collected in different categories and at different time frames, often from different individuals. It is very credible, as the process always includes some method to isolate the effects of the consulting. Not all firms are using these seven measures, but it is an ultimate goal of many firms.[3]

Communication is also an important issue. Routine communication throughout the project is critical. Reporting results through a variety of changes is necessary to reach the stakeholders. Subsequent chapters will address these measurement and communication issues.

Check Your Skills

Consulting requires a specific set of skills that may be different from those demanded in other types of work. Although almost everyone does some consulting no matter what the profession or job description, a full-time consulting effort demands distinct skills. While other skills can be helpful in the consulting task, the following are among the most important skills needed for the successful consulting practitioner.

Communication Skills

Perhaps the most important skills for the full-time consultant are communication skills, both written and oral. Consultants must be able to communicate effectively with potential clients—listening, understanding their needs, articulating the solution, proposing projects, and reporting results.

During the project, the consultant must routinely communicate with the client in an open and honest fashion, and when the project is complete, the consultant will generate a report. Writing skills are crucial. What the consultant documents essentially reflects his or her work and reputation. Oral communication skills are also crucial when the project is completed, so that the process and results are understood and the recommendations for action are based on a compelling case.

Observation and Feedback Skills

During the consulting project, the consultant must observe, listen, and be aware of the different inputs, positions, balances, and misunderstandings. The consultant must be a careful listener and be able to provide information to the client and other stakeholders to ensure that both groups understand the consultant's observations and analysis. Sometimes feedback is informal, and sometimes it's structured, but in any case, it is almost always routine during a project.

Problem Solving and Analytical Skills

At the heart of most consulting projects is the ability to help the client solve a problem, grapple with an issue that seems insurmountable, or explore an area that may be new territory. The consultant must be able to sort through the issues, uncover potential causes of problems, and allow the interaction between the factors to lead to solutions—solutions that are incremental and practical. Some projects will require significant data analysis using a variety of systems and routines. The consultant must be familiar with these techniques or at least find someone who can provide these services. At a minimum, the consultant must understand the analysis and be able to reach conclusions.

Independence

A consultant often works independently, and frequently without the structure of typical and articulated job duties. The consultant often must initiate activities and set and stay within schedules, essentially working autonomously. He or she must therefore be a self-starter and capable of working without close supervision.

Organization

Successful consultants must be highly organized. They must work through checklists, to-do lists, and other planning tools. They must adhere to schedules and project management tasks, using a range of templates and tools to keep themselves and the project on track—avoiding sloppiness, procrastination, and tardiness. Otherwise, clients and others will justifiably be upset.

Understanding Feelings and Relationships

Consultants must understand other people's feelings and be empathetic, appreciating the human dynamics at play within myriad issues and concerns. Consultants must also understand their own strengths and weaknesses and how these may influence others during the process.

Relationship Building

The successful consultant must build relationships with individuals and teams. When working with a group, the consultant must make sure that each person is engaged and that the group functions as a productive team.

Create an Exit Strategy

Early in the process, ideally from the very beginning, it is important to focus on an exit strategy—the way in which the business will eventually phase out or change hands. Unfortunately, this is usually not given sufficient attention in the early phases, and as a result, problems develop later. Sometimes a consultant wants to sell the business but because of early decisions, finds that the business is not as marketable as expected. As ownership changes hands, even to different members of a family, there often are financial, legal, and tax implications that need to be addressed. Lack of planning can create costly and emotionally charged complications. Several avenues are available that prescribe the fate of a business, which we will discuss later.

Have Patience

Patience is a cornerstone to success. Consulting practices are not developed in three months or six months, but often take years to achieve success. In our publication of successful consulting practices, we required at least a two-year track record of successful operation for a practice to be included in the book.

For most consulting firms, it takes at least two years to reach an initial index of success—breaking even financially and maybe even turning a profit, if they're lucky. An impatient person will not be a successful consultant. While impatience with one's own skills or application and abilities may serve a useful purpose for the consultant's own growth, building relationships, developing clients, and developing a database of successful projects will take months and years to generate and mature. Patience is needed throughout the process.

Figure 2-1   The Path to Success

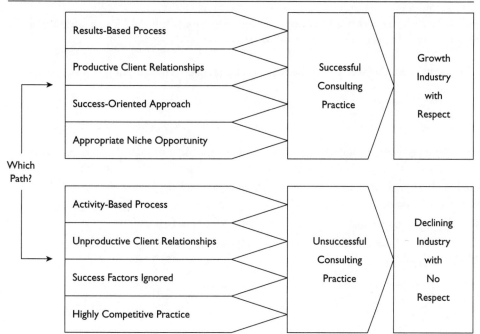

Final Thoughts

In this chapter we explored the basic factors essential to success in consulting. Each must be considered when starting a consulting practice or as a reminder while operating an existing consulting practice. Collectively, the various factors form an important framework in initiating the consulting practice and in delivering services as the practice grows.

While there is no absolute prescription for achieving success in consulting, we attempted to illuminate some of the key issues involved in developing a successful consulting practice. Our focus has been on small consulting practices, even one-person operations. In sheer numbers, such small practices represent the vast majority of consultants.

As mentioned in the previous chapter, consulting does not necessarily have a great reputation, and many consultants fail in their initial try at this occupation. It does not have to be that way. We are seeing many important changes in the consulting profession. As Figure 2-1 shows, a consultant can choose the path that leads toward success and helping the industry as a whole, or the route that has proven to be unsuccessful and contributed to the decline of the industry.[4]

The path to success involves not only the success factors set out in this chapter, but also rests upon four important principles:

1. The approach must be results-based throughout the process.

2. There must be very productive client relationships.
3. Skills and attitudes must be grounded in the expectation of success.
4. There must be a niche opportunity, either providing a service that no one else is offering or providing a service that is much better than others do now.

When these exist, we help build successful consulting practices and help our industry grow.

Notes

[1] Patricia Pulliam Phillips (ed.) and Jack J. Phillips (series ed.), *In Action: Building a Successful Consulting Practice* (Alexandria, Virginia: American Society for Training and Development, 2002).

[2] Christopher W. Hart, *Extraordinary Guarantees: Achieving Breakthrough Gains in Quality & Customer Satisfaction* (New York: AMACOM, 1993).

[3] Jack J. Phillips, *The Consultant's Scorecard* (New York: McGraw-Hill, 2000).

[4] Ron A. Carucci and Toby J. Tetenbaum, *How to Build and Sustain Lasting Client Relationships* (New York: AMACOM, 2000).

DEVELOPING THE BUSINESS PLAN

Perhaps the most important step in creating a successful consulting practice is developing an effective, livable business plan. Although some individuals regard this as an unnecessary step, or a process only required for investors or bankers, a properly used business plan can make a critical difference in the ongoing success of the organization. To achieve this, the plan must be developed following specific guidelines and with the right spirit and process in each step.

In this chapter we will show how the business plan is developed, presenting a step-by-step format for crafting the most important document for the consulting practice. A sample detailed outline of the plan is included.

Importance of the Business Plan

To understand the purpose of the business plan, you must first understand the *need* for the business plan. Is it being developed as a management tool or to secure funding? Is it being developed to achieve certain objectives or specific milestones? Is it being developed to impress various stakeholders? Whatever the reasons, the plan itself is critical. By definition, the business plan is the framework, strategy, resources, and the means necessary to develop a successful consulting practice. This definition begins to position the importance of the plan.

Is it necessary? This is an important question to raise. After all, there might well be resistance to developing a document that averages 20 to 40 pages. In fact, just the process of developing the plan encourages the principal owners (consultants) and other staff members to think strategically about the business. It also requires examination of all important aspects of the business and anticipating challenges and obstacles, and can be used as a tool to collect input and stimulate ideas from various stakeholders— particularly those who will be most involved in the consulting practice.

The result is a living document that clearly addresses the strengths and weaknesses of the consulting practice while communicating the visions and expectations for the future. If investors or loans are needed, this document provides the information necessary for the investment or lending decision. The business plan also serves as a tool for measuring the progress as important milestones are achieved and, through its revision, becomes a historical document highlighting how things have evolved and changed from the beginning to the present.

A business plan is not just for new consulting practices; it also should be in place for existing practices. While it is essential for a start-up business—because the plan shows how the practice will thrive and grow—it shows how the existing practice will be sustained, grow, and become even more successful in the future. Thus, it should be a living document for all types of consulting practices in any stage of maturity.

For Whom Is the Plan Written?

It's helpful to identify the stakeholders. Table 3-1 shows the major stakeholders who would be interested or involved in the development of the business plan.

Perhaps the most critical stakeholder is the owner of the business. The business plan provides him or her with a tool to develop and manage the business and help it grow. It also is an excellent tool for consultants and the support staff to provide input when they help to develop the plan. The support staff includes all employees other than the owner or consultants. For a small consulting practice, this may be a very small group. For a one-person consulting practice, there are no staff members, but there may be in the future. In the one-person situation, the "staff" could include those providing important outsourced services such as bookkeeping, transcription, typing, and office support functions.

The investors obviously will need a copy of the plan, since they are concerned with the success of the business. The plan forms a basis for their decision to invest in the practice. But since few consulting firms actually have investors, these could be stakeholders who are not active or involved but might be in the future. In any case, the plan should be written as if there will be an investor in the future, since this will add that perspective in the plan's development and presentation.

Various partnerships and alliances that are created in the business may be another important type of stakeholder, so long as the information in the plan is not sensitive. Most partners need to know how your business is growing, what is planned, and the key issues, challenges, and opportunities. In some cases, certain customers may be a key audience. This is particularly important for consulting practices that have just a few large customers—customers so important to the practice that it's helpful for

Table 3-1 The Role of Stakeholders in the Business Plan

Stakeholders	Develop the Plan	Review the Plan	Approve the Plan	Receive a Copy of the Plan
Owners	✓	✓	✓	✓
Consultants	✓	✓	✓	✓
Support Staff	✓	✓		✓
Investors	✓	✓	✓	✓
Partners/Alliances				✓
Bankers		✓	✓	✓
Key Customers				✓
Other VIPs				✓

them to see how your business is being developed and how it will evolve. If the financial portions are sensitive, they can be omitted for those stakeholders.

Finally, there may be other VIPs who could be partners in the future, or professional colleagues and others who are interested perhaps from a mentoring or coaching standpoint. The business plan provides an excellent vehicle to show these parties how the practice ideally would evolve.

While the content of the document is very important, its effective use is paramount. It must include input from others and undergo regular reviews and adjustments. In effect, it becomes a living document that evolves as the business does, and it should stay in step with the current state of the practice.

Before beginning to write the document, there are questions that should be answered. Table 3-2 lists 25 questions that are fundamental to the development of the plan. Some of these issues were explored in the first two chapters, and we will fully explore them in this chapter and in the rest of the book. Also, some of these questions are fundamental to the basic reason for the consulting practice to be developed. Take a few minutes to study them.

An outline of the typical business plan is shown in Table 3-3. It covers all of the major topics and issues that must be addressed for the plan to be effective, efficient, and usable. It may be necessary to add more detail for larger, more involved consulting practices, while it may be shortened and abbreviated for smaller operations, such as a one-person shop.

As you can see the presentation of the business plan should be clean and professional. Table 3-4 provides a list of guidelines for developing this document.

It may be helpful to seek professional advice for certain issues. In some cases, legal advice might be useful in determining the best exit strategy, as well as insurance and estate planning. Legal advice could also be helpful in deciding on the most suitable form of business organization, and preparing and filing papers of incorporation or similar documents. And professional accounting advice may be needed for the financial portion of the plan.

Table 3-2 25 Questions to Answer Before Developing the Business Plan

1.	What is the nature of the consulting practice?	14.	What facilities are needed?
2.	What services are being provided?	15.	How will the business be managed?
3.	What values are important in the consulting practice?	16.	What professional support will be needed?
4.	What market does this practice satisfy?	17.	What is the staffing philosophy?
5.	What is the size of the market?	18.	What are the income projections?
6.	Who is our customer?	19.	What are the capital requirements?
7.	Who are our competitors?	20.	What are the cash flow forecasts?
8.	What is our niche?	21.	What is the balance sheet?
9.	What, specifically, are our services and their advantages?	22.	What specific milestones must be achieved?
10.	How will customers be acquired?	23.	What risks might we face?
11.	How will customers be retained?	24.	What opportunities exist?
12.	What resources are needed?	25.	What is the exit strategy?
13.	What technology will be needed?		

Table 3-3 Outline of a Typical Business Plan

Title Page

Table of Contents

Executive Summary

1. **Purpose and Approach**

   A. Mission
   B. Vision
   C. Values

2. **Market Demands**

   - Target Market
   - Segregation
   - Size of Market
   - Client Description
   - Competition

3. **Products, Services, Niche**

   - Greatest Strength
   - Niche
   - Position
   - Services
   - Products
   - Special Features

4. **Client Development**

   - Acquiring Customers
   - Retaining Customers
   - Marketing Strategy

5. **Operations**

   - Facilities
   - Equipment
   - Technology
   - Resources

6. **Management**

   - Key Individuals
   - Job Description
   - Staffing Philosophy
   - Professional Support

7. **Financial Plan**

   - Sales Projections
   - Cost Projections
   - Profit Projection
   - Capital Requirements
   - Cash Flow Statement
   - Balance Sheet

8. **Goals and Milestones**

   - Sales
   - Clients
   - Profits
   - Staffing
   - Facilities
   - Technology
   - Alliances and Partnerships

9. **Risks and Opportunities**

10. **Exit Strategies**

   - Sell the Business to Outsider
   - The IPO Option
   - Hand Off to Associates
   - Hand Off to Family
   - Shut It Down

Purpose and Approach

Mission

Every organization, whatever its size—even a single individual—needs a mission statement to show the purpose of the consulting practice or individual consultant. This is an enduring statement, a purpose for an organization, identifying the scope of its operation in product and market terms and reflecting its values and priorities. A mission statement will help a company make consistent decisions, motivate, build an organization entity, integrate short-term objectives with longer term goals, and enhance communications.[1]

Essentially, the mission statement should have 50 words or less, describe what the consulting practice should provide, define its customers, and differentiate the practice from other consulting prac-

Table 3-4 Guidelines for Developing the Business Plan

1. Keep it in the range of 20 to 40 pages.
2. Plan for easy updating.
3. Address the document control issue.
4. Select a professional format and style.
5. Use precise, straightforward language.
6. Avoid jargon and terms unfamiliar to most audiences.
7. Use simple but professional binding.
8. Use metrics for financial and customer data.
9. Simplify financial projections.
10. Have one person develop the document.
11. Secure input from others.
12. Use references and appendixes

tices. Here are some examples of consulting firm mission statements, with the type of firms identified in parentheses:

- Provide America's small construction firms with top quality consulting services, helping them understand and meet their compliance responsibilities, and applying construction law with integrity and fairness to all. (Small consulting firm)
- We translate advanced technologies into value for our customers as the world's largest information services company. Our professionals worldwide provide expertise within specific industries, consulting services, systems integration, solution development, and technical support. (Large consulting firm)
- Our primary goal is to help organizations we serve in business, industry, education, and government to become the beneficiaries of advanced technology by providing software and consulting services to help them meet their organizational goals. (Software and consulting company)
- To exceed the expectations of our customers through the delivery of superior service and continuous quality improvement that rewards our employees and enhances the value of our shareholders' investment. (Small utility consulting firm)
- We provide outstanding advice in mergers and acquisitions integration and a valuable consulting experience to chief financial officers. (Small niche consulting firm)
- We provide consulting services on accountability of projects, programs, and solutions, including return on investment, to businesses, governments, and nonprofits throughout the world. (ROI Institute)

Vision

The vision differs from the mission statement. It is a concise word picture of the organization at some future time and, as such, sets the overall direction of the organization. It is what the consulting practice

Table 3-5 Value Statements for a Consulting Practice

1. Provide complete customer satisfaction, including full refunds or no invoices to dissatisfied customers.

2. Provide quick responses to customer inquiries and requests, at least within one business day.

3. Enhance the loyalty to customers by providing them outstanding services that are fairly and competitively priced.

4. Treat employees with respect and dignity at all times.

5. Foster a creative spirit among employees, recognizing accomplishments, improvements, and project completions.

6. Build loyalty among employees to enhance retention and commitment.

7. Offer above-market pay for qualified, productive employees.

8. Link employee rewards to key performance goals.

9. Operate efficiently with cost control in mind at all times.

10. Operate with the utmost integrity and trust, following precise ethical guidelines.

strives to be in the minds of the key stakeholders and clients. Further, a vision is something to be pursued, while a mission is something to be accomplished. For example, for the ROI Institute in the above list, the vision is to be recognized as a global leader in accountability, including measuring return on investment for businesses, governments, and nonprofits.

Value Statements

The values stated represent the collective principles and ideals that guide the thoughts and actions of the consulting practice's owners and managers. Values often define the character of the organization and its beliefs, essentially describing what the organization stands for as it pursues its business. Table 3-5 suggests possible value statements for a consulting firm.

Market Demand

Target Market

It's critical to understand the market that is being served by the consulting practice. It begins by clearly defining the market. Is the target audience a particular type of organization (or a part of it)? Is it a function, a subfunction, a department, or even individuals? A precise definition helps consultants and would-be consultants fully understand the potential.

Another issue to consider is "segmentation." That is, can the market be divided into different categories, and would the consulting practice pursue only parts of that market? For example, "consulting services provided to chief financial officers of publicly held companies" defines a particular market from an overall perspective. But the target market may be further narrowed to "consulting services for mergers and acquisitions (M&A)." So the actual market would be the funds or budget allocated for consulting on mergers and acquisitions. The segment may be only a part of this budget. Is the consulting decision (1) to formulate plans for seeking out mergers and acquisitions, or (2) to actually integrate M&A into the organizations, or (3) to evaluate the success of mergers and acquisitions? This step defines the particular niche provided by the consulting practice, which we will discuss in the next section.

Determining the size of the market will be an estimate, at least initially. More accurate figures may be available later. Some estimates may be based on a variety of publicly available reports and journals and Internet searches, while others might be based on expert input or the best guesses possible. For example, consider a consulting firm involved in developing and implementing leadership development programs. This particular consulting practice does not actually provide the leadership learning sessions, but rather, determines the needs, designs the programs, and implements them. Now ask yourself the key question: "What would be the potential market for this in the United States?"

Table 3-6 shows how this value was estimated.

First, the total market for learning development is determined. This value represents total direct expenditures for organizational training and development in both business and government. The sources for this were *Training* magazine's industry report, the American Society for Training and Development (ASTD), and Merrill Lynch. By combining their estimates, which were very similar, the $100 billion figure is considered a reasonable estimate.

Next, the amount of the total budget allocated to leadership development is estimated at 11 percent, based upon input from both *Training* magazine and ASTD. Then, the portion of that budget that was used for needs assessments, design, and implementation is estimated at 15 percent, based upon input from several leadership development specialists. This leads to $1.65 billion of this portion of the budget. The amount of that budget that is actually outsourced to others, again taken directly from the leadership development experts, was estimated to be 35 percent. This leaves an approximately $578 million target budget, which defines the total estimated market in the United States for both business and government.

As this is entered into the business plan, it is important to note that the overall learning and development budgets are growing significantly each year—faster than the producer price index—as is the total amount spent on leadership development, which means it takes in a bigger part of the overall budget. Thus, there is increased attention on the needs assessment, design, and implementation portion of leadership development to ensure that the appropriate leadership programs are implemented, and as a result, this percentage is increasing as well. Finally, the proportion of outsourcing is growing. In essence, this $578 million should grow at a faster pace than the actual growth of total learning and development expenditures each year. As projections are made, this number can be adjusted accordingly.

Table 3-6 How a Potential Market Is Estimated

THE FINANCIAL OPPORTUNITY

Learning Development Market

Total Direct Expenditures	$100 billion
Total Leadership Development Portion (11%)	$11 billion
Portion for Needs Assessment, Design, Implementation (15%)	$1.65 billion
Portion Outsourced (35%)	$578 million

The Client

Another important issue is to define the actual client, the individual(s) responsible for purchasing the consulting services. This may be a particular job title, or a series of job titles within an organization, or it could be individuals in a particular function area. In the example above, the chief learning officer (the person who leads the learning and development function), the human resources executive, or the individual in charge of the leadership development programs, could be the target individuals for the consulting service.

Competition

Finally, another important area to consider in describing the market demand is defining the competition. The extent of current and future competition is an important variable to understand, and to quantify, if possible. This will require defining who the competition is as accurately as it can be provided and describing how it differs from your consulting practice. It may require scanning the market, discussing the competition with perspective clients, and perhaps making contacts with competitors.

The most important issue is how the consulting practice will address competition—particularly if it promises to be stronger and more intense in the future. Stakeholders should clearly understand such competitive threats, as well as what the practice will do to minimize them. Table 3-7 shows a typical competitor analysis outline to compare your consulting practice with key competitors along several dimensions—in this case, five.

Defining Your Niche

As mentioned in the previous chapter, one of the most important considerations in the early stages of a consulting practice is defining a particular niche. A consulting practice should be based on an opportunity created because of a particular competitive advantage. This could be something the consultant can

Table 3-7 Competitor Analysis

Competitors	Reputation	Comparison with Your Practice			
		Quality of Consultants	Results Delivered	Unique Advantages	Pricing
Competitor A					
Competitor B					
Competitor C					
Competitor D					
Competitor E					
Competitor F					
Competitor G					

do that others cannot do, or that he or she can do much better (with less time) than others. The niche must be selected based on one of these three issues: more expertise, improved quality of service, or lower cost.

The narrower the niche, the less competition there will be, but then, the market will be smaller. The wider the niche, the larger the market and, consequently, the more competition. This niche may have to be selected in the context of examining the total market possibility and the competition discussed above. For example, in the leadership development consulting opportunity, the focus is on needs assessment, design, and implementation. A narrower niche may be just needs assessment—providing a service that focuses on determining the leadership needs. Alternatively, the focus could be on design or on implementation. Smaller niches make the market much smaller, but the key driver must be the expertise and reputation for the consultant or consulting practice.

After the niche is clearly identified, the exact services are detailed. For example, the assessment services, design services, and implementation services are defined. This may also include software, which is in the form of a product, and it also may involve providing workshops to explain the process or teaching others to do it if part of the philosophy is to transfer skills to the organization. As the service or product is designed, determined, or defined, any special features or benefits should be detailed, showing how this service might stand out from others.

In summary, a good niche is an area:

1. In which you have extensive experience and skills
2. Characterized by a substantial market with substantial money
3. In which you have significant competitive advantage
4. In which competition is less, or at least not overly competitive
5. Accessible from the marketing perspective[2]

Client Development

The client development section of the business plan defines how the practice will develop clients and retain them in the future. Specific techniques, methods, and marketing tactics to acquire new customers should be outlined. Also, specific ways in which customers are retained to build customer loyalty should be highlighted. This exercise provides an opportunity to address the overall marketing, promotion, advertising, and public relations strategies—all in the name of developing and retaining key clients. Essentially, this part of the plan becomes the marketing plan. Because of the importance of this issue, we devote an entire chapter of the book to it.

Operations

The operations section of the plan is substantial for an ongoing operation with hundreds of employees, but it would be minor for a small consulting practice with just one consultant.

The operations section identifies the way in which the business is actually operated. It will define specific processes or systems that are important to success and how they are utilized, whether automated or manual. It describes the equipment currently in use or planned for purchase and how it will be utilized. The section would include statements on the use of technology. (For some consulting firms, technology will be an important, and perhaps even critical part of the delivery, and should be defined in terms of scope, use, and cost.)

The operations section will also define office space requirements and specific facilities needs. This could range from a consultant working at home, to having multiple offices for consultants. The approach to acquiring and owning facilities would be described (lease versus purchase), and finally, the various resources needed to make the organization function, such as significant outsourcing arrangements, subcontractors, or suppliers, would be identified.

Management

Another important part of the business plan details how the consulting practice will be managed. This section should describe the job scopes or descriptions of key management staff. For a small consulting practice, the manager is the consultant. For larger practices, managing partners and other leaders in the organization are the key management staff. This section should also define the staffing philosophy in terms of outsourcing or employing additional staff and the additional professional support that might be needed as part of the delivery of services. Finally, the section provides an opportunity to describe management philosophies, management control systems, and other issues important to understanding how the practice is governed.

Financial Plan

For some stakeholders this is the most critical part of the business plan. In describing the financial aspects of the business, it presents sales projections, usually for a three- to five-year time frame, and projects significant cost items and future profits. These can be combined in the form of an income statement showing revenue, expenses, and profits. The financial plan would detail the capital requirements and how they will be funded, show cash flow anticipated for the three- to five-year period, and present balance sheets for that time frame. An entire chapter is devoted to this topic.

Goals and Milestones

At the heart of a business plan are the specific goals and milestones. These provide the focus for the key stakeholders, particularly the owners and the employees who must meet specific targets, and include goals for monthly, quarterly, and annual sales. The number of clients might also be included here. Client growth is important, and the different types of clients may be underscored. If appropriate, rollout of new products and services would be included in the timetables.

Profit goals also are included. If it is a start-up consulting practice, profits may not be generated for several months or even a couple of years. The goal is to minimize losses and bring the practice to profitability as soon as possible. Staffing targets may be established as additional staff members are recruited and new consultants are added, according to specific timetables. Growth of offices or facilities is included as well. New equipment and technology are detailed, with time frames for purchase and implementation. Alliances or partnerships are included.

This part of the plan should be reviewed routinely by the management and staff so adjustments can be made. The goals it details often reflect the performance expectations of key staff members.

Risks and Opportunities

The business plan also should include any potential risks. These risks may involve technology developments that would threaten consulting opportunities, the emergence of large consulting firms that could dominate the market, or the potential loss of business through outsourcing or offshoring of work. Risk assessments require a good understanding of the market and how it may evolve in the future, based upon developing trends.

This section would also address significant opportunities, representing the upside potential, detailing how things may change or develop that could benefit the practice in the future. For some firms this exercise may involve scenario planning, where a small number of possible scenarios are described, both good and bad. For each one, the impact on the business is examined, along with the firm's reaction to it. Table 3-8 shows a sample structure to capture this information.

Exit Strategy

Although sometimes overlooked, part of the business plan should detail specific exit strategies applicable to both eventual and unforeseen changes in the ownership of the business. There is often a reluctance to address this issue because it seems so far away and thus not necessary to include in the business plan. However, planning can make a huge difference.

The exit strategy should be considered ideally when the firm is first established. If not, it should be developed soon, so that plans can be made and the relevant legal issues addressed without duress.

Table 3-8 Scenario Planning

Risk and Opportunities	Impact and Action	
	How it will affect the business	What we will do about it
Adverse		
Scenario 1		
Scenario 2		
Scenario 3		
Positive		
Scenario 1		
Scenario 2		
Scenario 3		

As the old saying goes, "Only two things are certain: death and taxes." Both should factor into the exit strategies. If an owner dies, there will be a change of ownership, and thus the exit strategy selected may create tax consequences for the acquiring party.

Essentially there are six options for exit strategies:

1. Sell the business to an outsider. This could be a company looking to expand the services they provide by entering your market, another consulting firm looking to expand their market share, or someone interested in stepping into an ongoing consulting business. If this strategy is selected, the focus is on making it attractive to another buyer, which would drive some of the strategy, some of the product lines, and some of the performance goals.
2. As the business grows, consider an initial public offering (IPO). This is taking the business public, and through a small offering, making it available or public purchase. For this to occur, the consulting firm has to be of considerable size, probably in excess of $100 million in annual revenue, and must be successful enough to attract sufficient investor attention. If this strategy is selected, the important thing to remember is that profit and growth attract investors.
3. Hand it off to associates. Let the people who actively provide the services purchase it. This can be done through a simple change of ownership, distributing shares among employees, selling them to employees using stock options as a vehicle, or developing an employee stock ownership plan (ESOP). Such arrangements can get quite complicated, though, and may require the help of an investment counselor, a corporate tax lawyer, or a CPA.
4. Hand it off to family members so the ownership continues through the next generation. If this option is pursued, there are several steps that can be taken to minimize the tax consequences. However, problems sometimes surface, since the other family members may not be as capable as the original owner(s) and may not have sufficient interest to continue its successful growth. This, unfortunately, leads to negative but all too familiar results.
5. Simply close the business, perhaps referring the consulting opportunities and contacts to other colleagues in the industry. Such a drastic move usually is taken only when there are no other viable options, or when there are no other family members or associates who logically would be considered for hand-off ownership.
6. Let the practice die slowly. Let the business deteriorate as the principal owner or owners retire. This essentially requires cutting back on marketing and servicing clients until there are no more clients. Unfortunately, many small consulting practices end this way.

Because there are so many options, they should be addressed in the business plan, where various defined strategies and tactics can help move the business toward a suitable exit strategy.

Evaluating the Business Plan

After the plan is developed, it should be reviewed by the appropriate stakeholders, and adjustments could be made. This may be a time to bring in several tests to check for the soundness and appropriateness of the plan.[3]

Elevator Test
This test suggests that the business plan could be condensed into a very simple and straightforward statement. In other words, someone should be able to describe the business and what it is intended

to accomplish in the time it takes to ride the elevator. If it takes much more time than that, it may be overly complex and difficult to get others excited about it.

Three Rules Test

This essentially suggests that as the business plan is developed, stakeholders should ask themselves the following question: "What are the one to three things that are going to determine success?" Although the business plan is complete with details of these issues, the most important and critical ones need to surface here, and it is important that they are sufficiently addressed in the business plan.

Client Test

Put yourself in the position of a customer and ask yourself a range of questions. Would I purchase this consulting service if I were in the client's situation? If so, why? If not, why not? As a client, could I find others who could offer services that are equally unique? Am I satisfied for the price I am paying for this service? Finally, can I make this purchase decision without an extensive amount of education? Can I quickly make this decision based on what I know now?

Worst-Case Scenarios Test

This would mean, for example, examining the possibility of a huge competitor entering the market and taking away clients, or of your associates or partners beginning to compete directly with you and taking much of the business with them. The question to ask yourself is, "What would be my approach to this, and how could I survive?"

Cost of the Business Test

If this is a new start-up consulting practice, costs were projected and may be understated. Historically, costs are understated and revenues are overstated. Therefore, ask the question: "If I double my cost, is this still a good business proposition?" If the answer is yes, then it's a good plan. If not, there may be some issues to address.

Dependency on a Supplier or Client Test

Quite often, consulting practices are built around one or two initial clients, or on a particular industry with just a select few possible clients. The rule of thumb is that no single client should account for more than 35 percent of the revenue stream. If there is a heavy dependency on a single supplier or customer, then the obvious question is, "How do we deal with this and reduce the dependency in the future?"

Can It Survive Test

For entrepreneur consultants, where the business is built around one individual, the obvious question is, "Can it survive without me?" What would happen if the principal consultant unexpectedly dies or is incapacitated? Can it survive without that person? That is the key question. If the answer is no, then the business plan must address what is being done to safeguard against such worst-case scenarios.

Diversity of Services and Product Base Test

Other products provide multiple streams of income, not only from different clients, but from different industries, maybe even through diverse service offerings. Some consulting firms add product lines to their consulting services, in the form of software, equipment, job aids, books, and other products that can be marketed along with the consulting services, thus providing multiple income streams and ensuring that it is not a one-trick organization. These tests are critical in making sure that the business plan is appropriate and reflects the information necessary to survive.

Living the Plan

The final step in the development and use of the business plan is the ongoing review of the plan, including checking the milestones and timetables, reevaluating the assumptions and materials, and making adjustments as necessary. As has been said before, this must be a living document that is constantly changing as different assumptions emerge, different facts become known, and market conditions change. The plan itself should be revised on a periodic basis—usually annually, but sometimes more often if the business operates in a fast-growing market. It is important for the plan to remain current and to be as flexible as possible.

Final Thoughts

This chapter focuses on the most critical step a consulting firm can take: developing a business plan. Whether it's a start-up consulting practice or an existing one, the business plan becomes a central document that drives the business, keeps it on track, and sharpens its focus. It addresses various opportunities and possibilities and prompts the staff, managers, and other stakeholders to continually think through important issues, evaluate challenging scenarios, and offer new ideas to improve the practice and its operating environment. If developed properly and used appropriately, the plan can be the most important element for success.

Notes

[1] Jeffrey Abrahams, *The Mission Statement Book Revised: 301 Corporate Mission Statements from America's Top Companies* (Berkeley, California: Ten Speed Press, 1999).

[2] Robert Bacal, *The Complete Idiot's Guide to Consulting* (Madison, Wisconsin: CWL Publishing Enterprises/Alpha Books, 2002)

[3] Bruce Judson, *Go It Alone: The Secret to Building a Successful Business on Your Own* (New York: Harper Business, 2004).

FINANCIAL ISSUES

Now for the hard part: the finances. This is an area that most consultants prefer not to enter, yet having a solid grasp of financial issues can make the difference between success and failure.

In this chapter we will explore the basic monetary issues and financial statements needed to run the business effectively and, hopefully, profitably. And we will discuss the concept of capital. Whether the consulting firm is new or existing, capital is an important issue. For new firms, there will be a need for start-up capital; for existing firms, working capital is needed, along with capital to fund growth. We will go into the difficult issue of pricing consulting services. A variety of pricing strategies are presented. And finally, we'll conclude with the responsibilities, for finance and accounting, of ensuring that appropriate staffing is in place to address the financial issues adequately.

Financial Fundamentals

Finance and accounting do not have to be complicated, and you do not need a degree in finance or a CPA background to manage the finances of a consulting practice. We'll go into the fundamentals of finances first. Those familiar with these issues may skip to the next section.

Income

The first and probably most important concept is income. The income that appears on an income statement is the actual sales or revenue. Thus, the terms "income," "sales," and "revenue" essentially mean the same thing; it is the money received for the consulting services. In addition to consulting, income may be generated from auxiliary services, such as workshops or publishing. Ultimately, it is the revenue for a determined period of time—monthly, quarterly, and annually.

Expenses

Expenses are usually divided into two parts. The direct expenses are those that are involved directly in delivering the product or service. For consulting, it is usually the salaries paid directly to the consultant.

If a contract consultant is used, the direct expenses are the actual amounts paid for those services. If products, such as books, are sold and there is a cost of the product, it is listed as the cost of goods sold. The other expenses are operating expenses; essentially all the other costs of doing business, ranging from advertising to utilities.

Profits

Now to the most important measure: profits. Profits are usually reported three ways.

- Gross profit is income minus direct expenses. This is sometimes called the "operating margin," and it reflects the gross profit made on the services or products sold.
- When the other expenses (operating expenses) are deducted, the net profit, or net income, before taxes is the remainder. (The taxes paid to various federal, state, and sometimes local governments are income taxes. However, sales tax and property taxes are considered part of the operating expenses.) This amount can be even further divided into two categories: operating income and net income, if there are other sources of income beyond the consulting operations.
- Profit, or net income after taxes, is the ultimate bottom-line measure. Sometimes the word "profit" is called net income, and sometimes a distinction is made between "ordinary income" and "extraordinary income." For example, the sale of an office building that adds income for the consulting practice is not ordinary income, but rather, extraordinary income.

Assets

The assets of the organization are usually divided into two categories: current assets and fixed assets.

Current assets are considered to be short-term or liquid assets. In other words, these are assets that can be quickly converted into cash. The most obvious current asset would be the amount of money in the checking account. Another category is what clients owe you, which is called "accounts receivable."

Fixed assets are considered to be more long-term, and thus cannot be readily liquidated to generate cash. These often include office buildings, real estate, and equipment that cannot necessarily be sold quickly. This category could also include automobiles or other vehicles used in the business.

Liabilities

The liabilities of the consulting practice include all debts and obligations owed by the business to suppliers, creditors, banks, and other parties. The most obvious liability is the accounts payable, which includes the amount of money owed to suppliers and other vendors for the services and materials used in operating the business. This also would include notes payable, which is money owed on a short-term payback cycle and usually involves bank notes, vehicle payments, and possibly even mortgage obligations. Finally, this category includes accrued payroll and withholding, which is money owed to employees but not yet paid to them.

Liabilities are further divided into current and long-term. Current liabilities are those that must be paid within a one-year time frame. Long-term liabilities span longer than one year.

Capital

The term "capital" refers to the amount of money you need to spend on productive items, usually with a life of more than 12 months, such as equipment, vehicles, computers, fixtures, office buildings, and other real property. Capital can be provided directly by the owner and represents the owner's capital. This is sometimes referred to as "owner's equity," or "stockholder's equity," and is made up of the initial investment in the business, as well as any retained earnings that are reinvested in the business. Sometimes others interested in investing in the business can purchase and be provided with equity in the form of shares of stock in the business. The total liabilities and equity in the organization must equal the total assets, and this represents the balance sheet.

Depreciation

The concept of depreciation is based on the fact that an asset loses value after purchased. Each year the asset loses value, until it no longer has value to the business. Measuring the loss of value of an asset is known as "depreciation."

Depreciation is considered an expense and is included in the operating expenses. Land is not considered an expense, nor can it be depreciated, since land does not wear out as equipment, buildings, and vehicles do.

Invoices

Invoices are the documents that provide the income stream for the consultant. The invoice is the official document that tells the client how much they owe in direct consulting fees and reimbursable expenses. Invoices become accounts receivables as soon as they are issued, and the accounts receivables become current assets for the company. When accounts are past due, they go into collections mode, where a variety of efforts are made to collect the amount due. If it is not collected, then it's deducted as a bad debt expense.

Cash Flow

Cash flow presents the inflow and outflow of cash to the business. It is extremely valuable because it reflects the amount of money on hand. This is essentially a recording of cash that flows into the business when invoices are paid and cash that flows out of the business when operating expenses are paid.

Income Statement

This is perhaps the most important statement. It is also known as a profit and loss (P&L) statement because it ultimately shows the amount of profits or losses generated during a given operating period. It is sometimes referred to as an "operating statement" and is typically generated monthly and summarized quarterly and annually.

For some consulting organizations, the income statement is simpler than that of other businesses because there is no inventory or cost of goods sold. However, other consulting firms offer products

Table 4-1 Income Statement

	Income Statement12 months ending December 31,2006
A. ORDINARY INCOME	
Consulting services	$4,456,000
Workshops	2,888,000
Speaking fees	528,000
Publications	1,241,735
Total Income	**$9,209,735**
B. DIRECT EXPENSES	
Salaries	1,548,792
External consulting services	3,249,315
Cost of books	785,911
Gross Profit	**$3,625,717**
C. OPERATING EXPENSES	
Advertising	45,933
Automobile expenses	28,510
Bank service charges	892
Books and resources	5,715
Copying and printing	229,417
Donations	3,924
Dues and subscriptions	6,595
External support services	11,988
Equipment leases	1,255
Insurance	11,439
Interest	45
Licenses and permits	2,154
Office supplies	74,324
Payroll—Staff	694,321
Payroll—Benefits, Staff	232,934
Postage and delivery	121,004
Professional development	92,795
Professional fees	23,850
Rent	86,400
Repairs and maintenance	18,105
Taxes—Sales	1,245
Taxes—Property	2,315
Telephone	29,483
Travel and Entertainment	
Airfare	178,278
Entertainment	45,112
Ground transportation	38,931
Lodging	207,585
Meals	67,398
Travel and entertainment—Other	5,317
Total Travel and Entertainment	542,621
Utilities	
Gas and electric	6,752
Water	4,896
Utilities—Other	454
Total Utilities	12,101
D. TOTAL EXPENSES	**$2,279,365**
E. NET ORDINARY INCOME BEFORE TAXES	1,346,325
F. TAXES	403,897
G. NET ORDINARY INCOME AFTER TAXES	942,428

for sale, such as books and software. When this is the case, there must be accounting for the cost of goods sold, the resulting revenue that is generated, and the value of inventory on hand.

An example of an income statement is shown in Table 4-1.

Accounting Software

It is critical to find an accounting software package that is useful and appropriate for the consulting practice. Many are available. Two of the most popular are QuickBooks and Peachtree Accounting. They are based on generating the proper statements and following generally accepted accounting principles. Each software supplier presents a variety of options for purchasing. Software will make the accounting process much easier, and software packages are very affordable.

Purpose and Use

The income statement is the principal tool for the consultant (or owner of the consulting firm) to understand how well the business is operating. It shows the income, the expenses, and the profits. It provides a tool to increase revenues, improve operating margins, control costs, and improve overall profits. The income statement can be used to find out what areas are operating within budget or over budget. Income and expenses can be separated by the particular types of consulting service or products offered. Examining income statements over time reveals trends in operating expenses, consulting income growth, and profitability. The income statement also is required for taxes, prospective investors, and potential lenders.

Income

Let's examine the different items on an income statement by considering an actual example from an existing consulting firm, as shown in Table 4-1. This firm provides consulting services, but also conducts workshops that in turn drive the consulting business. In addition, the principals in the firm write books that are used to support the workshops and consulting practice. The principals often speak at conferences and charge a fee for most speaking engagements.

There are four categories of ordinary income (listed in Part A). Ordinary means income directly related to the business. Extraordinary income is income generated through means other than the basic operation of the business—for example, a gain on the sale of an office building. In our example, there is an annual income of $9,209,735, also known as revenues or sales, for the entire year.

Direct Expenses

Expenses can be presented as direct and indirect, or direct and operating. Direct expenses are those that are most directly tied to the specific source of income. Obviously, for consulting, these would be the salaries of the consultants. In Table 4-1, Part B, some consultants are employees of the consulting firm, and others are external independent contractors. The salary total of $1,548,792 for consultants directly employed by the organization and of $3,249,315 for external consulting services represents the total direct costs of the individuals in providing the services. And then there is the cost of the books: $785,911. The three subtotals, added together, constitute the gross profit.

There is some variation as to what goes into direct expenses. For example, if there is a support staff directly tied to specific projects, and their total costs are absorbed, then they could be included here. The important point is to understand what goes into these costs and how they can be changed or managed over time. The gross profit for this organization, often called the operating margin, is $3,625,717.

Operating Expenses

The largest category of expenses is what is considered to be operating expenses. These are the expenses for maintaining the business.[1] In our Table 4-1 example, they are typical for a small- to medium-size consulting practice. The accounts are listed alphabetically, but could be listed in any order desired.

The advertising expenses include all those expenses directly tied to marketing, promoting, or advertising the services. These could include developing and printing of brochures, mailing brochures, hosting receptions, buying ads, and other advertising costs. Automobile expenses include expenses for company owned vehicles. The bank service charges are the fees charged by the bank to process the checks, and otherwise maintain the financial records of the organization. Books and resources represent the books purchased to be used or consumed by the business. In this example, some books are purchased for resale and are included in the direct expenses. Resources could include various benchmarking studies, reports, and other information that may be helpful in developing workshops, conducting consulting, or speaking at conferences.

Copying and printing is self-explanatory and is significant for this organization because of the number of workshops conducted. Printing professional-quality workbooks and handouts is quite expensive. This item also covers the cost of printing final reports for clients. The donations are the professional or charitable contributions made to various organizations. These not only include contributions to organizations such as the American Red Cross and the United Way, but also foundations that may be supported by the firm that could be helpful in the future.

Dues and subscriptions include dues to professional societies and subscriptions to professional magazines. In this example, this is significant, because of the publishing aspect of the company. This firm subscribes to 40 different publications to provide a research base for developing the books.

External support services would be any support needed, such as short-term administrative support or contract labor. It does not include the consultants, which are included in the direct expenses. Equipment leases represent the money paid to lease specific equipment, which can include software subscriptions or copier leases. Insurance reflects the insurance premiums paid by the organization and can include coverage for liability, theft, and casualty. Interest represents the part of interest that is paid to lenders. In this particular organization, interest is very low because there is virtually no debt.

Licenses and permits reflect business permits required to operate the company, as well as license arrangements to use a methodology or software. The sum is very low in this organization. Office supplies represent all of the necessary consumable materials used in the business, including paper, envelopes, paper clips, etc.

Payroll includes the salaries for all the support staff (i.e., all individuals not in the direct expenses). The "Payroll—Benefits" reflects all employee benefits, including health care premiums paid by the company, retirement plan contributions, and other benefits. Postage and delivery include all shipping costs, as well as postage for mailing materials to clients or prospective clients. Professional development includes the costs for training and preparing the staff, including the consultants. For this organization, this category represents roughly 4 percent of total payroll. Professional fees are the fees paid to accountants, attorneys, and other professionals who provide advice to the business.

Rent represents the cost for the offices. In this case, three facilities are owned by the principal consultants, but leased to the business at a competitive rental price. The repairs and maintenance category represents the repairs for the office and equipment, and routine maintenance for vehicles and equipment.

"Taxes—Sales" is included because books are actually sold, and this firm is required to pay sales taxes, but only for sales within the home state. "Taxes—Property" is the property taxes paid on office equipment (computers, servers, copiers, etc.) considered fixed assets. Telephone expenses include not only the direct lines, but also long distance and teleconferencing costs.

Travel and entertainment represent several different categories, including airfare, entertainment, ground transportation, lodging bills, and other expenses. Because there is significant travel involved, as with many other consulting firms, this part of the operating costs may be significant. Entertainment usually includes the cost of meals, items, or services for clients, business associates, and prospective clients. Ground transportation usually includes taxis and rental cars, and reimbursement of auto expenses. Lodging covers expenses for accommodations connected to travel, and meals are the business-related food and beverage costs. The "Other" category involves travel expenses not covered in the other categories such as tips and tolls.

The utilities are often divided into different categories, in this case natural gas, electricity, water, and other utilities, to calculate a total cost for all utilities. These are often just the utilities for the office space only.

The total operating expenses are noted in Part D.

Net Income

When the operating expenses are subtracted from gross profit, the calculation yields a net ordinary income before taxes. This is the operating income of the organization. State, local, and federal taxes are then subtracted to give the net income (or profits) of the consulting firm. This is probably the most important measure, but it must be examined in the context of trends and current conditions within the company. Profits may be low if, for example, there has been tremendous recent investment in developing new products and services, or in training and developing new staff members.

Balance Sheet

The second most important financial statement is the balance sheet. The term "balance" comes from the fact that the assets must be balanced with the total liabilities and equity, as described below. The balance sheet is essentially a snapshot of the financial condition of the consulting practice at a particular time, usually at the end of the accounting year. Most consulting firms use a calendar year, but essentially any time period can be used.

Purpose

A balance sheet will help the consulting firm assess the financial strength and capability of the business. It shows the capability to not only to sustain the business, but grow and expand in the future. It also indicates the ability to absorb shocks, changes, and adverse effects. The balance sheet can help identify trends, particularly with the accounts receivables and payables. As described later, accounts receivable is an area that must be given attention so that they do not create problems and, ultimately, become uncollectible.

As with the income statement, the balance sheet is an important document for lenders and prospective investors. It helps investors decide how much to invest and lenders decide how much to lend. For suppliers, the balance sheet shows the strength of the firm and may be helpful in deciding how much credit to provide.

Assets

Table 4-2 shows an example of a balance sheet from the same consulting firm described in Table 4-1. The balance sheet lists the assets and the liabilities and equity. The assets shown in Part A are divided into two categories: current assets and fixed assets.

Current Assets

As shown in Part B, the current assets usually involve four areas for consulting firms. The first is the actual cash in the checking account. It is important to ensure that there is always enough cash to cover

Table 4-2 Balance Sheet

Balance Sheet 12 months ending December 31, 2006	
A. ASSETS	
B. CURRENT ASSETS	
Checking	$ 175,848
Savings	1,723,457
Accounts receivable	1,143,924
Notes receivable	0
Total Current Assets	**$3,043,229**
C. FIXED ASSETS	
Buildings/equipment/vehicles	$1,545,895
Less: Accumulated depreciation	325,780
Total Fixed Assets	1,220,115
Intangible assets	140,500
D. TOTAL ASSETS	**$4,403,844**
E. LIABILITIES AND EQUITY	
Current Liabilities	
Accounts payable	$438,972
Notes payable	
Accrued payroll and withholdings	79,832
Total Current Liabilities	**$518,804**
Long-term Liabilities	
Note payable (Shareholder)	$500,000
Total Liabilities	$1,018,804
Equity	
Common stock	1,535,000
Retained earnings	1,850,040
Total Equity	**$3,385,040**
F. TOTAL LIABILITIES AND EQUITY	**$4,403,844**

the checks that must be written. It's also important to keep the checking account from being excessive (i.e., most banks do not pay interest on the checking account balance). Consequently, most firms will create a savings account. This is still liquid cash available to be transferred in and out of the checking account. It could be a money market account or some other type of investment vehicle where the money can be removed quickly.

Accounts receivables represent one of the most important items on the asset side of the balance sheet. They should be monitored routinely and managed appropriately, with the goal of minimizing the amount as much as possible. The current assets category for most consulting firms is notes receivable, representing the loans that the organization has made to other individuals or organizations, but which are payable within the year. For example, this could be a loan to a partner to develop the capability to represent the consulting firm in a particular area. In this specific organization, there are no loans to any individual or organization. Although the checking account balance is quite high, with the processing of the payroll and other routine payables, it may need to be at that level. The savings account is higher than you normally expect in a current asset category and represents an amount of cash that could be used for growth.

Fixed Assets
Buildings, equipment, and accumulated depreciation are the typical fixed asset categories. The buildings represent property owned by the firm. Office equipment represents equipment purchased and used by the firm and includes company-owned vehicles. The vehicles may be separated from office equipment in another category, just as land may be separated from buildings in a separate category. The accumulated depreciation is the depreciation charged on the fixed asset to date. It is subtracted from the fixed asset value, to get a total of fixed assets. Another possible asset category is the intangible assets. This usually represents intellectual property that has been purchased, or goodwill that has been placed on the books for some particular transaction. In the case of this specific firm, the intangible assets represent the purchase of software.

Liabilities and Equity

Liabilities
The liabilities are divided into two categories: current liabilities and long-term liabilities. For most consulting firms, the most important current liability is the accounts payable. This amount shows the money owed to vendors, suppliers, and contractors. Notes payable would be the actual short-term borrowing that may be in place to cover cash flow needs. These are notes payable in less than one year. The accrued payroll and withholding is the payroll that has not been paid at the time on the balance sheet, but is actually due to the employees. The long-term liabilities typically include long-term loans. In the case of this particular firm, there is a shareholder loan of $500,000, representing money loaned to the firm from the principal owner when the company was founded.

Equity
The equity category represents ownership in the company, and there can be several kinds of equity ownership. Common stock is typical for consulting firms. When stock is actually issued, it is placed on the balance sheet. In this particular firm, considerable stock amounts have been issued with a value

of $1,535,000. Another category of equity is the retained earnings. These are earnings invested in the business after any specific deductions or a specific distribution to shareholders, such as dividend payments. Retained earnings, in this example, have grown considerably, to $1,850,040. The total equity is the sum of the stock and retained earnings. Finally, the total of the liabilities and equity is the sum of the current and long-term liabilities and the total equity. For the sheet to be in balance, this number must equal the total assets.

Cash Flow Statement

In a consulting business, as with any business, cash is king, and the cash flow statement shows how cash is flowing in and out of the business. A faulty cash flow statement can spell the demise of the most successful-looking consulting firm. The cash flow statement shows how much money is on hand and available to take care of the business expenses. Although the income statement and balance sheet may suggest that there's a profit because consulting projects have been completed, the cash might be tied up in accounts receivable, or in the inventory (e.g., in the purchase of books).

The cash flow statement begins with listing the money on hand and available on short notice. This would include money in the bank, in both checking and savings accounts, and money available from various lenders.

Next, add the cash receipts from consulting revenue generated for the particular month from all sources. List the total of the beginning cash balance and the cash receipts from consulting revenue as the total cash available. From the total cash available subtract the monthly operating expenses in all accounts payable. This provides the total cash disbursements amount. Subtract the total cash disbursements from the total cash available to achieve the net cash from operations for the month. Carry this net cash from operations to the next month, and that becomes your new beginning cash balance.[2]

Accounts Receivables

A fourth financial statement—in terms of importance—is the accounts receivable list. This reflects the money owed to the consulting firm and translates into action to ensure that it is under control. The purpose of the accounts receivable report is to show the status of all outstanding invoices. It is an excellent management tool to make sure there are no problems with certain invoices and to do what's necessary to minimize the number of invoices that are in the past-due category. This requires routine attention so that the accounts receivable is not too large. Accounts receivable can easily get out of control if they are not managed properly.

In an ideal world, accounts receivable should all be paid within the first 30 days, but for a variety of reasons, payments are often not generated that quickly, and in some cases payments may be delayed as much as 60 to 90 days, particularly if the client is a government organization. A typical report usually places invoices into four categories: (1) invoices issued within the last 30 days, (2) invoices issued in the past 30 to 60 days, (3) invoices issued within 60 to 90 days, and (4) invoices over 90 days old. The older the invoice, of course, the more it becomes a problem requiring action, as described in next section.

Invoicing and Collections

Minimizing Problems

At the heart of the revenue generation is the invoicing process for clients. Invoicing problems can be minimized by taking several actions:

1. Use a standard process when the invoice is issued and have one person, usually the person responsible for finance and accounting, manage invoicing.
2. Start the invoicing process when the contract is actually negotiated. An up-front agreement spelling out specifically the fees and expenses covered will make nvoicing much easier later in the process. Too often, problems with invoicing stem from misunderstandings in the beginning, in terms of fees and how they are calculated and the expenses that are covered.
3. Keep track of the time and people involved in the project. This may involve time sheets, if the payment is based on an hourly rate, or the need to keep rack of the consultants on a project. Good timekeeping helps not only to develop the invoice properly, but keeps track of the efficiency of the consulting process to deliver the finished project.
4. Track expenses carefully. Each consultant involved in the project should understand what is covered and not covered, and this varies with the client. Some clients will reimburse all expenses; others may limit reimbursement to certain amounts, such as a per diem basis on travel.
5. Invoice on a timely basis. Waiting too late to invoice a client creates problems for both the consulting firm and the client. Many clients are operating on budgets, and failure to provide the invoice at a particular time may create budget problems for them. Also, minimizing the "age" of receivables makes a great case for invoicing as soon as possible. In some cases invoicing is completed in stages. These milestones, defined in the up-front commitment, indicate when invoicing will occur, and each milestone should trigger the generation of the invoice.
6. Use a system of control, making sure each invoice is assigned a unique number for tracking purposes. That number becomes a reference to the client throughout the system and is absolutely essential.
7. Explain all the charges, fees, and expenses. The invoice itself should explain as much as possible, without becoming too cluttered. Also, it may be helpful—if not always advisable—to include a cover letter with the invoice to help prevent misunderstandings. This can avoid frustrations as the client tries to understand what has happened and can minimize follow-up communication back to the consultant.
8. Ensure that the client has received the invoice. Too often it is assumed that the client has received it when, in far too many situations, that is not the case. The problem could be that the invoice was addressed incorrectly, that it is lost in the mail, or that it was delivered internally to the wrong person. For e-mail or internet billing, the communication may get lost in the transmission. Although this may not be the appropriate step for every invoice, particularly if they are small, the significant ones need the personal attention of follow-up to confirm that the invoice has been received.
9. Check with the client to make sure everything is okay on the invoice. This can be conducted in conjunction with the follow-up to ascertain whether they received the invoice. This provides the client an opportunity to make sure that there are no problems, and it helps pave the way for timely and efficient payment of the invoice.

Addressing Problem Invoices

For most consultants, the nonpayment issue is not that critical. If the relationship is appropriate and the project was successful, there should be no problem in receiving payment for the bill. However, sometimes the specific contact leaves the organization, the project was not as successful as the client thought it would be, or for some reason the client may not want to pay for the project. In these cases, delays may be a problem, and ultimately payment may become an issue. Most of the issues can be resolved with discussion and perhaps with some adjustment, either in the invoice or the service delivered. Because the consulting process is so personal, when there is a problem, the lead consultant or the owner should call the client directly. This personal attention may help resolve the issue.

Next, let the client know that it is past due, and if there is some penalty invoked, explain that penalty, and by all means stop work on other projects if there are any in progress. Ultimately, send the invoice to a collection agency. Most agencies will collect the money and charge anywhere from 20 to 40 percent. For extremely large amounts, you may want to consider legal action and going to court. Fortunately, for most consultants this is a rare occasion. For example, in the 13-year history of the ROI Institute, no bills have ever been turned over to a collection agency or proceeded to legal action.

Setting Fees and Pricing Strategies

One of the most mysterious and sometimes confusing issues is setting the service fees that should be charged. Four strategies are available.

Financial Need

Sometimes the most obvious approach is to price fees based on what is needed to make the business successful. This involves the following steps:

1. Estimate the annual expenses for the firm. If it is a one-person consulting practice, this is all of the expenses anticipated to occur that year. If it is an ongoing business, it's basically the expenses from the previous year.
2. Add to this amount the profits before taxes that would be desired. It is helpful to be realistic, particularly if it's early in the start-up process, since there may not be any profits. Add these two amounts, and that sum is the total annual revenue that must be driven.
3. Divide this number by the anticipated working days each year. This can vary significantly with consultants. To work 48 weeks out of the year, taking vacations and holidays, would yield 220 workdays on a five-day week. For most consulting firms, if half of the days can be billable on consulting projects, it would be acceptable. So, divide the total amount in Step 2 by 110 (the number of billable days), and this becomes the desired daily rate.

Fees Based on Desired Salary

A slightly modified approach from the one above is to determine the desired salary, based on similar corporate work, a previous assignment, or what is necessary for a comfortable living. This should be adjusted for direct employee benefits. For most individuals this would be in the 20 to 30 percent range for a small consulting practice.

Add to this desired salary and benefits the anticipated expenses. This would be in the range of two to three times this salary. For small consulting practices, a factor of two times this salary could be used because of the inexpensive facilities. For larger firms, where there are buildings and other expenses, three times salary may be more appropriate. This total amount is then divided by 110, to calculate the desired consulting rate.

These two approaches are similar, but the second approach avoids having to detail all of the expenses.

Fees Based on Market Averages

Another way is to determine market averages based on what others are charging. These realistic data are sometimes difficult to obtain, since consultants often do not like to reveal the specific fees they charge. A consultant charging low fees may inflate fees out of concern for what accepting low fees may mean. Others, who charge high fees, often do not want to share that information for fear that it may create the appearance of overcharging the client. Either way, estimates, based on a variety of survey benchmarking data, as presented in Table 4-3, suggests the fees for small to medium-size consulting firms. (There are so many different factors that can affect these rates, so the numbers in the table are ballpark figures.)

The first level in the table represents those who are completely new to consulting; however, they are experienced in some process or have an appropriate knowledge base (or they should not be involved in consulting). At level two, this person has some experience; he or she not only has expertise in a process, but also has at least two years of consulting experience. At level three a senior consultant has at least five years or more of consulting experience. Level four is an expert consultant with 10 years of experience.

These fees are based on one-on-one or small group consulting and do not include facilitating workshops. Teaching or training is not necessarily consulting, which often commands a higher rate because of the multiplicative effect (i.e., clients are usually willing to pay more for teaching than for one-on-one consulting). The teaching requires some preparation that is often factored into that consulting rate.

Fees Based on Client Capability

Sometimes fees are based on what the market will bear. In these cases, the fees are either raised or lowered based on certain circumstances. There are some legitimate reasons for adjusting fees, which we'll go into.

Table 4-3 Market Data Ranges for Consulting Fees

Experience Level	Description	Daily Fee Range
1	New, entry-level consultant	$1,000–$2,000
2	Some experience, with at least two years of consulting experience	$2,000–$3,000
3	Senior consultant, with at least five years of consulting experience	$3,000–$4,000
4	Expert consultant, with at least 10 years of consulting experience	$5,000–$10,000

Reasons to Lower Fees

There may be a reason to lower the fee when a specific project is being undertaken to develop future business. There is anticipation or even a promise that additional work will follow if the current project is successful. Or, perhaps this project allows the consultant to move into a new market or area where there is much additional business. Another reason to lower price is that the project is unfamiliar to the consultant or represents new territory, and there will be some learning. Also, it may be helpful to lower fees when the results can be applied to other projects. In essence, there will be leverage of project knowledge across similar projects and an opportunity to make up the fee difference on those projects.

Finally, it is reasonable to lower fees when the client is unable to pay and it is desirable to help them. This is particularly true for nonprofits. For example, many consultants with successful businesses offer their services for little or no charge to nonprofit organizations and sometimes to governmental units.

Reasons to Raise Fees

There are some legitimate reasons to increase fees as well as lower them. In some cases the project is extremely valuable, very high profile, and may make a huge difference for the organization. It may be appropriate to charge more with the anticipation of delivering a much better product. Also, the ability to pay is a factor. Some organizations are rich with resources and willing and capable of paying more. They do not question the fees, and they expect excellent projects. Still, in other situations it may be a project that is not desirable. No one really wants to do it, but because it's an existing client, there may be an obligation to complete the project. In these cases, a slightly higher fee may be appropriate. Finally, when the project is urgent, it may demand a higher fee. Essentially, an urgent project may mean that other projects will have to be delayed, adding inconvenience and perhaps even some additional time with those projects. In that case, a higher fee may be suitable.

Pricing Strategies

As the fees are set, other issues about pricing strategies need to be considered.[3] When coupled with the method of setting the fee, these strategies will provide a comprehensive framework from which to charge clients for the work performed.

Daily vs. Hourly Rate

Some consulting firms prefer to work by the hour and charge the hourly rate to the client. While these rates are negotiable, they are usually fixed in the proposal, and the hours assigned to the project are charged directly for that hourly rate. Other consultants prefer to work on a daily rate, assuming that all of the consulting can be completed in chunks of one day at a time. In these situations, a half day may be feasible.

Both approaches have some advantages. The hourly rate may be more efficient in terms of keeping track in billing all of the time on the project. The daily rate is a little easier to manage from the record-keeping standpoint, but it has its disadvantage in that sometimes people want to buy just an hour or two of time.

Fixed-Price Project

Instead of paying by the hour and the day, some firms prefer a fixed-price project (i.e., a price for the total completion of the project from the beginning to the end). When this is the case, the project agreement must detail all of the items that will be delivered, as well as the timing of the delivery. (This is covered in a later chapter.)

The fixed-price project has the simple advantage of not necessarily needing the recording of individual hours worked, but only the expenses incurred. The consultant can work when necessary or convenient to get the project done. If the consultant can complete the project quicker than anticipated, then it becomes a more lucrative project. This leads to an obvious disadvantage. Fixed-price projects often take longer to complete than anticipated, thus making the process unprofitable. If there are problems with a project, additional hours may be needed to make the project acceptable to the clients.

Retainers

In some situations the client will pay a retainer for the individual. This is a fixed price on a monthly, quarterly, or even yearly basis to provide a certain number of consulting days. The retainer price may be a little lower, because it is guaranteed, and there is some possibility that it will not be used. When this is the case, it can create a windfall for the consultant. The disadvantage is that the client may request work when the consultant could be busy on other projects, consequently creating some scheduling issues and stretching the capability to provide quality services.

Variable Pay

Sometimes the consultant may place part of the pay at risk. This is an important trend, which we cover in detail in a later chapter. With this approach, the consultant charges a certain minimal base pay and has an opportunity to receive a bonus if certain results are achieved.

Cascading Rates

Consulting firms with a variety of staff capability may offer a series of cascading rates depending on who is doing the work. Table 4-3 shows the market averages for fees charged by consultants at four different levels of experience. The firm could establish rates for certain individuals, and staff the projects with those levels of individual consultants, thus providing an economical approach without losing top-level expertise.

Fee Increases

Over time, fees often increase, and this can create a dilemma for existing clients. Fee increases should occur infrequently, maybe even with years between fee increases. Otherwise, the client may be concerned that the fees are going up much faster than they should. Fees may increase for three reasons:

1. The cost of doing business is higher, and therefore demands a little higher fee.
2. As consultants become more experienced, they can justify a higher rate, and thus an increase in a particular cost.
3. As a firm becomes more experienced, it becomes more valuable and more of a known commodity, and therefore increasing the rates may be desirable and can be acceptable.

Pricing Ethics

It is important for the pricing to be discussed and detailed as much as possible. Having hidden charges or being reluctant to discuss prices creates an air of suspicion about the firm. Identifying individual fees on a contract by the person directly assigned to a project is one of the best ways to alleviate those concerns.

There is also an ethical issue about charging different customers different prices. As mentioned earlier, there are some legitimate reasons for doing this. As long as those situations are understood and followed, they will be easy to explain when challenged by a particular client. Clients have a way of discussing these issues with each other, and sharing rates may be one item of conversation. Consistency and fairness are the keys.

Use of Independent Contractors

The issue of growing a consultant practice is a difficult one to address. It is unlike growing other businesses, where immediate talent is available. It may take months or even years to develop a consultant who can deliver the same capability as the original owners. With this huge investment of time and money in the individual, it is devastating when they leave to start their own consulting practice. One way of managing this growth is to find consultants who are already experienced specialists and to use them as independent contractors. The independent contractor is not an employee and therefore is not subject to employee benefits and the legal attachment of the employment relationship.

When to Use Contractors

The contractual approach is used when there is a need to manage the growth and developing internal consultants might not be feasible. It is also used to keep payroll costs low, so that consultants are paid only for the time they are working on a project. Using a contractor is also a way to bring in specific skills that may not be available with internal consultants and to manage peak workloads when multiple projects are tackled at the same time, taxing the current staff's capabilities.

Requirements

The requirements to classify a person as an independent contractor require addressing a number of issues. Table 4-4 shows the kinds of questions that must be answered before deciding if independent contractor status is appropriate.[4] It may be helpful to consult a CPA or tax attorney and IRS guidelines.

As the name implies, independent contractors must be independent and not directly under the supervision of the consulting firm. They must do work for other firms and not in any way be treated as employees of the organization. There are some advantages for the independent contractor. Essentially the consulting firm does not have to pay the FICA taxes; the independent contractor pays an equivalent self-employment tax. The independent contractor can deduct business expenses. However, using independent contractors just to lower tax bills is inappropriate. Independent contractors should be pursued only for the purposes outlined above.

Advantages and Disadvantages

There are several advantages to using independent contractors. As suggested earlier, this may be the best way to manage the growth in the organization, acquiring critical, unique skills needed to manage large projects—particularly the overload—and taking on new projects that are beyond the full capability of the organization. Because the consultants are not employees, there are fewer anxieties and frustrations (i.e., there is no challenge to keep them fully engaged). If they are not working and

Table 4-4 Independent Contractor Questions

- Does the hiring firm or the independent contractor determine when, where, and how work is performed?
- Is the hiring firm providing the independent contractor with training?
- How do the independent contractor's services integrate into the business?
- Are the services rendered by the independent contractor performed personally by him or her?
- How does the company hire, supervise, and pay the independent contractor?
- What is the continuing relationship between the independent contractor and the firm that hired him or her?
- Does the hiring firm set the working hours for the independent contractor?
- Does the hiring firm require the independent contractor to work full-time?
- Does the independent contractor work on the hiring firm's premises?
- Is the work order or sequence of work performed set by the hiring firm?
- Does the hiring firm require written or oral work progress reports from the independent contractor?
- Does the hiring firm pay the independent contractor by the hour, week, or month?
- Does the hiring firm pay travel and other business expenses on behalf of the independent contractor?
- Does the hiring firm supply the tools and equipment necessary for the independent contractor to perform the task?
- Does the independent contractor have a significant investment interest in the hiring firm?
- Does the independent contractor realize profits and losses from the hiring firm?
- Does the independent contractor work for more than one firm at a time?
- Does the independent contractor make his or her services available to the general public?
- Does the hiring firm have the right to discharge the independent contractor?
- Can the independent contractor terminate his or her arrangement with the hiring firm without liability?

Adapted from David Kintler, with Bob Adams, *Adams Streetwise Independent Consulting: Your Comprehensive Guide to Building Your Own Consulting Business* (Holbrook, Mass.: Adams Media Corp., 1998).

providing a service, then there is no payment. This essentially lowers administrative costs for the consulting firm, and perhaps some of the legal costs associated with the employment relationship. Under this scenario, a great independent contractor can be added to the staff as an employee after the work is reviewed and there is some success.

The disadvantages of using an independent contractor are that there is less flexibility and less control; since there is no direct supervision, the quality of the effort and the time the contractor is available may pose problems. Also, these consultants may not be loyal to the firm—since they are not ongoing employees—and may not be committed to providing the kind of service the firm desires. Also, they may attempt to leverage their work for their own gain in the future. They are not always part of the team and may refuse to do any of the back office or support work that is often a part of consulting projects. They only want to work for the period of time when they're being paid and are unlikely to provide any additional data or information at other times.

Financing the Business

Another important issue is the funding of the business, which is not only an issue in the start-up phase, but also for ongoing operations—particularly when growth is planned.

Amount Needed

The amount of money needed is based on the anticipated business. The income statement and balance sheet presented as Table 4-1 and Table 4-2 early in this chapter are developed on a pro forma basis to show the anticipated operations if this were a new business. In the start-up scenario, the investors, lenders, or other interested stakeholders are provided the anticipated expenses, revenue, and the subsequent profit or loss, and funding is requested. Pro forma income statements are usually developed for three years, perhaps five years if more serious levels of financial input are sought.

To obtain this initial capital, as well as manage the ongoing operations until the business becomes more profitable, a cash flow statement may need to be developed. Developed on a pro forma basis, a cash flow statement shows the anticipated cash inflow and cash outflow of the business. It also shows when the business turns to a positive cash flow, which is very important. In addition, capital may be needed to finance additional growth as new consultants are added, new service categories implemented, or expansion takes place to other geographic areas, or even internationally.

The balance sheet may be presented on a pro forma basis to show the proposed or anticipated condition of the business through successive years, again generally across a three- to five-year time frame. With the necessary funding amount based on pro forma statements that show the anticipated performance of the consulting firm, it's important for the calculations to be fair and realistic, and for conservative assumptions to be used in the analysis.

Equity

Sometimes the funding for the business is based on selling stock. Initially, the funding may be based on owner equity, and the owner provides the funding. Later, others may become interested. Potential investors may include family and friends, business partners, even venture capital firms. In some cases consulting firms have grown and were offered to the public through an initial public offering (IPO). Although this is unlikely for small firms, it may be an ultimate goal for a few.

Obtaining capital from friends, family, and business partners may be easier than obtaining venture capital. The friends and partners will need the pro forma income statements, pro forma balance sheet, and pro forma cash flow statements, but venture capital firms are often more difficult to handle. Because they are in the business of evaluating potential start-up companies or new growth opportunities, there is much competition for their funds. Consequently, they have developed some tough-minded approaches.

Presentation to a venture capital firm is in the form of the business plan developed in Chapter 3. A very effective business plan with the appropriate financials on a pro forma basis will go a long way in attracting the interest of venture capital firms. However, they are very shrewd and often have seen almost every trick of the trade. Table 4-5 lists the top 10 lies that venture capital firms hear.[5]

Debt

In some cases loans could be a way of obtaining additional funding. Although the initial owner might make a loan to the company, other potential lenders are business partners, banks, financial services firms, or commercial banks. A local bank is a logical place to start. Also, more small consulting firms are turning to the U.S. Small Business Administration (SBA) for help. The SBA loans are government-sponsored with low interest rates, and may be appropriate under certain circumstances. While there is often much paperwork involved, it may not be much more than is required by some of the financial institutions.

Table 4-5 Top 10 Lies Entrepreneurs Tell Investors

Lie #1:   "Our projection is conservative."

Lie #2:   "Gartner says our market will be $50 billion in five years."

Lie #3:   "Microsoft is signing our contract next week."

Lie #4:   "Key employees will join us as soon as we get funded."

Lie #5:   "Several investors are already in due diligence."

Lie #6:   "McKinsey is too old, big, dumb, and slow to be a threat."

Lie #7:   "Patents make our business defensible."

Lie #8:   "All we have to do is get 1 percent of the market."

Lie #9:   "We have first-mover advantage."

Lie #10: "We have a world-class, proven team."

Adapted from Guy Kawasaki, *The Art of The Start: The Time-Tested, Battle-Hardened Guide for Anyone Starting Anything* (New York: Portfolio, 2004).

Table 4-6 Distinctions Between Debt Financing and Equity Financing

Debt Financing	Equity Financing
Lenders are risk averse	Equity investors accept higher risks
No loss of ownership	Involves giving up some ownership
No explicit loss of control	May reduce control
Must be repaid	Does not have to be repaid
Increases cash outflow	Decreases cash outflow
Reduces cost of capital	Increases cost of capital
Increases return on equity (other things being equal)	Reduces return on equity (other things being equal)

Adapted from Richard Stutely, *The Definitive Business Plan: The Fast Track to Intelligent Business Planning for Executives and Entrepreneurs,* 2nd edition (London: Financial Times/Prentice Hall, 2002).

The choice of debt versus equity financing is a difficult but important one. Table 4-6 shows some distinctions between the two. Essentially, debt does not require that you give up control of the business, but the loan payments increase the cost of operations. Giving up ownership reduces your operating costs, but it requires sharing some control of the business.

Responsibilities for Finance and Accounting

To end this chapter, it's appropriate to consider who is responsible for the finance and accounting area in a consulting firm. Even in a one-person firm, the finance and accounting tasks must be accomplished either by the individual or by contract with firms that do these tasks for small businesses.

Certified Public Accountant

Every consulting firm needs a certified public accountant. This person represents the most critical investment since they can make the difference between success and failure. Thus, the accountant must be knowledgeable in accounting, current with recent changes in rules and regulations, trustworthy, and very experienced, particularly when it comes to consulting, if possible. The person must be impartial and willing to challenge you, but at the same time willing to be creative as long as it is legal.

Your accountant must be considered part of your long-term strategic team. The worst thing that could happen is to change CPAs regularly. This person will be representing you, after all, should you be challenged by the taxing authorities. Essentially, the CPA is a business advisor in finance and accounting, and maybe even in some of the legal issues that determine the appropriate corporate structure. More important, he or she will be the expert on taxes and will actually complete the tax return for most consulting firms. This individual is also available for routine financial planning, keeping the business fiscally sound and in compliance with the various laws and regulations, and minimizing the actual tax burden. And always, they should be available to provide advice on any of the issues related to the finance and accounting.

It is a bonus if the CPA is also a tax attorney, and this is a combination available to many. An individual who is both a CPA and a lawyer provides the added legal twist to the experience base and can actually represent you in court, if necessary.

Internal Finance and Accounting

Most consulting firms employ an internal finance person who generates the statements outlined in this chapter and keeps track of the total financial system. For larger firms, this is a complete professional and administrative staff. The duties of the internal staff must be clearly outlined to show how they are integrated with the external CPA. Their specific duties include managing invoices, developing reports, generating statements, handling collections, and performing many of the processes described in this chapter. These duties are usually specified for the entire team. The finance and accounting staff certainly should be capable, knowledgeable in current regulations, and have the utmost in ethics and integrity. Their trust and confidences are critical.

Entire Staff

Essentially everyone in the consulting firm is involved in some financial aspect of the business because every activity performed shows up somewhere as a cost or revenue item. The more that each employee understands about financial performance, the better they will be able to help manage the finance and accounting of the firm. For some employees, if not all, there should be a bonus tied to the financial performance of the business. Of course, all staff members should have a cost-control and cost-containment mentality and, above all, should be held accountable for cost and revenue in every activity.

Managers and Owners

The managers and the owners of the firm have the additional responsibilities of reacting to cost statements and managing the business in a way that keeps it profitable and healthy. One of the first challenges is to define the record-keeping system and ensure that it is proper, efficient, and understandable. This includes identifying the financial statements needed, as well as their frequency; setting the accounting period; and deciding if the firm should operate on a cash or an accrual basis (i.e., at the end of the year, is the performance of the firm determined by the cash received, or is it based on what it has

Figure 4-1   Hierarchy of Financial Responsibilities

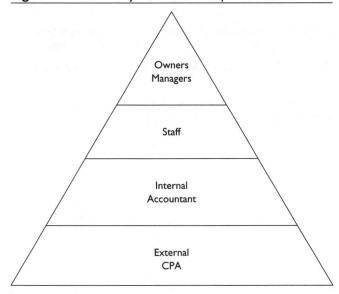

accrued?). The owners and managers must understand what the financial statements mean and review them periodically. More important, they must react to them and act to ensure that problems are corrected and steps taken to keep the firm healthy and profitable.

Figure 4-1 shows the hierarchy of these financial responsibilities. The most important responsibility is the external CPA as a trusting and trusted advisor. The second most important group is the internal accounting staff. Next are all the employees, and finally, the owners and managers. This hierarchy places the financial responsibilities in the proper perspective. If the other parts of processes are working properly, the owners and managers will have an easier job.

Final Thoughts

This chapter has addressed one of the most challenging and difficult issues of managing a consulting practice—the financial process. It explored the basic financial statements needed and the financial issues that must addressed to have a successful, profitable business, as well as the various challenges in raising capital, managing the collection systems, understanding statements, setting fees, and using independent contractors.

Notes

[1] Elaine Biech, *The Business of Consulting: The Basics and Beyond* (San Francisco: Jossey-Bass/Pfeiffer, 1999).

[2] Frank Fiore, *Write a Business Plan...in No Time* (Indianapolis, Indiana: Que, 2005).

[3] Robert Bacal, *The Complete Idiot's Guide to Consulting* (Madison, Wisconsin: CWL Publishing Enterprises/Alpha Books, 2002).

[4] David Kintler, with Bob Adams, *Adams Streetwise Independent Consulting: Your Comprehensive Guide to Building Your Own Consulting Business* (Holbrook, Massachusetts: Adams Media Corp., 1998).

[5] Guy Kawasaki, *The Art of the Start: The Time-Tested, Battle-Hardened Guide for Anyone Starting Anything* (New York: Portfolio, 2004).

[6] Richard Stutely, *The Definitive Business Plan: The Fast Track to Intelligent Business Planning for Executives and Entrepreneurs*, 2nd edition (London: Financial Times/Prentice Hall, 2002).

CHAPTER 5

LAUNCHING OR RELAUNCHING YOUR BUSINESS

This chapter is appropriate for both new and existing consulting firms. For new practices, it provides insight into the elements that must be in place prior to the launch of the new business and immediately afterward. For existing firms, it shows how to revitalize, restart, reinvent, or relaunch the consulting practice. Sometimes it's helpful to make a fresh start—a new approach—and do things differently.

We will provide input and insight into such issues as designing an appropriate Web site, creating the proper business image, landing that first big client, and establishing a board. We'll also explore critical marketing efforts, including the importance of effective networking in the early stages of the business.

Creating an Effective Web Site

A Web site is one of the most valuable tools for a consultant. It offers a relatively inexpensive yet powerful opportunity to describe what you do and how you do it. Designed properly, the Web site can create a compelling marketing advantage; poorly conceived and mismanaged, though, it can work in the opposite direction and may even project an image worse than having no Web site at all.

Purpose of the Web Site

The purpose of the Web site, first and foremost, is to project a professional image of the consulting firm. The Web site is essentially a reflection of the organization. How it's designed, how it looks, how it's navigated, and the information it delivers dramatically reflect on the organization. The Web site also serves as a forum to educate your audience—especially if that audience is unaware of your particular consulting niche—by offering trends, insights, white papers, and articles. It is an opportunity for the audience to quickly understand what you do, why your services are valuable, and, if possible, how those services are validated by credible research.

The Web site is also an opportunity to provide easy access to information. The navigation should be painless; the information should be organized properly so people can find what they need quickly. While content includes more about the organization, such as references and case studies, the information must be easily accessed. Ultimately, the Web site is there to help drive business. It should not have a hard-sell approach or be too flashy, but if it works properly, it will entice others to learn more and perhaps to get more engaged in the organization and at least follow up in some way.

Building and Hosting the Web Site

A very important early issue is the naming of the Web site. Ideally the name should reflect the name of the organization or perhaps a principal product or service. Additional information on naming the business is presented later in the chapter. It is not recommended to use an individual's name, but a firm name that reflects as much as possible about what the organization does.

Another issue is whether to build the Web site or have it built by a specialized company—and there are many of them. For larger firms, that is not an issue. For smaller firms, a legitimate option may be to build your own site using a software program such as Microsoft FrontPage or Macromedia Dreamweaver. The professional appearance of the Web site is critical, and an internally developed site may not present the desired image. External suppliers know this issue well and can help considerably.

Still another issue is finding a host. Sometimes your Internet service provider can serve as a host. In other situations a firm that builds the Web site might host it. Larger firms often will host their own sites.

These issues should be resolved based on economics, feasibility, and convenience.

Content Is King

The trend in Web sites is more content than flash. Although there needs to be much white space on your Web site pages, they should also be full of content, and not necessarily contain movement or be heavily populated with animated figures. Remember, this is not a brochure. It is designed to bring attention to what you do and who you are. Above all, the Web site should be content rich with plenty of free and valuable information. This is particularly important for consulting firms.

Table 5-1 shows the type of content that should be on the Web site.

The items in the table should be valuable, timely, and most of all, free. Not only will this information excite Web site visitors, it might also prompt them to tell others about their positive experience or even forward your Web site address to potential future prospects. This may be your most important way of building awareness and understanding of what you do and how you do it. Content should be

Table 5-1 Samples of Information on an Effective Consulting Web Site

- Articles about the consulting process provided
- Articles about the need for the consulting processes
- Trends that indicate the need for the consulting process
- Benchmarking data about the use of the consulting process
- Key studies showing applications in a variety of settings
- Research that shows the need for the consulting process
- Quiz to test the amount of knowledge about the process
- Self-assessment about where the organization stands on the particular issue

organized in such a way as to enable fast retrieval, fast navigation through the site, and to help users quickly and effectively understand the key issues about your practice.

Design

The appearance of the Web site is very important. It must look professional and represent the image of the firm. It should be colorful, with excellent design features and, as we noted above, have plenty of white space. The navigation must be easy and fast. It must be search-engine-friendly, so that the Web site is picked up quickly and often by various search engines, and there must be a means or method to track visitors and analyze the activities of those visitors, including the time spent on the site.

Although it is a little risky to discuss best practices in terms of Web content design, the best practices in Table 5-2 are offered by David Meerman Scott, from the book he wrote on the subject.[1] These best practices are for the most part self-explanatory, but a few may need some clarification.

Ideally, according to Best Practice 1, there should be some assessment of need. For a consulting practice, this may be the initial analysis that led to the need for the service, but it also may involve input from a variety of clients and from those who may be potential users, so you understand what they would need to see on a particular Web site.

Best Practice 2 is a given. To be consistent, one person should place all of the content on the Web site and be involved in creating it.

Best Practice 3 ties very closely to this, since there must be someone who is willing to be the content person. Best Practices 4 through 6 involve the mechanics of the design. Number 7 is a very important issue, using photos from actual situations and clients. This may include showing client headquarters—not just the name, but the headquarters building with a clear logo. It may be photographs from working sessions featuring one or more key consultants.

Table 5-2 Best Practices in Web Site Design and Use

1. When launching a new site, start with a comprehensive needs analysis.
2. Speak in one voice to create a consistent site personality.
3. Dedicate editorial resources to create consistent and informed content.
4. Encourage browsing by using appropriate self-select paths.
5. Use a separate URL or blog to provide targeted content.
6. Push content to users to pull them back to your site.
7. Do not forget images; original photos are powerful content.
8. Consider making proprietary content freely available.
9. If you serve a global market, use global content.
10. Include interactive content and opportunities for user feedback.
11. Use content to trigger viral marketing.
12. Link content directly to the sales cycle.

Adapted from David Meerman Scott, *Cashing In With Content; How Innovative Marketers Use Digital Information to Turn Browsers into Buyers* (Medford, New Jersey: Information Today, Inc., 2005).

Best Practice 8 has and will be advocated throughout this book (i.e., providing free information to clients or to prospective clients). Number 9 is a must for the global market. Numbers 10 through 12 are logical practices to create the appropriate marketing opportunities.

In summary, the Web site will be an important marketing tool and should be created ideally before the practice is launched, or should be reviewed in a relaunching situation. There are many ways to tackle the issue of a Web site and its design, and there are many publications about creating a Web site.

Networking

Networking is a powerful process for selling consulting services. It may be one of the most important if not effective marketing channels. According to Keith Ferrazzi, author of *Never Eat Alone*, networking is the number one strategy for building a business—particularly in a personal business such as consulting.[2]

Why It's Important

Networking is critical because consulting is a service, and a service is a personal process. In the consulting process, an important part of the decision to approve a consulting project is made on the basis of relationships. It is not like buying a product based on the product features, but rather, provides a service offered by an individual, and the relationship of that individual to the client—however brief it may be—is an important part of that decision. Often, the client's trust and confidence in the consultant is an important part of that decision, which further reinforces networking as the most productive marketing channel.

How to Do It

There are many ways to make networking work for consulting. Table 5-3 shows 20 networking possibilities. Although many of them are self-explanatory, a few deserve some underscoring.

For example, the time to develop the network is before you actually need to use it. For a new consulting practice, the network should be established prior to launching a practice, and for existing consulting firms, a network should be functioning before the fruits of the network are actually needed. You must do your homework to make sure that you clearly understand how your consulting is used, where it's used, and who makes the decisions—all of the issues covered in Chapter 3.

Next, the individuals and venues must be selected carefully to make sure that you are networking in the right places. Selecting the meetings, associations, and individuals are critical. When there is a gatekeeper trying to control or manage the time of the individual you need to see, you need to be able to manage them, work with them, and befriend them. They should be your ally as you seek to spend a few minutes with the individual you've selected.

Lunches make great networking opportunities. Always have lunch with someone in your network, locally or during travel. Deciding which conferences and association meetings to attend to use networking is important. You want to be at the conferences the best clients and decision makers attend. Using the network, raising critical issues, listening and being alert, and taking a stand are all critical issues. Occasionally you want to expand your circle and get beyond where you are now—by finding those people who may be a prospect for your next consulting services, the next level of decision maker, or the next industry where you might want to focus.

Table 5-3 Networking Checklist

Action	NETWORKING STATUS Not Doing This ← → Very Successful at This				
	1	2	3	4	5
1. Develop it before it is needed.	☐	☐	☐	☐	☐
2. Do your homework.	☐	☐	☐	☐	☐
3. Pick your venues carefully.	☐	☐	☐	☐	☐
4. Select the people wisely.	☐	☐	☐	☐	☐
5. Manage the gatekeepers.	☐	☐	☐	☐	☐
6. Use lunches routinely.	☐	☐	☐	☐	☐
7. Leverage your passions.	☐	☐	☐	☐	☐
8. Work the conferences.	☐	☐	☐	☐	☐
9. Expand your circle.	☐	☐	☐	☐	☐
10. Connect with connectors.	☐	☐	☐	☐	☐
11. Raise critical issues.	☐	☐	☐	☐	☐
12. Listen and be alert.	☐	☐	☐	☐	☐
13. Take a stand.	☐	☐	☐	☐	☐
14. Recommend resources.	☐	☐	☐	☐	☐
15. Follow up faithfully.	☐	☐	☐	☐	☐
16. Provide valuable information.	☐	☐	☐	☐	☐
17. Explain your practice.	☐	☐	☐	☐	☐
18. Provide contact information.	☐	☐	☐	☐	☐
19. Build your own network.	☐	☐	☐	☐	☐
20. Evaluate progress.	☐	☐	☐	☐	☐

Adapted from Keith Ferrazzi, with Tahl Raz, *Never Eat Alone: And Other Secrets to Success, One Relationship at a Time* (New York: Currency Doubleday, 2005).

This also involves connecting with the connectors—finding people who are networked well so they can broaden your horizons quickly, through a multiplicative effect, and who can recommend resources, provide information, offer free information, and follow up faithfully. Failing to follow up will quickly kill the relationship. Explain your practice and describe what you're doing and what you can do. Provide appropriate contact information, so that they always know how to contact you easily and quickly.

Consider building your own network of clients. This may sound far-fetched for some organizations, but it has been accomplished with many organizations. It becomes a user group in the marketing sense. The ROI Institute featured in this book founded an ROI network, a group of users who are struggling with implementing the ROI methodology. Supported by the ROI Institute, the network quickly grew into an independent user group, and now claims more than 600 members. This becomes a valuable tool for marketing indirectly.

Finally, evaluating your progress is important so that you can see where you've made progress and where you haven't. When using Table 5-3, it may be helpful to score the instrument. Assign numbers from 1 to 5, using the five categories based on where you are with the item. The perfect score, which is probably unachievable, is 100; the lowest, which would indicate doom and gloom, is 20. Listed below are suggested scoring ranges:

- 80 to 100. Networking is exceptional. You have done all the things you need to do to make networking effective, and you have shown outstanding progress. This should translate into direct consulting business.
- 61 to 79. You are making progress. You've had some solid wins, and things are progressing nicely, but there is room for improvement, and efforts are needed.
- 41 to 60. You have realized some success, but most of the networking efforts are not producing the kind of returns you need. You must continue to focus; otherwise, networking is not going to pay off for you. Much improvement is needed.
- 20 to 40. Networking is almost nonexistent. It must get started quickly or networking will never be an effective tool for you.

Make your assessment each year to see how well you are making progress on this important issue of building the proper networks that ultimately drive your business.

Cautions

As you explore networking, it's helpful to think about the cautions—some things that could create problems. First, do not overdo it. Do not let networking become a burden for others. Try to determine when you're being too pushy, forceful, demanding, or showing up too often. Know when to back off of the relationship and maybe leave it alone or visit it less frequently. Be careful about making commitments to the people involved in your networking.

Effective networking usually means that you will do some things for the people in the network. If you overcommit or underdeliver, you'll destroy the network you have worked to build. Failing to follow up may be the quickest way to kill the network. If you do not do what you said you would by a particular time, the relationship will go sour. The situation may be worse than having no relationship. Despite these cautions, this can be one of the most important ways to grow your business.

Building Your Board

A situation facing every consulting firm is to determine the proper way to receive advice from others. There are both formal and informal ways in which this can be done. Advice is needed, not only at the beginning of the consulting practice, but throughout the practice as well, as it grows, develops, and expands.

Essentially there are three approaches that can be taken. One of the following should be appropriate for your firm:

- A board of directors, which is formal and part of the legal structure in the incorporation of the company.

- A board of advisors, which is a formal board (i.e., experts listed, communicated) yet has no legal responsibilities.
- A board of experts from an informal perspective, made up of individuals who may provide you advice, but not through an official role. They may not even realize that they are on your board of experts.

Board of Directors

Some consulting practices want a formal board of directors, particularly when the consulting firm is incorporated as a Subchapter S or Subchapter C corporation where a board is actually required. The board does not have to be external to the owners. It could be all internal. However, to use a board of directors as advisors, it may be best to have a formal structure with outside directors.

These directors are knowledgeable experts in some way or phase of business. They are supporters or influential individuals. They are legally appointed to the board, and there is a way in which board members are actually added and removed. The advantage of this approach is that these individuals often have a stake in the process. They understand their role and are there to help make decisions—hopefully, making better decisions than could have been made previously. They have a fiscal responsibility to ensure that the firm is being managed properly, and they feel obligated to speak their minds and take a stand. Sometimes these board members are provided company stock or stock options, increasing their commitment to the organization and making their stake in the process more valuable or more significant.

The disadvantage with this formal board of directors is the legally required issues. There is formal reporting, and the board members have a liability, which means that good board members may not want to serve because they are vulnerable to being sued. The firm must have liability coverage to protect them. Also, they do have some control, although not enough to necessarily take over the organization, unless somehow the other board members have majority ownership. Board members have to be listened to. It is hard to ignore them, because they have a responsibility to fulfill their role.

Formal Board of Advisors

A formal board of advisors usually consists of experts or supporters who have excellent name recognition. They are people that can help you and influence others to help you. Your board of advisors should be impressive to your clients. There is often minimum involvement for advisors, and every effort must be made to keep their involvement in the financial areas to a minimum.

The advantage of this kind of board is that it is a way to network with and get the support of individuals you need in a productive network. The disadvantage is that the individuals may not take their role very seriously. They may feel that they are more for show than for actual advice because they have no way to make decisions.

Informal Board of Experts

For some practices, particularly for small consulting firms, the informal board approach may be best. These are trusted individuals who can serve as personal advisors in different areas of the business (i.e., legal, financial, marketing, technology). There is nothing formal at all about the structure, and those who are involved in this informal board often do not realize that they have a role. They are only used when they're needed, and they may be replaced routinely. Since they never knew that they were on the board, there is no problem with replacements. The board is invisible to others since they are not listed anywhere (i.e., they do not know about their role or the role of others).

The advantage is that this may be the best way to obtain outstanding personal advice. This board will provide input as a friend, as a trusted confidant. The disadvantage is that since they do not know that they're shaping your business, they may not realize the consequences of their advice. And since they may not realize that you may be taking their advice and translating it into action, they might not think through the process as well as you'd like. Their advice may be off-the-cuff, a top-of-head reaction, instead of a thought-out response that might be more useful and more valuable. Still, this can be a valuable approach, and many entrepreneurs say it is the best approach.

Consider the Three Possibilities

In summary, every consulting firm needs a board. The right board depends on the amount of control you want to retain for the owner. Figure 5-1 shows the control relationship. Under an informal board of experts there is no control; the owner has all of the control. Under the formal board of advisors, there is some control, but not much. With a board of directors, there is much control, and the owner begins to lose control. If the majority of the board is against the owner, they have the total control.

Figure 5-1   Various Board Options

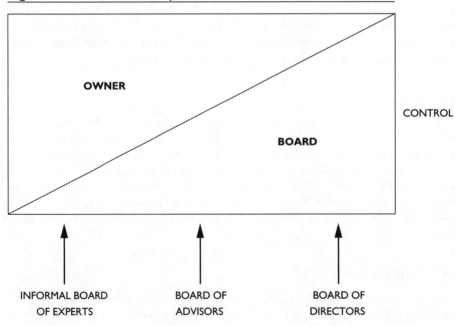

Creating the Proper Image

Building image is important, not only in the Web site, but in items such as names, logos, brochures, and communications; they all are important.

Getting Started

For consultants launching their own practices, an important early challenge is to choose an appropriate name for the organization. There are several approaches for doing so, but perhaps the most obvious one is to use a name that reflects the primary stakeholder or consultant—John A. Lawson and Associates, for example. The word "associates" suggests that other individuals are involved in the practice, but the name makes it clear that John Lawson is the principal consultant.

This approach has some disadvantages. The most obvious is that it may suggest to some that there is only one person in the practice—or that even if there are many associates, there is only one who really matters—and it may be difficult to hand off work to someone other than John Lawson. Also, as the business grows to the point where it may become an acquisition target for another consulting firm or similar organizations, having an individual's name associated with it may be a drawback, since there often is reluctance to buying a business that is heavily dependent on one individual. Additionally, some believe that naming a business after its owner serves only to stroke his or her ego. Consider what would happen if the firm grew and the owner died. Would it make a difference?

Others use part of their name but combine it with a word or phrase indicating the nature of the business. For example, Pride Consulting, led by president Frank B. Pride, is a somewhat less egotistical name but doesn't give up the principal's name altogether, and it signals that consulting is the type of service provided. Another example to consider is Wallace Training Cost Recovery Company, which, as the name implies, is a practice that specializes in recovering or obtaining reimbursements for money spent on training grants, training credits, and training incentives. Essentially they work with government agencies to secure the proper tax credits or refunds for companies when they use certain government programs and policies. This name brings in the original owner and more detail about the service provided.

Consider a name that reflects a service while making it independent of the ownership. For example, the company The Difference Maker, Inc., founded by Steve Kaplan,[3] provides a wide range of consulting services and business tools to help companies succeed, particularly in the area of marketing and attracting large clients. Steve has implied that his firm makes a difference, hence the name. Or consider the company name Management Systems Consulting Corp., which implies that the business provides consulting services and management systems.

While there are several options, the selection of a name essentially boils down to these considerations:

1. Should the name of the individual be included?
2. Should the service or product offered be included in the name?
3. Does the name imply geographical connotation, such as Global Strategic Consultants?
4. Will the name last for a long time?

There are obvious pros and cons. We recommend selecting the name based on the service it delivers. It's less restrictive and avoids the trap of being linked to an individual's name.

A case in point: We built a consulting firm called Performance Resources Organization that focused on helping organizations improve performance with a variety of resources, but principally through consulting. Each word was important. "Performance" reflected what we were trying to provide. "Resources" suggested that we did more than just consulting, that we conducted workshops, authored and published books, and created various tools and templates. "Organization" was selected to give the firm an easily identified acronym: PRO. Although that obviously was and is an overused term, it did help shorten the name with an appropriate acronym. This firm was purchased for several million dollars by a company listed on the New York Stock Exchange. Had it been named after the original founder, it would have been difficult to consummate that purchase.

Another issue is the logo. A logo should reflect the name of the organization and perhaps the services offered. It may be helpful to seek the input of a marketing professional or a creative consultant who offers several designs.

The logo selected must be clean, understandable, and project a great professional image, and it should be included on all communications, marketing materials, and especially in the print media. The name of the company should be registered and perhaps even trademarked if possible, as should the logo. Business cards and stationery should include the logo, reproduced in the same size, typeface, and colors. When used consistently on all of the company's materials, it creates a desired brand. Over time, you want clients to perceive the image of your company as meaning or standing for something, which often is a part of the vision and values as described in Chapter 3.

Brochures and Print Material

Regardless of the type of consulting practice, print material must be developed. Although much of the material may be sent over the Internet, hard copies will be printed out and preprinted versions will often be available. One of the first documents is a portfolio fold, which is a document that contains other brochures and pertinent information, and includes a place for a business card. Portfolios are used at meetings, briefings, and workshops and provide an opportunity to present a variety of materials in a professional manner.

Next there is an overview brochure that describes what the organization provides. It contains a profile of the organization, what service is provided, why it is important, the particular approach taken to provide the service, and maybe a few samples of work product. This brochure is always left with clients and prospective clients. The next possibility is a brochure about a specific service. Many consulting firms offer different services and provide a brochure on each particular service.

Another possibility for print material is article reprints. Ideally, these could be articles written by consultants or where the consultant is interviewed. In some cases—when the firm is just getting started— these articles reflect the need for the service offered.

Another possibility is reprints of ads. Some consultants take out full page ads in conference programs or targeted professional or trade magazines. An ad reprint is a handout that not only shows what a service provides and the organization offers, but reminds them that it has been advertised in this particular publication.

Short case studies can also be very effective. A case study is a summary of a successful consulting project which is evaluated to show the contribution made, preferably in terms of a financial return on investment. This can be a very impressive marketing effort, particularly if it includes references to individuals who readers can contact for more information. Testimonials and references are sometimes provided on a separate document where clients describe the value of the consulting services.

Print media can vary considerably, but are important in conveying the proper business image. Printed materials must be written professionally, always using the organization name, logo, and tagline.

Communications

The communications should always reflect the business image. Telephone communications should be very professional, clear, and precise. Telephone systems should be user friendly, with the voice mails as professional and consistent as possible.

E-mails may be the most frequent way of communication, and they should be professional too, always reflecting business image. The signature on the e-mails for different individuals of the firm should include the company name, tagline, address, and various contact information.

Business correspondence by mail, which is becoming a rarity, should have an excellent business appearance, always using the company stationery and appropriate envelopes. Some clients, particularly senior executives, still prefer communication with direct mail as formal correspondence.

Legal Organizational Structure

Several options are available to legally establish a consulting business. If it is a new firm, the options are usually different from those who've been in business for some time; although the organizational structure can change.

Sole Proprietorship

The simplest form is to operate as a sole proprietor. This is usually the best option for a part-time consulting business. In the United States the tax obligations are considered in with the personal income. For income taxes, the consultant files a separate form, Schedule C, which is profit or loss from business. Many consultants still use this, even as they grow larger, and essentially there is no income limit.

Partnership

If partners are involved, a legal organizational structure called a partnership can be created. This has some tax advantages; it could be set up as a limited liability partnership, but with more flexibility to operate independently.

S Corporation

Many consultants prefer to operate as a Subchapter S corporation. Essentially this is a separate corporation with a board of directors operating independently. However, the profits and losses of the corporation flow through to the personal income of the owners. Thus, the liability of the corporation essentially flows through to the ownership.

C Corporation

Larger corporations typically follow the regular Subchapter C corporation, which has the advantage of being completely separate. Most large consulting firms probably would follow this schedule. There is no liability necessarily to the individual owner, but just to the shareholders of the corporation. Professional advice from your CPA or attorney is recommended for this area of your business.

Timing of the Launch

Preparing for the launch is critical and sometimes involves months if not years of groundwork. Managing this transition is one of the important success factors for consulting organizations.

Transition to Consulting

Because of the difficulties of securing a viable flow of clients and sustaining the business, it's important that those considering becoming consultants make a gradual transition to the business. Gaining experience on the job and translating that experience into part-time consulting is perhaps the ideal way. But this might well pose difficulties for those who are employed full time. In lieu of this, writing articles, making presentations, and, in some cases, writing books can help build the credibility needed to make the transition into the consulting business.

It may be helpful to prepare a transition plan—a plan of action to move toward becoming a consultant with a fully operational consulting practice. A transition plan would indicate specific activities, projects, and accomplishments in preparation for launching the business. After the business is launched, the business plan, as described in Chapter 3, becomes the governing document.

The schedule of processes, actions, and accomplishments that constitute the transition described in this section will ensure that the start-up is effective and successful.

The actual launch date may be connected to some particular event—perhaps at a milestone in a full-time job, such as eligiblility for retirement, or when the prospective consultant is fully vested in his or her 401(k) plan. Some take advantage of the company's downsizing and volunteer for a workforce reduction. Still others may tie the timing of the launch to the economy making sure that the business is in demand (preferably peak demand). Others may look at a particular time of the year, such as during the spring season. For example, it is difficult to launch a consulting business in December, the busiest time of year, since it would be difficult to get the necessary attention and interest.

Above all, during the transition period and the launch, one must have a family commitment. The family must be prepared for the tough work involved, the long hours, and the struggles, anxieties, and stress that go with building the business.

Secure Commitments for Work

In an ideal world, the launch of the consulting practice would coincide with actual work projects, committed from a prospective client, with the practice launched at the time work actually begins. This would mean starting with fee generating projects to fund the business from the very beginning.

In fact, some individuals leaving the corporate world manage to secure contracts for work they're performing there, essentially flipping their current job into an external consulting contract. This is occurring more often as organizations seek to reduce the actual headcount in their organizations while keeping the talent available. For the individual moving toward consulting, this of course makes the transition much smoother. Another way to secure that first contract is to contact professional colleagues and secure commitments. Making those first contacts in advance is ideal.

Financial Preparation

In the previous chapter we presented details on the financial aspects of the business. As an early exercise, it's helpful to forecast the actual expenses needed for two years and secure enough capital—either from owner equity or a loan from the owner to sustain the business for that period. If a consulting firm can survive financially for two years, it can usually keep going. The alternative is a loan made in the beginning, which places the business in a strain from the start. Not only must it survive the two years, but it has a debt to pay off, which will continue to put a strain on the young practice.

Location

For a start-up business, the first location is usually fairly obvious: a home office. Developing an office at home may require some changes in mind-sets and work schedules. Some individuals are good at working from home, and others have difficulty dealing with the distractions. An office secluded from other parts of the house is best, so that the consultant can work uninterrupted, and without disturbing family members.

Managing the time, setting priorities, staying focused, avoiding distractions, and practicing efficient communications are challenges with a home office that must be addressed. Some migrate from a home office quickly to an office suite. There are possibilities for office suites in office complexes, essentially a place for a one-person office with administrative support. This arrangement provides an address, a location, and a place away from the home to work, but it adds an extra expense.

Others will migrate quickly into leased office space, typically to accommodate additional consultants and support staff. Sometimes leases are structured with an option to grow in the future as the practice expands. And still others take the route of purchasing a commercial building, leasing office space to the consulting practice, and leasing any additional space to other tenants. If there is sufficient owner capital, this arrangement creates an excellent source of additional income and can go a long way toward putting the organization on solid financial footing.

As the business continues to grow, other challenges will unfold regarding location. This may require an analysis of the markets that need to be served. If most of the clients are clustered in a certain part of the country—on the West Coast, for example—this may require relocating the business to the West Coast, or at least opening a major office there. In some cases offices are located in different geographical regions to better serve the customer base. Given the ease of working remotely and the need to have consultants located close to specific markets, it may be helpful to have individual consultants stationed in different parts of the country, though not necessarily in fully staffed offices. Such important office-space and expansion considerations will evolve and develop and should be a part of the business plan as described in Chapter 3.

Staffing

Staffing for a small start-up consultant practice is straightforward. It starts with a part-time practitioner, who transitions to a full-time consultant with a part-time administrative assistant (yes, you may need administrative help). Then it grows to include full-time administrative personnel and other consultants, followed by additional administrative assistants and support. Determining the proper mix of support staff is an important consideration.

Then again, with so much communication carried out via e-mail, and given the increasing power of software and desktop publishing packages, some consultants never require administrative assistants. After all, many corporations have eliminated administrative support on an individual professional employee basis. Even managers and executives sometimes do not have support staff anymore. However, to multiply the effectiveness of a consultant is an important issue. If a consultant can spend less time on administrative processes, then he or she can spend more time delivering consulting.

Written communication, responding to telephone calls, conducting limited business development activities, preparing proposals, and developing final reports can all be performed by qualified support staff that can be paid at a lower rate than the consultant is earning. Thus, it makes sense to use a support staff, but determining the right amount can be a challenge, and it may require some experimentation.

As the office grows, the issue of adding consultants will have to be explored, and should already have been explored, at least to a limited degree, when developing the business plan. The challenge is to find one or more consultants who can deliver the same service as consistently as the original consultant or existing consultants. These consultants must earn the respect of the client team, be credible with their work, and above all should not leave the consulting practice to create a competing practice. This is difficult, but has to be faced if the office is going to grow.

Mental Preparation

As described in the first two chapters, the consultant must be prepared mentally for the consulting work. Consulting success is much harder to achieve than success in a previous corporate job. There is much hard work with long hours, and the consultant must have a strong work ethic, be highly organized, and do what is necessary to make it successful. This may require essentially forgoing the social life for some time while getting the business started.

The Launch Date

Sometimes the date is important. The time of the year or the time of the month may be a consideration. The timing may need to coincide with a conference where the clients will be attending. Perhaps it should coincide with the first project. These are all possibilities in setting the date so that the business is launched at the best time.

The Actual Launch

While the actual launch is usually a very important event, it must be deliberately planned to be the type of event desired by the firm and needed for the client base.

Big Splash or Low Profile?

Sometimes it's helpful to make a big splash, particularly if the consultant is trying to bring attention to the new business, a new opportunity, a new process, or a new service. There are many potential clients who need to know! Others prefer to maintain a low profile, launching the practice quietly and informing only those who are targeted as immediate client prospects. Both ways have their advantages and disadvantages.

A big splash provides excellent exposure quickly and instant name recognition to a specific audience. On the downside, it is expensive and may be ineffective in reaching particular audiences. The low-profile approach has the advantage of being inexpensive, and it tends to position the practice as more subtle and conservative, which may be important for the target clients or the atmosphere of a particular community or industry. However, some prospects might not get the message and client opportunities may be missed. Both approaches must be weighed carefully in deciding the direction to take.

Issue a Press Release

A press release is an important step in getting the announcement to the proper audience. The content will depend on the nature and scope of the practice, and the information should reflect the need for the practice, as well as the experience of the consultant. Figure 5-2 shows a sample of a press release for a new consulting practice.

The content should be straightforward, concise, and written in a style that effective press releases follow. The distribution should be carefully considered. It must reach the target audience, which might

Figure 5-2   Sample Press Release

Veteran Educators Launch Consulting Practice

FOR IMMEDIATE RELEASE

NEW YORK, Feb. 14—Veteran educators Vincent Monet, Meredith Fore, and Charles Leeding announced today that they have formed a specialized consulting practice to serve selected clients in the area of corporate training and development.

The company, Monet Fore Leeding LLC, will be based in New York, N.Y., with offices in Progress, California, and Opportunity, Illinois.

"The company will focus on providing superior customer service," said CEO Vincent Monet, a former university professor. "We want our clients to know we mean business." According to President Meredith Fore, a former high school principal, Monet Fore Leeding will be more than just the company's name. "It's our promise to our clients," she said.

Charles Leeding, Senior Vice President of Research, once worked as a football coach and driving instructor. He said he looks forward to working with the firm's clients. "Just because they may be in the training business doesn't mean that they themselves can't learn," he said. "And we stand ready to help them."

For more information on the services offered by Monet Fore Leeding, call 1-GET-LEEDING (1-437-533-3464), or visit http://www.monetforeleeding.biz.

well require sending it to magazines in the professional field and to newspapers that serve the client base. Be prepared to be rejected by major media. This is not an event that large newspapers typically are willing to pick up. If your practice is serving a local market, it may be helpful to try smaller community newspapers, where the content typically is more reflective of news and events in the immediate area.

Prepare a Press Kit

A press kit would include the press release and other related print material. It may be delivered personally to newspapers or sent to appropriate magazines that serve the industry. The press kit is sent to a smaller audience than the actual press release. It is not necessarily sent electronically, but delivered as a package. A press kit provides background information and may actually spark an interview to describe the service offered and the need for the service. This is particularly appropriate when there is a niche consulting process that would attract a lot of interest, is a novel business, or whose potential clients are high profile organizations.

Develop Launch Materials

The materials used may vary, but they typically involve several essential items. The invitation or announcement is important (i.e., inviting potential clients to a reception or just an announcement of the business). This is not necessarily the press release, but could be in the form of an e-mail or letter. A fact sheet may be needed to discuss the need for the practice, why it is a concern, why this practice can address this issue, and who is involved in the consulting.

A variety of print materials described earlier may be made available to those who need it or sent along to others when and if the need arises. Business cards must be printed, along with stationery and other materials containing the logo, the name of the practice, and the taglines that project the desired image.

Advertising specialties may be an important part of the launch. Having a giveaway item left with prospective clients, ideally reflecting something about the business, may be appropriate. For example, in a consulting practice that focuses on helping individuals save time on the job, an hourglass might portray the proper image. In a practice aimed at uncovering and creating direct cost savings in the administrative area of a business, a large paperweight resembling money might be provided. At a firm that focuses on wellness and fitness, a stress reliever ball would attract attention and create name awareness. A company focusing on measurement systems could provide a ruler. Of course, there are the traditional mugs, umbrellas, and pens that may be appropriate.

Advertising

In addition to the announcement and press release, advertising may be appropriate. Direct mail might be called for. If the audience is broad, this is expensive but may be appropriate. It can help with name recognition. Sometimes an ad announcing the consulting practice may be appropriate, particularly in a professional publication, as might sponsorship at a conference, a part of the conference, a cocktail reception, or a particular speaker. The sponsorship usually provides an opportunity for the consultant to discuss the new practice or write an appropriate message that reflects the new practice.

The Personal Touch

Few things are more important than the personal touch during the launch of the business. This might mean personal visits to potential clients—very short visits to explain what is going on. Personal phone calls to prospective clients, particularly building on contacts from the past, may be appropriate. Personalized letters (not form letters with the name added) may attract additional attention, as well as personal e-mails.

Reception

Should there be a formal reception? This step depends upon the audience targeted for the consulting. If the audience is all local in a particular area, it might be helpful to host a reception at a hotel, business club, or some other special event location. It could be held at a conference, inviting selected conference attendees who are prospective clients to come to a reception to discuss the new consulting practice. An association meeting is another possibility. Consider a client-hosted reception (i.e., having a satisfied client to launch the business, with the reception hosted by the client but paid for by the consultant). Table 5-4 shows a checklist of things to consider as the new business is launched.

Table 5-4 Checklist for Launching the Practice

- ☐ Determine profile of launch.
- ☐ Print stationery and business cards.
- ☐ Prepare an appropriate press release.
- ☐ Develop appropriate print materials.
- ☐ Develop press kits.
- ☐ Deliver press kits to key magazines.
- ☐ Send press releases to appropriate newspapers, professional magazines, and trade publications.
- ☐ Consider an ad in the appropriate media.
- ☐ Prepare a compelling announcement.
- ☐ Consider direct mail announcement.
- ☐ Sponsor a part of a conference.
- ☐ Purchase appropriate ad specialties.
- ☐ Call key prospects about the announcement.
- ☐ Announce with personal visit if possible.
- ☐ Send personal letters with announcement.
- ☐ Consider a reception with announcement.
- ☐ Be prepared for no response.

Be Prepared for No Calls

Even with all of the preparation for the launch and conducting the actual launch, the consultant needs to be prepared for little or no response. With so many consultants, and with tight budgets, it is unlikely that many people will respond unless it's a burning issue for a particular person. This can be disturbing or frustrating for new consultants. While disappointing, it takes some time and many efforts to continue to develop the awareness of the need for one's services, get to the right audience, and develop a successful practice.

Find a Big Client

According to Steve Kaplan, author of the book *Bag the Elephant*, the key client is like a big elephant.[4] It is very smart, has a great memory, and is very slow to move and change; it requires a lot of feeding and can be disastrous and even deadly if the circumstances go in the wrong direction. A big client is often key to the success of a small consulting firm. Although this may be perceived as out of reach by many, it may not be the case. Acquiring a big client takes a very determined effort.

Why a Big Client?

A big client provides several major advantages. First, there is the financial impact. The big client can sometimes sustain the entire consulting firm for a period of time, a year or so, and it may continue. Also, obtaining a key client provides self-satisfaction for the consultant or for the consulting team, and the key client will often be the most important reference to use to leverage that work to other clients. Key contacts at the big client may become a referral. The prestige of working for this large organization can be important to the respect and credibility of the firm. It may be the first stepping-stone for tremendous growth.

How to Do It

Bagging the big client requires some deliberate effort. Table 5-5 provides a checklist for securing a big client. Although some of the steps are self-explanatory, a few may need more detail.

The first step is to take deliberate efforts to understand the big organizations, since they don't operate the way smaller organizations do. Understanding the culture, politics, and bureaucracy is a great beginning in this process. Identifying those areas where the big client may be a particular target organization, or even identifying a specific individual in the organization, is important.

Making the contact and beginning to work with the client are the obvious next steps. Part of this may be to offer a prebriefing, particularly if the consulting practice offers a niche product or process not readily available from others. Finding that key champion is important since this is the person who will ultimately make the decision and turn into an advocate internally. Cultivating that champion and continuing to work with him or her is important. Working with the bureaucracy and following procedures in terms of purchasing, contracting, and delivery may be a challenge. Some turn this into profit by getting the client to pay for actually performing activities prescribed by their bureaucracy.

Table 5-5 Checklist for Securing a Big Client

- ☐ Understand large organizations.
- ☐ Create a feasible target group.
- ☐ Select the right consultant.
- ☐ Make the contact.
- ☐ Offer a free briefing.
- ☐ Identify internal champion.
- ☐ Cultivate your champions.
- ☐ Learn to deal with the bureaucracy.
- ☐ Ensure the client feels at home.
- ☐ Do whatever it takes to get the project.
- ☐ Make it a top priority.
- ☐ Drop the negative resistance.
- ☐ Have fun along the way.
- ☐ Negotiate from strength.
- ☐ Don't settle for just one.

The remaining approaches are common sense steps: Stay with a client, make it a top priority, and do whatever it takes to remain persistent without becoming overly aggressive and irritating. And, yes, have fun along the way. When you land the big one, though, do not settle for just one; try to get another big one. The first one is the hardest; the second is easier.

The Risk of Big Clients

Although big clients do bring many rewards to the table, it's important to also understand the inherent risks. If you mess up the deal, for instance, you may destroy that relationship for the future, and perhaps other relationships if word gets out. Bad news travels fast, and in the big circle of big clients, a botched attempt may spread and eliminate the opportunity to work other clients.

Obtaining a big client is much like the reaction to a narcotic: You feed off of that client and develop an addiction—particularly if the client gives continued business. But the client could go away abruptly, leaving a tremendous hole in your revenue stream. Putting all of your eggs in one basket is rarely a good idea in business.

Another issue is being able to deliver, which is often a key concern for big clients and is frequently brought up in conversations. Can the delivery be made? Is the capability there? Is the staffing appropriate to handle it? Remember, there is no previous track record for the big client, so there is not much of a track record.

Finally, big companies often make demands—sometimes excessive demands—on short notice and they do not mind making you jump through hoops to keep them satisfied and happy.

Be Remarkable

Perhaps it is fitting to end this chapter with a discussion about being different. Earlier in the book we discussed the importance of having a niche product—a service that no one else can do as successfully as you can. Sometimes, however, it even needs to be more. It needs to be remarkable. According to Seth Godin, author of *Purple Cow: Transform Your Business by Being Remarkable*, the marketing landscape has changed.[5] You must be remarkable; you must be different to be successful. Everyone else who can offer the same service, the same product, and in the same way, becomes very boring in a boring world.

Why Be Remarkable?

Consultants are everywhere. It is a fast-growing occupation dominated by individuals and firms that are destined to fail. For almost any service imaginable, there is someone who can offer it. Consequently, your service must be unique, it must be presented differently, and it must get attention, because clients today have many choices for solving problems. Clients are hard to reach; they are not readily available and will not necessarily respond to many of the traditional marketing methods. Mass-marketing is not going to work in most consulting environments; therefore, the approach, service, attention, delivery, and follow-up must be unique. Simply having a successful client and betting on that success to create new successful clients may not work. The old rules simply do not work as well.

How to Do It

First and foremost, make sure that the service, or the delivery of the service, is unique. This has to build on experience and expertise. The expertise is a given to go down this journey. Find out who is listening, who's interested, and what it is they want to hear. What is the important way to present this?

Find satisfied clients and get their opinion as to what can be done to let others know about the service. You may be surprised. They may tell you some things that you did not expect. It may be the way in which it was presented, or described, or actually delivered, or the way in which the uniqueness is packaged.

It must be differentiated from the services others offer, and one-on-one relationships are more critical than mass media. Look for new ways and new twists. Consider even the novel idea of promising results, presenting that as a guarantee, and be willing to tear up the invoice if the results are not there. (This issue is discussed further in later chapters.) You might even try the concept of variable pay, where the pay depends on the success of the project. Consider providing an extra service, unanticipated; deliver something beyond what was planned in the contract. Consider the unexpected evaluation of your service showing that you are successful in a credible, objective way. That makes it different and unique, which goes a long way toward creating your own purple cow.

Final Thoughts

This chapter explored launching or relaunching a consulting practice.

For new businesses, we presented details that are important to initiate the business—to launch it. Although the timing of the launch and the launch itself are important, the groundwork that is needed—proper preparation, networking, building a Web site, offering a unique product or service from the beginning—is critical. It's also important to pursue a large client in the early stages of the process.

For organizations that have been in existence for some time, this chapter provides helpful ideas for planning a relaunch, at a special time such as recognizing a milestone anniversary. Create new things, do some things differently, and implement new approaches, but treat it as a relaunching of the business.

Notes

[1] David Meerman Scott, *Cashing In With Content; How Innovative Marketers Use Digital Information to Turn Browsers into Buyers* (Medford, New Jersey: Information Today, Inc., 2005).

[2] Keith Ferrazzi, with Tahl Raz, *Never Eat Alone: And Other Secrets to Success, One Relationship at a Time* (New York: Currency Doubleday, 2005).

[3] Steve M. Kaplan, *Bag the Elephant! How to Win and Keep Big Customers* (Austin, Texas: Bard Press, 2005).

[4] Ibid.

[5] Seth Godin, *Purple Cow: Transform Your Business by Being Remarkable* (New York: The Penguin Group, 2003).

CHAPTER 6

BUILDING BLOCKS FOR CLIENT DEVELOPMENT

This chapter is intentionally called Client Development to set it apart from labels such as Marketing, Sales, or Finding Clients. From the consulting perspective, the process of identifying clients and shaping their perception about the consulting practice essentially develops the client. Once the client is engaged in a project, client development continues, since current clients may be the most important marketing tool available.

We will go into the many ways in which clients are developed, starting with the different ways to attract clients, make them aware of the consulting practice, and position the consulting practice appropriately in the minds of the clients. We'll discuss which marketing approaches and techniques are most effective as they relate to consulting. And we'll discuss how to keep the clients flowing, turning them into profitable disciples of the business.

Because client development is incremental, given the gradual development of clients, many of the strategies suggested in this chapter take time and often become more complex as they grow. Consequently, it presents what might be called the "building blocks" of a consulting practice.

Client Development Opportunities

With so many opportunities to develop clients, the challenge is to select the correct approach. And because the marketing of consulting is much different from the marketing of retail products, the approach to client development is much different. Let's examine a few issues.

Marketing vs. Selling

Perhaps the most important distinction is the definition of marketing versus selling. Selling is the actual transaction—closing the sale, when a customer actually buys a product or service. For many products, the sale is at the end of the cycle, but for consultants, it is often the beginning of the cycle. Marketing is a process of presenting information about a product or service, creating an image about the product and service, and providing all the information necessary to make a purchase decision. Marketing is about awareness and brand building as much as enticing people to sign the purchase order.

Marketing Principles

As it relates to consulting, marketing has six basic principles:

1. Exposure and recognition are critical. Prospective clients must understand that the consulting practice exists and know the consultant(s) who deliver the service.
2. Targeting a focused client base is essential. The consulting practice is usually narrowly focused because of the uniqueness of the service and the niche it is attempting to develop. Consequently, marketing must be focused on a very specific target audience.
3. Marketing must build the appropriate image. Much of consulting is based on cost and perceived value—two areas that cannot come from an advertisement or exhibit. It must come from a clear understanding of what can be provided and who is providing the service.
4. Cost effectiveness is an important consideration. If marketing is not focused correctly or is not achieving the desired responses, it may be too expensive. Thus, the cost of marketing activities must be carefully weighed against the responses obtained from them.
5. The effectiveness of various approaches should be measured to reflect their effectiveness. Some channels, processes, and approaches produce more results than others—both long and short term. It is important to collect and understand this information.
6. Consistency is critical. A brand needs to be developed, supported, and sustained. There must be a consistent message and image throughout the process.[1]

Passive/Indirect Approaches

Selling consulting is unlike selling a product at a retail store; the marketing and selling processes differ dramatically. The most effective marketing approaches are more indirect, passive, and personal in their connection to the client or prospective client—and there are dozens of approaches in this category. Fortunately, they often require low time commitments and little expense. We will cover this in detail.

Personal Approaches

The outcome of a successful consulting project often hinges on the relationship between the client and consultant. Because of this, the personal approach to prospecting, selling, and client development is critical. A consultant must become familiar enough with the client's needs to be sufficiently involved, and to provide the personal touch that is needed throughout the process. This approach is underscored throughout the chapter.

Paid Advertising and Direct Mail

Depending on the consulting practice, direct mail and paid advertising may or may not be effective. Paid advertising in the appropriate area may provide excellent name recognition, exposure, and branding. Direct mail, when used judiciously to the proper target audience, may be cost effective while at the same time provide exposure and name recognition. Using e-mail has the same effect. The most common and practical direct mail and paid advertising approaches are covered in this chapter.

A word of caution: Telemarketing is not suitable for consulting. Some would argue that telemarketing is not appropriate in any industry, but this rule certainly holds true for consulting. Having a telemarketer call to sell consulting is one of the quickest ways to destroy a consulting business.

Creating a Client Development Process

Client development is the lifeblood of the consulting practice. A systematic, step-by-step process is needed; it cannot be left to chance or random events. Take the time to design a plan and stick with it. This will ensure a consistent process that can be adjusted or modified to make it better.

Create Your Own System

The beginning point for creating a system is to determine the best marketing strategies. Different techniques can be worked systematically. While there may be many processes involved in building name recognition, creating exposure, obtaining referrals, and ultimately developing a brand, the goal is to obtain a face-to-face meeting with the client and turn that meeting into a future prospect.

Figure 6-1 shows the new client development system recommended by Steve Kaplan, author of *Bagging the Elephant.*[2] This process has been modified to reflect the approach used by the ROI Institute and is designed to build upon an introductory mailing to a specific target audience.

As the figure shows, the target for the mail campaign must focus on specific, likely prospects. This mailing will include an article or information that draws attention to the consulting practice as well as a request for a phone call. The phone call, though brief, is designed to glean information to revise the database and ensure that this is a valid prospect. If it appears that this contact does not qualify as a future prospect, the name is either removed from the database (killed) or moved to inactive status. If a meeting is scheduled, the objective of this phase—the sales cycle—is complete. If no meeting is scheduled but there is still some interest (or no lack of interest), the process continues.

An additional mailing where testimonials and a white paper are sent, or more information of value to the client, would be appropriate. This is then followed up with a phone call that would push for a meeting. At this point, three options are available: A meeting is set and the process continues; there is no meeting, the contact remains a prospect, but nothing else is done at the time; or the contact is "killed."

If no meeting is scheduled, but the individual or organization is still a prospect, the prospective client should be included in future mailings, e-mail distributions, newsletters on current status and activities, etc. In essence, they become a prospect for updates and contacts only. If something develops in the future, additional mailings are in order. Kaplan, for example, suggests three mailings leading to three phone calls, but his focus is on getting a huge client. A judgment call has to be made on how much personal follow-up is needed to arrive at a face-to-face meeting.

Whatever the method, it is important to have a logical, rational, step-by-step approach to develop new clients. It does not have to be documented in every step, as indicated in Figure 6-1, but it must involve follow-up with every major direct contact. Obviously, there is a great deal of indirect process,

Figure 6-1   New Client Development Flow Chart

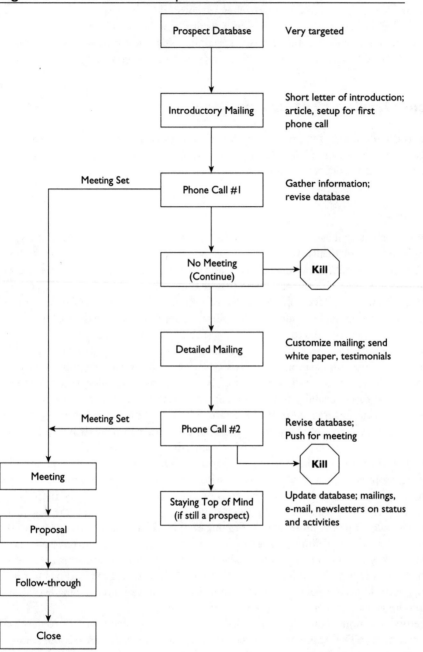

Adapted from Steve Kaplan, *Bag the Elephant! How to Win and Keep Big Customers* (Austin, Texas: Bard Press, 2005).

such as writing articles, giving speeches, and using clients, all of which are discussed in more detail later. These are working in the background to generate new prospects. When a prospect presents itself, the new client development system kicks in.

Using the Internet

It is hard to imagine a consulting practice without heavy use of the Internet. Imagine trying to run a business without a phone. Some perceive the value of the Internet in the same way—it must be one of the most important communication tools and an important part of the marketing approach.

Web Site

The Web site is the key connection to the business through the Internet. To be an effective marketing tool, it must be well organized, helpful, full of easy-to-read content, and easily accessible. Some detail around Web site design was described in the previous chapter.

Blogs and Discussion Lists

With so many blogs available on almost every conceivable topic, it is helpful to pay attention to the bloggers. The bloggers can help you, ignore you, or hurt you. They can bring what you do into the blog, and you can assist the process by getting clients to make comments, add comments yourself, and essentially following the current discussion issues. It can also ignore you. This would be a call to action to ensure that you are involved. In some cases it can hurt you, particularly when some individuals are discussing your consulting practice, methodology, unique advantage, or any articles or books you have written. Ideally, a negative discussion needs to be confronted by neutral individuals.

A discussion list is another useful tool to get others involved in your consulting issues and practices. Sharing what you're doing and adding your comments, advice, suggestions, and thoughts about particular issues can create name recognition and provide additional needed exposure.

A word of caution on both blogs and discussion lists: They can become time consuming, particularly the discussion lists. Trying to stay in touch with discussion list activities may not be worth the effort. Also, many consultants have found that the people who are involved in detailed discussion lists are not clients but competitors. If the clients are not reading the discussion, it may make little difference in your practice. Discussion list activities should be acknowledged in some way. If the discussion is adverse, the negativity should be corrected; otherwise, be careful.

Newsletter Publishing

The Internet makes newsletter publishing affordable and practical. Some consulting practices create a newsletter with useful, helpful, and value-added information, and make this available to the clients at no cost. This information must be perceived as valuable; otherwise it becomes marketing propaganda, or spam for some potential clients. A newsletter requiring much effort may not be cost effective unless there are many current or prospective clients and the newsletter is a principal way of keeping in contact with them. If so, this is an excellent way to update them on changes and improvements, needed services and additions, as well as to provide useful tips, trends, research, and other related innovations.

Communicating with Potential Clients

E-mail can be a very cost effective way to provide new clients with much needed information. It may be the source of the introductory mailing, suggested in Figure 6-1. E-mail can also be sent to other prospects to announce services, provide updates, or offer more information about the consulting firm. It is helpful to distinguish this type of e-mail from what may be considered spam from some clients. Start with an eye-catcher and get right to the point. The less they have to read, the sooner they will get the message. In some cases the e-mail may just bring up an issue and provide a Web site link. The key is to have a very small, focused mailing list and provide useful information for the reader.

The Internet in the Consulting Process

The Internet is the most useful tool for consultants as they develop and submit proposals, maintain routine communications with the client, and deliver interim and follow-up reports. Some organizations will not accept proposals except through the Internet. This is the most effective way to keep the client posted on progress, barriers, and issues around a consulting project. The Internet and a Web site may be very helpful in communicating the final report, although a face-to-face meeting is preferable and will be described in a later chapter.

Using Direct Mail

One of the classic ways to market is through direct mail. It may be helpful for a consulting firm, where there is a tremendous emphasis on securing new clients or gaining exposure in a broad market. Direct mail is an efficient method of advertising since it takes very little time to prepare an effective piece. The delivery is almost automatic: The message is sent out either electronically or through the postal service. This high-level exposure provides the recognition that is sometimes needed for a consulting practice—particularly a new practice. Though it may not work for some, at least on a cost effective basis when the market is narrow and clients are few, direct mail can be a part of a brand-building process to provide exposure for the company name and share its unique methodology.[3]

Types

Direct mail can be in the form of a simple marketing letter introducing a product, service, or the company. It may include an attractive, compelling brochure focusing on the products and services. It may bring attention to a particular type of interest such as research, trends, or some announcement that is important to the profession. The direct mail may instruct participants to go to a Web site, write or call the company, or return a business-reply card. These decisions are based on understanding the culture of the client and what is most likely to work in this process.

Making It Work

For direct mail to be successful, it must be targeted to prospective clients. These client lists can be purchased through a variety of sources belonging to associations or otherwise developed in some way. The direct mail piece must be attractive, but not too flashy. It should catch the attention of the client so it does not automatically end up in the "junk mail" pile. Professional help may be required from a marketing or promotional firm.

The important issue is to control cost because direct mail can be expensive, particularly in the form of printed materials sent through the postal service. E-mail will be much less expensive, but may not get to the client because of spam blockers or other techniques used to control unwanted mail.

A test to determine the effectiveness of a direct mail piece might be helpful, such as a few friendly clients providing their reaction to a particular piece. The key to success is focus, focus, focus. Focus on the right audience, keep it precise and to the point, and if the piece fits the culture of the group, the response should be positive.

Concerns

As mentioned earlier, this may not be cost effective for some consulting firms; for most consulting, it is not the best way to sell a product. It may bring attention to the firm and to the process, but the direct mail itself will rarely result in a sale. In fact, direct mail sometimes turns off clients, since they view it as a desperate move rather than a legitimate marketing process. And too much direct mail can be irritating and fall into the category of junk mail or spam.

Using Paid Advertising

Parallel with the direct mail approach is to purchase advertising space. Paid advertising has been effective in selling many types of service processes. It is often considered an efficient way to reach a large number of potential purchasers. It brings name recognition and exposure. In the early phases of a consulting firm it may be necessary to let large numbers of people know about the firm's existence, particular processes, or unique trademark advantages. It often takes very little time to develop the ads, and it's efficient in terms of the actual time of those involved in the consulting practice. It is helpful in the branding, which is very important to building a long-term, sustained image of the firm.

Trade and Professional Publications

A variety of publications are appropriate for paid advertising. One of the most focused efforts would be an advertisement in a conference brochure where the conference attendees are clients or prospective clients. Another focused audience would be journals and magazines in the profession that is likely to reach prospective clients. Trade magazines in a particular industry that is being targeted can be helpful if the subscriber is the decision maker.

For a broader audience, business publications—local, regional, or national—may be helpful, although their advertising rates generally are more expensive than those of special interest publications. Local newspapers are usually not effective, but may be helpful if the advertising is restricted to a particular part of the newspaper that might be viewed by clients (i.e., the business section). General-interest newspapers are less advantageous because of their wide focus and lack of targeting to a particular audience. Directories may be efficient because of the low cost of most listings. Buyers guides, often developed by a trade association, may be helpful too. The yellow pages is not usually a viable option. Few prospective clients go to the yellow pages to look for a consultant.

Sponsoring a Program

One of the most effective ways to use paid advertising is to host or sponsor an event or activity within a conference that clients and prospective clients are attending. Sponsoring a keynote, break-out session, luncheon, reception, or an award may be appropriate. This not only connects your name to the event, but often includes a full- or partial-page ad as part of the sponsorship. This has the advantage of reaching those people who share your interest and might be attending the conference to find a consultant with your level of expertise. In a way, such advertising provides something of value to prospective clients.

Tips

Developing an effectively focused and compelling ad may require help from a professional marketing or communications firm. The ad must be consistent with previous messages, using the logo and tag line. Branding is always an issue in these ads. The proper balance of content and flash is important so that the ad catches the attention of and communicates helpful information to the prospective client. The critical issue is to ensure that the right group sees the ad and that a specific response, such as a call to action, is a consequence to the ad. This is the case whether a prospective client is visiting a Web site, asking for a document, or requesting a white paper or benchmarking report; this contact can be made through telephone, e-mail, fax, or direct mail.

The biggest concern with paid advertising is the cost involved. Paid advertising is expensive, and unless it is targeted directly to the audience, the process may be inefficient in reaching the right group. Consequently, it may not be cost effective for most consultants.

Building Related Tools and Products

One of the most important client development activities is to build products and services related to the consulting practice. These not only enhance and support consulting, but can drive significant revenue as well. Related tools provide a steady stream of revenue when consultants are not delivering work for the consulting practice. This is more important for smaller firms because if consultants are not driving revenue, there is no revenue stream. In addition, related products and services complement consulting and may be the decisive advantage for securing a consulting contract. The related products and services can vary but usually fit into six categories, which we'll go into below.

Workshops

The most logical supporting process is workshops that offer the consultant's methodology. These workshops should be available to both clients and prospective clients. For some consultants, this is the principal lead-generating process—getting individuals to pay to attend the workshop to learn what the consultant does. The risk is that a participant may learn enough about the methodology to apply it without the help of the consultant, but this is usually a minimal risk.

Software

When the consulting solution needs to be automated, software is sometimes required or essential. Many consultants recommend a commercial software package they have found helpful, or they contract with a software provider in a reseller arrangement. Some consultants develop their own software and sell it along with the consulting process. Still others use a variety of existing software and offer consulting to show how the software can be used.

Equipment

For some consulting projects, equipment may be needed to implement the solution, and the purchase of equipment might come through the consulting firm. In this scenario, it is important to maintain credibility and objectivity. Ideally, the consultant should offer a variety of equipment options and let the client select the one that is most appropriate. As part of the solution, the consultant may install or implement the equipment.

Books

Books can be complementary to consulting processes and often represent one of the most effective ways to sell the consulting. Most well-known consultants will author a book about their methodology and use it as an important lead-generation tool as well as a revenue generator.

Benchmarking

In some situations, benchmarking involves collecting data from organizations addressing a particular topic or issue at hand and presenting this to clients in terms of best practices. This service can be provided for a fee and represents an important or significant revenue generating process while supporting the consulting services.

Research Reports

Similar to benchmarking, research reports show how others are using various processes and tools offered by the consultant. These reports can show the success made and the challenges involved in implementing the processes offered by the consultant. For example, a research report might show the ways in which firms are utilizing the consulting solution, the successes of the solution, or the barriers to its implementation.

Figure 6-2 Sample Breakdown of All
Products and Services

Making Related Products Part of the Process

The pie chart in Figure 6-2 shows the breakdown of other products and services offered by the ROI Institute, a global consulting firm. While the largest source of revenues is consulting, there is a significant amount of revenue generated with workshops that support the trademark process, software that supports consulting, books that explain the process, and research and benchmarking that also complement the process. For a new consulting firm, this may appear to be a daunting task and initially may involve only one additional related product. For a small independent consultant, this is absolutely essential.

These other services generate revenue when consulting is not being delivered. The advantage of using related products is underscored when considering the complementary aspects of the services described.

For example, a consultant who develops books and other publications will use these materials as references or texts for a workshop. The basis of the books and the workshop leads to the sale of the software that supports what is being taught in the workshop and is being described in the books. All of these generate leads for new consulting opportunities, and the consulting opportunities generate more experience to be included in more books and publications or revised editions of them. It becomes an important cycle, where one process feeds another, making the related products and services an integral part of a flourishing consulting practice. Figure 6-3 illustrates the complementary relationship.

Using Workshops to Develop Clients

As described earlier, workshops can be complementary while driving revenues. They can also build expertise and recognition for the consultant. Public workshops can provide all the marketing advantages of any type of promotional or advertising medium.

Figure 6-3   Related Products and Services

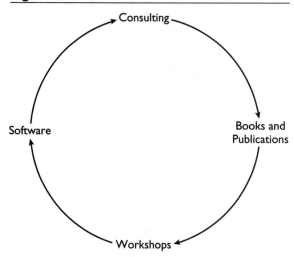

The Challenge

Workshops represent a different product line. A good consultant may not necessarily be a good facilitator; presenting workshops may require developing new skills. If the workshops are not effective and facilitated in an expert manner, future attendance will fall short of expectations and may negatively influence consulting. One challenge is to develop the skills for effective facilitation. Another challenge is to organize the workshops. For public workshops, this may involve securing facilities, arranging for catering services, taking registrations, and marketing the event to ensure that the desired number of people attend.

Many consultants do not have the support or the desire to do all this. In those situations, it may be helpful to partner with an existing workshop provider. For example, the American Management Association can be used as a vehicle to offer workshops. Essentially, AMA advertises the workshops, coordinates the registration, and the consultants show up to make their presentations. Since AMA pays a relatively small fee to the facilitator, this has the advantage of providing low cost marketing while generating a small amount of income, and relieving the consultant from the responsibility of marketing, registration, and logistics. Several types of workshops can be offered. Figure 6-4 shows the typical range of workshop possibilities.

Briefings/Short Workshops

The most logical place to begin is with client briefings or short workshops to prospective clients—up to and including half-day workshops. These may be offered for client groups or within client organizations. The goal is to make sure that the client understands the services by providing new and valuable information. This is not simply a sales pitch or marketing presentation; in fact, marketing should be very subtle. This is information that a client or prospective client needs.

Figure 6-4 Building Blocks for Workshops

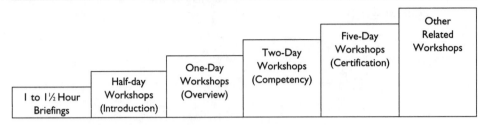

Competency Building Workshops

An extension of a half-day workshop would include workshops of one-, two-, or three-day durations where significant competencies are developed. The challenge is to develop a greater understanding of the processes the consulting firm can offer. In some cases this will involve teaching the client to implement the processes—eliminating the need for the consultant. While this may appear to be intuitively self-destructive, it usually has the opposite effect. Often, the more informed and capable you make the client, the more business it will develop. The client will need more information, take the process to a higher level, or bring the consultant in to review the work.

Certification and Certifying Others

In some situations the consultant may certify others to conduct the same type of work offered by the consultant. While this appears to be shifting the role of consulting from an external provider (the consultant) to an internal consultant, it may have the opposite effect. Having more individuals certified in the methodology can create more interest in and need for assistance from the consultant. Essentially, it is teaching people how to fish, rather than giving them a fish. When clients know how to implement the process, they will continue to use the consultant to validate and review their work. They may also bring the consultant in to expose others to the process and handle the difficult or politically sensitive assignments. Some firms develop a full array of workshops to support existing consulting or to launch a new service.

Business Development Through Writing

Writing may be one of the most critical skills for a consultant, and it can be an important success factor in client development. Writing for the general public is important for enhancing credibility for the consulting practice and for the individual consultant. It shows the expertise and validates the knowledge of the consultant. It provides exposure and recognition that is often needed to market the consulting practice. It is inexpensive and can be highly effective.

Not Everyone's Cup of Tea

A good consultant may not necessarily be a great writer, although writing is one of the critical skills necessary for success, as we mentioned in Chapter 2. Almost every consulting assignment leads to

Figure 6-5   Building Blocks for Writing

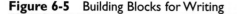

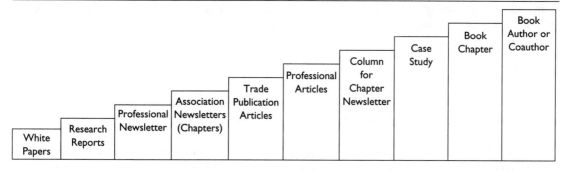

some type of report or impact study, and good writing skills are needed. Using those skills and continuing to develop them for public consumption can provide the promotion, recognition, and marketing needed to sustain a consulting practice. The key is to start small and grow—working up to writing one or more books. Improvement along the way is an important part of the process; getting better with each new article or each new assignment is a way to make this successful. Figure 6-5 shows the stepping-stones to building a writing career to supplement the consulting practice.

Internal Documents

A logical starting point is to develop internal reports. These could be white papers, research reports, or benchmarking reports, written in a way that attracts and holds attention, and that conveys a large amount of information to the audience in a compelling way. These can be transformed into other documents later.

Newsletters

Newsletters are an easy outlet for publishing. Many industry publications, associations, and consulting practices offer newsletters to their clients. In addition, newsletter articles are not subject to the same editorial conditions or criteria that exist for professional journals.

Articles

A very visible approach is to write articles in trade magazines geared to a particular industry or profession. Professional magazines and journals are great outlets, and the editors are always seeking new sources for articles. Obtain the manuscript guidelines for the publication, and follow them closely, taking into consideration the style, format, and appearance of the existing articles.[4]

Columns

Some consultants migrate to writing a column for the local chapter in a newsletter of a professional association or a professional magazine. A regular column goes beyond an article and consistently provides excellent name recognition, issue after issue. It also provides the consultant an opportunity to display the range of projects and issues addressed in the consulting practice. The challenge is that it may be difficult to provide routine articles over an extended period of time because new material is always needed and deadlines come often.

Case Studies

Case studies offer excellent opportunities to showcase the consulting practice. Authoring case studies that represent actual consulting assignments shows the success of the consulting practice, brings recognition to the client (if the name can be mentioned), and creates a desire to have a similar success. The practical slant is very important. There are many outlets for case studies. Trade magazines and professional journals are always looking for printable examples. They make an ideal accompaniment to a workshop. They can be published in books or even special casebooks.

Book Chapters

Preparing a chapter in a book is another stepping-stone. Many edited books are comprised of pieces written by experts and reflecting an industry topic. Knowing what books may be available and having the right contacts may generate an opportunity to author a book chapter. Letting an editor know that you can provide a chapter as needed when a particular book is updated might get you into the book or into the next revision.

Books

The ultimate writing experience is to develop a book that highlights the consulting practice. While this may appear impossible for many consultants, it's remarkable how often this is accomplished. Most business books are written by consultants promoting their concepts and their consulting practices. The top name gurus regularly write books—often pushing their consulting—and the consulting is generating more revenue than the books.

Doing this is easier than most people think. It's a matter of building through the progression and working with appropriate publishers. There are a variety of publishers serving almost all fields. Knowing who they are and obtaining copies of their proposal guidelines is a place to start. Also, consulting *Writer's Market*, finding particular publishers that serve the field, and securing details on how they pursue additional manuscripts, is another approach.

Business Development Through Speaking

Just as writing is an important business development tool, so is speaking. Addressing a variety of audiences creates additional exposure while generating leads for the consulting practice. Speaking to professional audiences increases the credibility of the consultant and the exposure of the consulting practice. It provides name recognition for both the consultant and the firm. It also validates the expertise of the consultant and displays the consultant's capability to a large number of people.

Figure 6-6   Building Blocks for Speaking

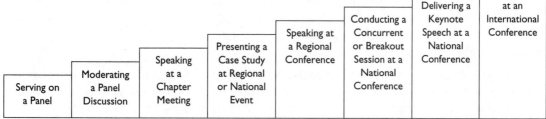

This May Be a Tough Assignment

Becoming a great professional speaker may be beyond the scope of the average consultant, although communicating is an important skill, as mentioned in Chapter 2. Being able to communicate to audiences—large or small—represents the beginning of a successful speaking career, often leading to consulting projects. This is a skill that can be learned and improved over time. It is important to start small and move up the building blocks described in Figure 6-6. Practice, practice, practice, makes this much more effective.

Panel Discussions

Perhaps a starting point is to agree to participate on a panel to discuss a particular topic related to the consulting practice. Panels are readily available at conferences and trade associations. This experience can be elevated, in some cases, to becoming a panel moderator.

Chapter Meetings

Another logical early activity is to speak at chapter meetings of professional groups, or at associations where potential clients may be in attendance. Active participation in the chapter may or may not be required, but chapters are always seeking speakers on topics of interest to their members. Although these organizations seldom provide compensation, this is an excellent marketing strategy.

Presenting a Case Study

Presenting a case study at a regional or national conference is another important step. Most conference organizers want case studies—real life examples of how someone has solved a problem, implemented a process, or taken advantage of an opportunity. Perhaps a case study presentation in concert with the client could add additional credibility while strengthening the consultant-client relationship.

Regional and National Meetings

Regional professional or trade groups represent other opportunities. Presenting a break-out session, a concurrent session, a cracker-barrel or round table discussion, are opportunities. Involvement provides the recognition needed and offers an opportunity to display knowledge and contribute to the profession. The ultimate prize is to present a keynote address to an audience. This usually comes only when there is a hot topic for the membership and the consultant has demonstrated the capability of conducting the keynote presentation.

International Conferences

Beyond the national are the international conferences, where the subjects or issues are discussed on a global level. Starting with concurrent sessions and ultimately moving to keynote presentations at large international conferences provides immense name recognition and the chance to show the credibility of your work.

The Subtle Approach

It is important to distinguish presentations from direct marketing. These presentations must be presented in a lively and engaging way with much value for the audience. The marketing is low key or almost nonexistent. Clients can make the connection that the speaker provides consulting services without a marketing pitch. Many professional organizers do not allow marketing from the lectern, and in fact it is not necessary. Simply providing contact information may be enough to make the desired connection.

Using Clients in Client Development

One of the most powerful ways to develop business is to let current clients do the work for you in both subtle and direct ways. This type of client development is extremely credible and is often perceived to be objective. One client is essentially convincing a potential client that you are offering a successful and valuable consulting service. For some clients the decisive decision-making factor may be that others have used the services and are willing to endorse or validate the success. This client involvement can take on a variety of processes. As shown in Figure 6-7, building blocks are appropriate for using clients in business development.

Figure 6-7   Building Blocks for Using Clients in Business Development

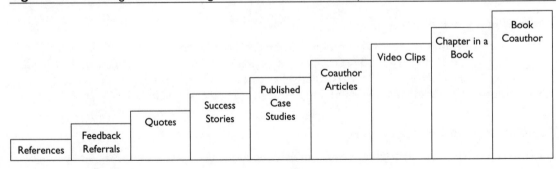

References

The first step would be the use of references from key clients. Before any reference is used, however, the consultant's relationship with the client should have been excellent and the project viewed as successful from the client's perspective. Reference lists of former or current clients can be targeted for a prospective client when they ask for references. A large general list can be offered to prospective clients with a note that you will furnish individual names if they want to contact someone directly.

Referrals

Beyond references, it may be helpful to seek referrals from the client. In this scenario, the clients are asked if there are others who may need your consultant services. When the names are provided, we suggest two approaches: (1) Ask if you can contact them directly and use the client's name as a referral, or (2) ask the client to communicate with prospective clients directly to tell them they may want to explore your consulting service. The latter is preferable, and it's likely that most clients who are very satisfied with the service you offered would be willing to do this.

Quotes

Building on the referrals would be a quote from the satisfied client. This is often a one paragraph description of the consulting success the client has experienced. It's important to have the quote written, including the name, title, and organization of the person who is providing the quote. A quote from an executive at a well-respected organization is more valuable. Above all, the person providing the quote must give the consultant permission to use it in certain types of advertising and marketing.

Success Stories

Every consulting assignment is a potential success story. When success is achieved, it can make an interesting story. When the client perceives the assignment as an unquestionable success, the consultant should document that the client is pleased in order to use the story internally in the organization. Also, it may be possible to provide the story to others externally. If the data is sensitive, a brief summary with the sensitive numbers removed may be helpful. The key point is to obtain permission to use it or to encourage the client to share it with others either through discussion or written communications.

Published Case Studies

Having a client write a case study for publication is another step in business development. The consultant may assist the client, or even offer the case study on a coauthor basis. The consultant would work with the client to find the appropriate publication in a trade magazine, professional journal, or book. The market is ripe for successful case studies, particularly in topics that have not been covered extensively in the literature. If there are no publishing opportunities, the consulting firm should consider self-publishing the case studies and offering them to other clients as additional sharing of information. More important, these case studies serve as a marketing tool for prospective clients.

Coauthoring Articles

Writing a joint article for a professional publication or a trade magazine can display the success of a process that has worked quite well. This goes beyond a case study and shows the importance of a particular process or service provided by a consulting practice. The topic must be of interest, and the consultant must work with the publication to ensure the article complies with manuscript guidelines.

Video Clips

A novel way to use a client in business development is to secure a video clip from the client explaining a part of the process. The client is taped discussing an issue that involves the consulting practice or part of a solution that comes from the consulting process. Essentially, the client is showing what they did to make it work or how they tackled a particular part of the process. The subtlety is that they are endorsing the process and recommending it to others. It may be helpful to write the script for these sessions and arrange for the videotaping to be convenient. Ideally, a group of clients might be interviewed or taped at a professional meeting or trade show. Arranging for a videotaping in a particular room can keep the cost of this approach very low. In addition, the video clips can be used in workshops or other promotional ways.

Chaptering a Book

Bringing the client into a publishing process, including coauthoring a chapter in a book, may be helpful. Obtaining a book contract and inviting different clients to write chapters is an excellent way to strengthen client relationships while developing business from others in the future.

Book Coauthoring

The ultimate development opportunity is to coauthor a book with a client. In this situation, the client should be very high profile and one that can be leveraged significantly to gain additional business. This is the ultimate client/consultant partnership. It is a huge endeavor but has worked for many publications. Many business books are written by a combination of a consultant and that consultant's client. Essentially, the client is endorsing the methodology and the consulting process, and the book becomes an important calling card for the next client.

Using Neutral Experts

The number of industry and professional experts is continuing to grow, with new categories added every few years. These groups can be a very inexpensive but credible resource for developing new clients. Information presented by published neutral experts is considered credible because these individuals are unbiased and have expertise on a particular topic. It is important to ensure that these individuals are perceived as both neutral and expert. Several methods, or building blocks, can be used to develop these experts, as can be seen in Figure 6-8.

Figure 6-8   Using Neutral Experts for Development

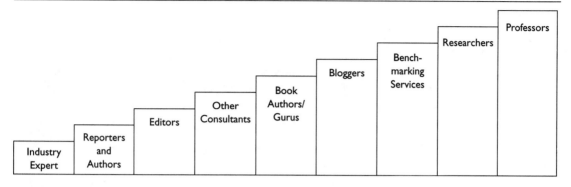

Industry/Professional Experts

In almost any profession or industry, there are people considered to be experts. Some are self-appointed, but others are recognized in the literature and industry. By being aware of your service, practice, or expertise, these experts may refer to you and your work or include your material in some of their publications, speeches, or reports. After all, they need continuing information to disseminate to their audience.

Reporters and Freelance Authors

Freelance authors who write articles for newspapers, newsletters, or magazines and other publications are always searching for ideas. Making them aware of trends, issues, and your work may stir up interest. Do not be surprised if the initial contact is not warm, friendly, and inviting. Just remember, they need sources, and it could be that they see you as another important source. Also, they need stories and angles, and you may provide that with your particular topic of experience.

For example, consider the experience of Marshall Goldsmith, who runs a very-high-profile consulting firm specializing in executive coaching. Marshall has gained much national press by developing relationships with editors and reporters of high-profile magazines or working with clients who have that connection. This has led to Marshall's firm being routinely listed in these magazines.

Magazine Editors

The professional magazines of the field offer a great opportunity for promotion. Magazine editors are always looking for sources, information, and reports. Providing information may help them write a story, feature your process, or explain a success you have experienced.

Other Consultants

Other consultants in a noncompetitive field may be helpful. These should be high-profile consultants or consultants in a complementary process. Essentially, letting them know what you're doing puts them in a position to refer clients to you. This could be arranged in a formal way, such as mutual referrals.

Book Authors/Gurus

People who write books need information. They need to know what others have done. For the mainstream books in your profession, it may be helpful to provide the authors of those books with information about what you do. This might entice them to include your expertise in their work. Having a guru write a story about you in a major publication can be a significant client development opportunity.

Bloggers

Bloggers permeate every field, and the person who is managing a Web log will need information about your expertise. Select a blog that is important to you and is one where your clients are participating. Join in the conversation, offer your information, or provide data to the blogger.

Benchmarking

Benchmarking studies are being conducted in almost every profession. Providing information to benchmarking groups involved in your field can be very important, and your input might enhance the likelihood that you will be included in the next report.

Researchers

There are many professional researchers, particularly in the Internet research field. Contacting the Association of Independent Information Professionals and understanding who is tracking information in your industry may be helpful. Making contact with them, familiarizing them with your Web site, and providing information about your methodology can ensure that you are included in some of their research reports.

Professors

An often overlooked resource for development is professors who teach a subject closely connected to your practice. Offering professors the benefit of your expertise, information, research, publications, and success stories provides them with additional material for their classes. They may invite you to participate as a guest lecturer, but more important, mention your name frequently. One of those students may become a client in the future.

Creating Alliances and Partnerships

For most businesses, this is the age of partnerships and alliances. Most successful businesses do not operate independently. Often they provide only a part of the solution. They rely on many partners who complement the processes and enable each of the partners to be successful. This is particularly true for consultants who do not have the resources to develop everything that may be needed to complement their work. Consequently, alliances and partnerships are becoming critical to survival and the ability to deliver services. Partnerships also represent an important way to leverage the scope and impact of consulting processes with minimum investment. It can be the growth engine for the future.

Complementary Processes

Figure 6-9 shows the building blocks to be successful at building productive alliances and partners. As the figure shows, it's best to start small and move to more involved and sophisticated relationships. Partners may be available who offer either products or services that complement the consulting practice. It may be a service provided prior to or after your consulting niche, or it may be a complementary process that leads to or uncovers the need for your particular services. Either way, these complementary processes can be extremely valuable in developing the business relationship.

For example, the ROI Institute, which provides consulting services to show the impact or success of a particular process, partners with other firms that offer complementary services. A large commercial bank system, for instance, decided to upgrade all of its software and hardware for the branch locations. Accenture, a large consulting firm, received a contract to manage the technology implementation project. Operating independently of the bank and Accenture, the ROI Institute was engaged to show the value of the project. Accenture became a partner because they offer complementary processes. In this case, they were performing much of the work that was evaluated by the institute.

Partnerships and alliances are an efficient and effective way to grow the business, reach new clients, and develop existing clients. It is often inexpensive and becomes a natural in the consulting environment. The important point is for the partnership agreements to have a win-win approach so all partners are benefiting from the relationship.

Technology Support

Another important partnering opportunity may be the use of technology. Many consulting processes utilize either existing technology or have technology developed specifically for implementing the

Figure 6-9   Building Blocks for Alliances and Partners

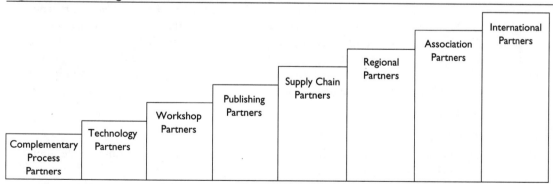

consulting solution. Some consulting firms choose not to invest in the actual technology development, but rather partner with a technology firm that has expertise in the area to offer special software for the consulting process or find existing software that can be used with the consulting process. In either case, the technology firm becomes a partner, and these partnerships can grow and flourish in the future. This has the added advantage of avoiding an investment in the technology.

Workshop

As mentioned earlier, workshops may be an important part of building capability awareness for a particular consulting service. As workshops are offered, many consulting firms do not want to maintain staff levels to engage in the required workshop administration, logistics, and coordination. Essentially, they want to avoid the business of marketing workshops, taking registrations, and working with hotels. Consequently, they find a workshop partner who has this as a primary business and will compensate the consultant for conducting the workshop. This works quite well for many consultants since it keeps staff at a minimum, exposure still quite high, and provides a process that builds the business. The downside is that workshop fees are often low when all of the risk is absorbed by a workshop partner.

Publications and Publishing

As mentioned earlier, publishing may be an important business development tool. When publishing involves booklets, books, or case study books, a publishing partner may be appropriate. This may be a major publisher willing to publish a book or casebook about the methodology, or the publication arm of a professional association that will publish case studies or books about a particular service of interest to its members. There are many other smaller publishers focusing on a market or niche. Finding that partner and working with them in productive ways may keep publishing costs to a minimum and also avoid the stigma that is sometimes associated with self-publishing.

Supply Chain Partners

Sometimes a consulting service is part of a chain of processes, and the consulting solution may involve the implementation of products, equipment, or technology. The organizations that offer these products could become partners with the consulting practice. It is important to maintain objectivity (i.e., not recommending or referring a product unless it is indeed the best product). Other supply chain opportunities may surface early in the process—the activities or processes that often lead to the need for consulting. For example, auditors and inspectors may uncover a situation that calls for consulting to correct a problem or unfavorable situation. In essence, these auditors and inspectors become partners of the process. It is important to ensure that the relationship does not represent a conflict of interest and that the processes remain objective throughout.

Regional Partners

When moving into new areas, it may be helpful to find a regional partner who can provide similar consulting services in a different city or state. This partnership precludes the hiring of additional staff or entering into contractual arrangements with a consultant. An existing consulting firm becomes the local consultant for a particular methodology or process. This is an efficient way to leverage and grow the business in lieu of consultant contracts and employment obligations.

Association Partners

When the consulting practice supports the processes where association members are involved, the association may become a partner. This is important when the association recognizes the importance of the service offered by the consulting firm. For example, Meeting Professionals International (MPI) sought a partner to help members measure the impact and return on investment in large meetings. They developed a partnership with the ROI Institute. The institute provides workshops, consulting services, tools, templates, and a variety of other services for MPI members, becoming an important partner for the association.

International Partners

As a consulting practice grows, the global market has obvious growth potential. Some firms begin with this perspective in mind and try to serve the global market. This has one advantage: It provides leverage over other firms in those countries. International partnerships essentially mirror the services offered by the consulting firm, but in that language and culture. International partners are tied by branding, maybe even common names, and become part of a professional network of users. This is often considered the ultimate of partnerships and brings a global presence to the consulting firm.

The ROI Institute, which offers a variety of consulting services around measurement, evaluation, and accountability, has developed partners in more than 35 countries. This enables the institute to increase its exposure to different types of organizations and cultures at very little expense and with many rewards in terms of royalties and license arrangements.

Associations and Exhibits

Although sometimes considered expensive, exhibiting at conferences and association meetings may provide important exposure and needed recognition to continue to develop clients and build the business. Exhibiting is important to attract attention from a particular audience. If attendees at the association or conference are potential clients (or are in the mix), the exhibit can bring proper attention to services offered. In addition, it provides a presence because, for some conferences and exhibits, who is *not* there is sometimes as important as who *is*. Not participating in a conference may be perceived as not being a viable part of the market.

Exhibiting can also provide immediate contact with potential customers in a brief interactive mode to begin to reinforce the message delivered, the value of the service, and the overall marketing approach. It may be a valuable process of learning about the client and improving the marketing strategy.

Joining the Right Organization

The message here is twofold: First, get involved and join the right association; second, consider exhibiting to those associations. The most important issue of determining whether to join an organization is from the client development perspective—picking the association where the prospective clients exist. This becomes obvious for some industries, less so for others.

For example, when the ROI Institute provides consulting services to meeting planners, it's obvious that the institute should be involved in the principal meeting planning association—Meeting Professionals International—and consider exhibiting at their annual conferences. However, consider the Accenture project mentioned earlier. Accenture was managing a technology implementation to a large banking network. Which association should Accenture join and support with an exhibit? Should Accenture exhibit at a financial services conference? Maybe. Should Accenture be involved in conferences where technology providers are in attendance? Maybe. Should Accenture be involved in professional associations involving marketing and client development? Maybe—maybe all of them.

The important point is to pick the one group where the appropriate focus exists and become actively involved in the association—if it makes sense to mix and mingle with the clients and stay informed of current issues and activities.

A second category for associations would be those where the technical processes are located. Take the consulting firm that provides telecommunications consulting to clients, helping them to decide how to configure their networks for maximum effectiveness. Most of the consultants are electrical engineers. For client development, these consultants may be involved in associations where the clients are likely to be in attendance. But at the same time, consultants may participate in professional organizations such as the Institute of Electrical and Electronic Engineers, where the process of what is provided is discussed from a technical perspective. Clients will not necessarily be there, but it provides an opportunity to understand the latest trends, issues, and techniques.

Still others may want to be involved in associations where other consultants are located. There are a few groups of consultants, such as the Society for the Advancement of Consulting, which is dedicated to the promotion and advancement of small consulting groups.

Active Participation

To get the most out of any association or professional society, participation is important. If the association or society includes prospective clients as members, active involvement becomes critical. This may take the form of local involvement to national events. It may involve serving on a committee, chairing the committee, acting as chairman, president, or even serving on the board of a national organization. Attending the conferences not only provides an opportunity to develop clients, but to learn and grow professionally.

Selecting the Right Place to Exhibit

The most important consideration when deciding to exhibit at a trade show, conference, or association meeting is to determine the number of clients that will be in attendance. Using the available data, determine the likelihood of getting business from those clients. Some organizations, such as the International Association of Exhibition Management, offer tools and templates to help consulting firms decide if they should exhibit at a particular trade show. It is based on the number of registered attendees, the number they anticipate visiting your booth, the percentage responding to follow-up, and ultimately making a sale. This benefit stream can then be compared to the cost of the exhibit to see if there is a potential return on this investment. A return on investment may not occur for some time—often one to two years.

In addition to the actual return on investment calculation, there are other benefits. One is the amount of learning that can take place to understand the issues, clients, culture, and interaction with those clients. Also, there are the intangible benefits such as the brand building, name recognition, and relationships. Just having a presence can be important to the profession. All of this has to be weighed against not only the direct cost, but also the time and expense to make it work. It will require preparation time, commitment to working the exhibit, travel time, and expenses, as well as the cost of the exhibit.

Making the Exhibit Work

To make the exhibit work, the process should be carefully planned with the objectives in mind—the reason to attend the conference. Booth design must portray a professional image, communicate the brand, and underscore the messages communicated during the conference. Giveaway items are very important, but should be chosen carefully; ideally, they should have value to the client as something they can use regularly. Each person in the booth should have business cards and other promotional material and be prepared to discuss results with key clients.

Remember, yours is one of many booths the clients are interested in visiting. Clients are interested in quick messages and results; the quicker you can get to results that can be delivered by consulting, the more attention it will attract. It is usually not recommended to go online in a booth because it takes too much time, involves more expense, and increases the chances of experiencing technology difficulties.

Ideally, participants registered for the conference should be invited ahead of time to visit the exhibit. An invitation should be connected to giveaway items or special information they may need. The individuals staffing the booth should be prepared for a tough, draining assignment, but it can be valuable in learning about the marketplace as well as developing clients. Above all, the individuals should always be professional, and every part of the experience should be consistent with the image and branding desired. Booth attendants should ask prospective clients for business cards, and there should be some follow-up mechanism.

Working a Trade Show

In addition to the exhibiting, a trade show provides an opportunity to learn more about the competition in the market. Working from a plan of which places to see and visit is necessary on a tight schedule. This provides an opportunity to check out the competition, scan for ideas, and identify where people are attracted. As these ideas and information are uncovered, this can be easily recorded in a pocket recorder. Be prepared for impromptu meetings with potential clients. Attend other sessions—particularly those presented by the competition—and *always* have business cards on hand.

Use Your Brand

In this and the previous chapter, several references were made to branding. This is an important part of client development. Branding provides a source of promise and value to clients, and it's critical to develop it, live it, and sustain it. As mentioned earlier, a brand is very important in terms of the image being portrayed in the materials, the messages, and the marketing. It also brings consistency to ensure the same message, image, and process. These days, connecting the organization to value is crucial. Clients are seeking value, particularly in the consulting process, and branding is one way to convey the image that your firm provides value. Another issue is underscored here: Make your brand very visible.[5]

Developing the Brand

To make sure the brand is developed properly, it should be placed on everything: written documents, giveaway items, final reports, and Web site communication. It should be on any document or item where the company's name is used. It should be communicated routinely and, where appropriate, included in conversations. It should be referred to often by the consultants and staff members.

Living the Brand

A brand that communicates a particular image will be destroyed if the consultants fail to live the image. If a brand is about delivering value, the consulting must deliver value. The concepts behind the brand should be internalized by the consultant and the staff, and the meaning should be practiced routinely. Above all, it should be reinforced, perhaps by including how well the consultant lives the brand in performance review, with the result reflected in the consultant's pay structure. When this happens, the consultants will live it.

Sustaining the Brand

For a brand to be effective, it must be sustained over a period of time. Changing a brand portrays the image of a firm trying to find its identity, and changes should be initiated only on rare occasions and long after the brand has been established. When a new service or product is rolled out, it should be consistent with the brand and have the brand information connected to it. The consultant's behavior should be consistent so that it becomes inherent in the training and development programs of the consulting firm. Clients should experience the brand, consistently over time as they become involved in subsequent consulting assignments. These efforts should ensure that the brand is sustained over a period of time.

The Personal Approach

This chapter would not be complete without emphasizing the need for a personal approach in marketing, though the importance of this was underscored in many of the marketing and client development techniques offered.

In contrast to selling a product or service in a retail store, consulting is personal, and the need to communicate personally is important in client development. Making personal phone calls to follow up a particular marketing piece or client development action is critical. A personal, face-to-face visit is preferable, particularly if that visit has the possibility of generating a proposal. However, most clients do not have time for chat sessions to talk about business opportunities. Thus, a personal visit may be difficult to schedule. If the visit can be a briefing on the latest trends, research, and perhaps even on your unique methodology, it may become acceptable. This personal touch can go a long way toward strengthening a relationship that can turn into a business opportunity.

The personal approach involves following up with communications. As the business grows, this becomes more difficult. Consider employing an efficient assistant, which can ensure follow-up. Sometimes service agreements contain a clause where the consultant commits to get back to the client within a certain period of time.

Personal follow-up with new clients to gauge progress is critical throughout the project. Following up and communicating with existing clients to check on continued progress may trigger a need for new activity. Meeting key clients at events or conferences, hosting dinners or lunches, or arranging specific meetings is another way to utilize communications to continue to build clients.

Marketing Mistakes

To make this chapter complete, it may be helpful to examine some of the mistakes made in an attempt to develop a client base. Table 6-1 contains a list of mistakes made by some of the best experts in the field. They are collective mistakes provided by some of the materials referenced in this book as well as the author and are reminders of what we should avoid as the client development process continues.

Final Thoughts

The variety of approaches and techniques presented in this chapter to create client relationships is the lifeblood of a consulting business. They are the building blocks, since much of client development builds on simple approaches and moves to the most advanced and complex. Many of the approaches presented here are based on indirect, passive marketing and powerfully create the need

Table 6-1 Common Mistakes

1. Making cold calls	9. Relying too much on the Web site
2. Attempting to be just any kind of consultant	10. Marketing only on a local basis
3. Reducing marketing when you have one or two big clients	11. Failure to use referrals from satisfied customers
4. Creating marketing materials internally	12. Sending brochures to a large mailing list
5. Relying too much on direct mail	13. Losing the personal touch
6. Sending spam e-mails	14. Failure to examine costs vs. benefits of a marketing approach
7. Missing the audience	
8. Listing in a business directory or yellow pages	

Figure 6-10   Client Development Checklist

	Always	Pursued Sometimes	Never
Use a systematic client development system	☐	☐	☐
Use the Internet to develop clients	☐	☐	☐
Mail selected items of interest to prospects	☐	☐	☐
Provide valuable information routinely to clients	☐	☐	☐
Publish articles in relevant journals and magazines	☐	☐	☐
Provide pro bono work to community/nonprofit groups	☐	☐	☐
Exhibit at trade shows and association meetings	☐	☐	☐
Secure interviews in newspapers and magazines	☐	☐	☐
Publish a book related to unique service	☐	☐	☐
List in directories and trade publications	☐	☐	☐
Advertise for visibility, branding, and leads	☐	☐	☐
Network with other consulting firms	☐	☐	☐
Join client industry/trade associations	☐	☐	☐
Employ professional publicists and agents	☐	☐	☐
Create complementary products and services	☐	☐	☐
Use workshops to generate consulting clients	☐	☐	☐
Request referrals from clients	☐	☐	☐
Request testimonials from satisfied clients	☐	☐	☐
Coauthor an article with a client	☐	☐	☐
Use a neutral expert to promote your service	☐	☐	☐
Use partnerships to leverage growth	☐	☐	☐
Promote your brand on every document	☐	☐	☐
Use a personal touch in communications and follow-up	☐	☐	☐

for consulting services. These often start out small and develop into more involved and comprehensive processes.

As a brief reminder of the vast array of possibilities, Figure 6-10 presents a client development checklist showing many of the techniques offered in this chapter. This is only the beginning of the possibilities.[6]

Notes

[1] Robert Bacal, *The Complete Idiot's Guide to Consulting* (Madison, Wisconsin: CWL Publishing Enterprises/Alpha Books, 2002).

[2] Steve Kaplan, *Bag the Elephant! How to Win and Keep Big Customers* (Austin, Texas: Bard Press, 2005).

[3] Elaine Biech, *The Consultant's Quick Start Guide: An Action Plan for Your First Year in Business* (San Francisco: Jossey-Bass/Pfeiffer, 2001).

[4] Mary Ellen Bates, *Building & Running a Successful Research Business: A Guide for the Independent Information Professional* (Medford, New Jersey: CyberAge Books, 2003).

[5] Catherine Kaputa, *U R a Brand! How Smart People Brand Themselves for Business Success* (Mountain View, California: Davies-Black Publishing, 2005).

[6] Alan Weiss, *Million Dollar Consulting: The Professional's Guide to Growing a Practice* (New York: McGraw-Hill, Inc., 1992).

CHAPTER 7

WRITING PROPOSALS THAT WORK

This chapter is devoted to the importance of creating proposals, which is the primary method of securing business for most consultants. The various approaches used to develop and present proposals, however, can make a crucial difference in pursuing and winning consulting assignments.

Highly detailed, complex, and comprehensive proposals are not always necessary; a simple letter of understanding outlining the project goals is sufficient in some cases. For a variety of reasons and in most situations, though, such a basic letter will not be enough, and a formal proposal is required. It is important to develop effective proposals. We will look at creating effective proposals, along with the critical steps necessary to ensure that the consultant fully understands the challenges of the project, gathers the needed intelligence, and includes all of the proven elements that winning proposals should contain.

The various proposal philosophies are described, as are the differing approaches for developing both simple and complex proposals—or something in between. Presentation strategies are addressed at the end of the chapter, along with a discussion of common pitfalls and challenges associated with the important functions of developing and presenting proposals.

The Role of Proposals

Two important facts about the consulting process typically emerge from any substantive discussion of proposal development:

1. Most consultants do not enjoy and may even resist writing proposals.
2. Most consulting projects require a proposal.

To some consultants, securing projects with a handshake agreement and minimal documentation seems convenient and inviting. However, this arrangement can be a recipe for disaster later, since projects can easily go astray due to unfortunate misunderstandings that might have been avoided with a mutually accepted written proposal.

The Only Way to Get the Business

For most projects, a proposal is required. In a growing number of situations, it is required through a formal process after a request for proposals has been issued. Thus, creating a proposal is the only route for many projects, and the larger the project, the more formal the proposal process is likely to be. Because of this, knowing how to complete the process thoroughly and consistently is perhaps the best determinant of whether the business will grow steadily.

As an Agreement of Understanding

One of the most important functions of a proposal is to help make sure that all of the parties are on the same page. The proposal sets forth what is needed from the client perspective, thus allowing the consultant to begin formulating a plan for how the need will be solved—in as much detail as the client desires. This facilitates a clear understanding of the project, its scope, timing issues, and costs, in addition to goals related to benefits, outcomes, and payoffs. The proposal also helps prevent misalignment, misunderstanding, and the potential deterioration of the consultant's image for missing the mark.

As a Compliance Mechanism

In some organizations, particularly in governmental units, the proposal is necessary even for very small consulting projects. It is an integral part of the contracting process and must be submitted to the appropriate government agencies as part of achieving compliance with applicable rules and regulations. Even if the client wishes to hire the consultant and has perhaps even entered into an informal agreement, the formal process may be required because of the need to be in compliance. Failure to follow the process may kill the project before it gets started.

As a Learning Process

A detailed comprehensive proposal, when approached in the manner suggested in this chapter, provides an excellent learning process. It is an opportunity to learn more about the situation, the needs, and what is desired by the client. It provides an opportunity to understand more about the market and the competition, and what is available, and to understand the capability and responsiveness of the consulting firm. Finally, it provides a great opportunity to build a history, which is often needed for the next opportunity.

As a Relationship Building Process

A proposal may be the beginning of a relationship (or the renewal of an existing relationship) with the client. When successful, how the proposal is developed and presented represents an important beginning of that relationship. A carefully structured proposal with specific objectives, deliverables, and product timelines provides an excellent structure and discipline to deliver the solution needed by the client. It also helps nurture and improve the client relationship.

However, if the proposal is one of many that have been obtained and if it is not successful, there is still an opportunity for relationship building. The challenge here is to find out what went wrong and to correct it for the future. This situation provides an opportunity to build a future relationship.

In short, the proposals are an important way of life. There are many great advantages of going through the proposal writing process. It is resisted because it takes effort, but the payoff is often in proportion to the effort. This chapter should provide some structure, processes, tips, and techniques to accomplish this very essential part of the consulting process.

Responding to a Request for Proposal

In some situations the proposal may be in response to a request for proposal (RFP). This is a more formal approach and inherent in very large projects. To be fair and impartial, some organizations will require RFPs for any proposal above an estimated project budget.

Helping Your Client Prepare the RFP

Many requests for proposals come out of projects that have been initiated informally between a client and the consultant. Perhaps the consultant has suggested and initiated or even planted the seed for a particular project. Or a client has a particular project in mind and has contacted the consultant because compliance with the RFP is necessary. In this case, the consultant has a unique opportunity to help shape the RFP.

It is not uncommon for clients to ask the consultant to help provide the recommended specifications for the project. Obviously, this provides the consultant with the unique advantage of providing specs that fit the particular niche or methodology offered by the consulting firm. To some, this seems to be unethical, creating an unfair advantage over others who may respond. For the consultant, who perhaps initiated it, or the client, who desires a particular consultant, this seems a logical process. This does not necessarily mean that the consultant in mind will automatically secure the project, but it does mean that the consultant has an opportunity to highlight the uniqueness of the consulting firm.

Is There a Ringer?

This type of process creates a problem for others who would respond. The first question to ask about any particular RFP: "Is there some consultant or some consulting firm destined to receive this project?" As difficult as it is to ask or even respond to this question, it needs to be addressed. Otherwise, a tremendous amount of time could be wasted on the proposal.

This is not to suggest that the activity is necessarily unethical; it may be that a particular consultant has a unique process, and the client is unaware of others that may be able to provide it. This open proposal process to the RFP provides an opportunity to see if others could provide the same service, perhaps even with some additional advantages or even at a lower cost. For those who are responding and are not in the loop, it's important to weigh the risks. Is it worth the effort if the RFP has been generated informally through a predetermined arrangement? It may be difficult for the client to even admit that this is going on, but digging and searching may help.

Searching for Clues

The proposal itself often provides clues of a previous informal arrangement. A specific methodology, process, and deliverable that might be unique to another consulting firm each provides a hint that an arrangement might exist. A complete reading of the proposal several times by different individuals can often uncover these hints. This additional reading may reveal not only that others are involved, but that there are underlying issues that have not clearly been reported.

Use the Checklists

While reading the RFP, it might be helpful to review the situation analysis checklist provided later in the chapter. This list poses important questions that may determine if others may be familiar with the situation. Asking them about the issue might uncover the information. Understanding all of the stakeholders involved and their particular roles is very important, and reviewing with the stakeholders may provide additional information. The section on gathering intelligence can be helpful in terms of identifying the people and framing the issues to confront, discuss, or explore. Seeking all of these items, which may not be clearly stated in the RFP, is crucial.

Challenging the RFP

In some situations the client may be ill informed. The client may be seeking a solution without the proper analysis to point to that solution, or the solution may clearly be incorrect, or there might be a much better solution to the problem at hand. In these cases, it may be appropriate to diplomatically challenge the assumptions in the RFP by offering some information that might be helpful to make the adjustment. This must be accomplished in a delicate way to avoid alienating the client. No one wants to be challenged or be informed that their analysis is incorrect. But if it is clearly off the mark, letting them know may be the best course of action.

Protesting the RFP

In most cases a protest is not recommended, but if the adjustments described above are not made, it may be appropriate. The protest can be made before or after the award is made. Unfortunately, protests often are initiated after the award is finalized, where the protesting consultant did not win the bid.

If a protest is lodged, it should be made before the actual contract is awarded. With the government, there are several ways in which formal protests can be filed with the Government Accountability Office (gao.gov). Also, there is the possibility of filing a formal lawsuit. This action may do more damage than good, and consultants must weigh the risk of the protest versus how it will affect their chances in the future. It may be best to walk away after a good effort is made to try to change the RFP.

Gathering Intelligence

Before tackling the issues involved in developing a proposal, much information is needed, and gathering intelligence becomes a critical skill. First, a good intelligence gathering system is needed with most projects. If it is in place and properly working, the RFP should never be a surprise. Information in an effective intelligence gathering process will involve both the topics addressed and the sources of information on the topics.

Intelligence Topics

Table 7-1 lists the information needed in an ideal situation. Some of these topics are very sensitive, and as result it may be difficult to uncover reliable details. Others are developed over time, working with other consultants in the marketplace and through contacts with the client. The information about the history of the client with the consulting issue is important. Essentially, we need to know how the problem evolved, what caused it to get to the point where it is today in this proposal, the relationship to other projects, or other ongoing activities that might be related to the topic.

Understanding your competition is crucial, which includes knowing the competitors who might be involved in the project and the extent of their relationship with the client. This begins to show the strengths and weaknesses of the competition. More important, as discussed earlier, is knowing whether the client has any sort of commitment to another consulting firm. Pricing and funding are two critical issues. Gaining insight into expected pricing would be crucial information. Is there a history of what they're willing to pay? Which department or division is actually providing the funding? This may provide critical insight in terms of what the budget might be, or what budget might be acceptable.

It is also important to understand more about the proposal. Several questions need answers. Are there any particular hot buttons in the proposal that must be addressed in a particular way? What are the success factors for the project? How will the proposal be judged? What has been done previously? What are the concerns and worries about the project, both from the perspective of the client and the consulting team? Who may have concerns about the project's viability? How urgent is the project? Does it need to be done even quicker than the time frame specified? Would this be an advantage?

Understanding more about the situation may involve other documents. Availability and accessibility become issues. Understanding the key stakeholders, defined later in this chapter, is important. Trying to understand the management commitment to the project is a tricky issue. Without commitment and support, the project will not be successful. The final issue is the perception of the consulting firm. Is there a current relationship? How effective has this been? This, at least, should be easily assessed.

Table 7-1 Intelligence Gathering Checklist

Client history with issue	☐	Funding mechanism	☐
Relationship to other projects	☐	Proposal hot buttons	☐
Competitors that may be involved	☐	Typical success measures used by client	☐
Commitment to another firm	☐	Concerns and worries about project	☐
Competitor relationship to client	☐	Urgency of project	☐
Pricing insights	☐	Stakeholders	☐
Related documents	☐	Client perception of consulting firm	☐
Management commitment to project	☐		

These and perhaps other issues are topics to explore to get into the proposal process. Information may not be available on all of them, but the more information that can be obtained, the better the proposal. Some of this information will be used in detailing the situational analysis and the stakeholder analysis described later.

Sources of Information

Information sources can vary significantly depending on the situation. The most obvious source would be the client, if the client is willing to provide information. Some of this information may have been obtained routinely over time. An understanding of the pricing, success factors, hot buttons, and similar issues may be readily available from the history of working with the client. If this is not the case, another individual may be able to discuss these issues. Other members of the client team involved may be able to shed some light as well. Those closest to the situation but not constrained about providing information, are excellent sources. These sources often come from informal networks with the client.

Sometimes the market will have information through informal networks, other consultants and professionals involved in the same field. Related documents may be available directly from the client or others familiar with this situation. Previous consultants who have worked with the client may be willing to provide data, although this may not be the case if they're competing for the project.

This exercise shows the importance of having an existing relationship before the RFP is actually presented. When this is the case, many of these answers are already known and the consultant is actively involved in the process leading to the proposal.

Proposal Philosophy

Proposals should be addressed with a certain philosophy in mind. The approach is important and must be consistent with not only what the client desires or needs, but with what the consulting firm is willing to offer and present. Having an effective philosophy should provide the consultant with an important edge. Several key issues should be considered when choosing a philosophy for the proposal that is likely to suit the client.

Meeting Needs vs. Shifting Needs

The first part of the philosophy is to determine how to address the needs outlined in the proposal. Should they be met as described, or should they be shifted or changed? In some cases the needs may not be on track, or they may be vague. The challenge is to convince the client that the needs should be more clearly defined, that there is an assumption of a different need, or that the needs should be specified completely differently. These are all possibilities, but it's important to reflect the philosophy of the consulting practice. While it's sometimes best to just do what is requested, an alternative approach is to discuss, explore, negotiate, or even challenge a need that appears to be inconsistent with logic. Additional information may be in order.

Results vs. Activity

As mentioned earlier in this book, there has been a dramatic shift to results-based consulting. Traditionally, consulting projects were based on activity: analyzing issues, performing tasks, implementing software, and completing action items. However, since more clients are seeking results, projects need to focus on outcomes. This philosophy, if practiced, should show up throughout the proposal, providing measures of business success, clearly defined objectives, and monetary benefits. Making the focus of the project more results-based is the key.

General vs. Specific

Some consultants would like for the proposal to be brief and vague. The more detail, these consultants argue, the more problems it can create, the more work they have to do, or the more difficult it will be to make changes in the approach. However, more clients desire specifics and details showing exactly how something will be accomplished and when it will be accomplished, by whom, and at what cost. Specifics usually win.

Cost Detail

When dealing with the cost of a project, an important dilemma often faces the consultant. How much of the cost should be detailed? It's tempting to show an overall cost without much breakdown, giving the client an opportunity to compare the total cost with those of competitors. However, providing details of the cost breakdown may improve the credibility of the proposal. This involves showing the time it takes to complete a task, the hourly rate of the individuals involved, and the costs of different tasks. With this approach, all cost details that add up to the final cost of the project are included and can be analyzed.

There is a reluctance to show this degree of detail for fear that the client may think parts of the project are overpriced or might want to cut parts of it. This can usually be addressed with some flexibility in the actual time and costs for each step. When considering these issues, clients typically want more data on costs. They are curious about how costs evolve. Detailed cost presentations usually win out over the less detailed proposal.

Logic vs. Topics

Should the proposal address the topics outlined in the proposal in the sequence offered, or as the entire project unfolds logically? The logic usually wins out. Ideally, the topics should be presented on a logical basis showing how the process evolves to obtain the desired results, using a flow chart or a step-by-step process. Almost any client would prefer a logical approach showing how things will be accomplished in an orderly sequence.

Green vs. Mixed Colors

This philosophy focuses on how the consultant will work internally to make sure that the proposal reflects the best thinking of the group. This builds on the creativity work of Edward de Bono. According to de Bono, six different colors of hats can be used to represent different styles of thinking. Focusing on a particular aspect of thinking at a particular time can reduce confusion.[1]

De Bono suggests that a team choose one of the six hats to wear at a particular moment. The green hat represents new ideas, concepts, and perceptions. In encourages deliberate creation of new ideas, alternatives, and even more alternatives. In essence, it seeks to identify a new approach to the situation. Using this approach, the proposal development team all wear the green hats to review the proposal to see if anything is left out, if anything could be added, if all issues have been approached, and whether alternatives have been explored. This maximizes the use of team input to make sure the proposal is the very best.

Create a Proposal-Development Process

Finally, it may be helpful to create and implement a formal proposal-development process. Figure 7-1 outlines one such process—used by a highly successful proposal-writing team—that goes beyond simply listing the steps in a logical form.[2] It guides users sequentially through the process, prompting them to think through the rationale in each specific step as they work toward the final document. Making regular use of a well-conceived, effective process minimizes the time required to develop proposals, reduces confusion, provides for greater consistency despite variables, and helps consultants create more informative, compelling proposals.

Understanding the Stakeholders

Stakeholders involved in a potential consulting project are critical to proposal development. Understanding who they are and their concerns can lead to specific items in the proposal. As many as seven different stakeholders may be involved in a project.

Requester

The requester is a person who initiates the project—who actually has asked for it. This requester may be the key client. It may be the individual who has had some informal discussions with the consultant. In any case, this is the individual who essentially initiates it.

Decision Maker

Although proposals may be evaluated by a team, there is usually a key decision maker. In simple projects there is only one client involved, and the decision maker is that individual. In more complex projects involving many individuals, the decision maker may not be readily obvious.

Contractor

This is the individual who ensures that the proposal follows the proposal guidelines. The concern is compliance, fairness, objectivity, and consistency. This individual will process the proposal and, following the rules, may decide if a proposal moves forward or not.

Figure 7-1   Proposal Development Process

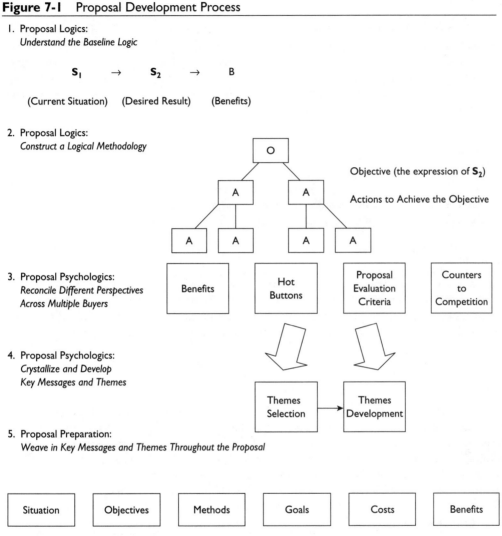

1. Proposal Logics:
   Understand the Baseline Logic

$$S_1 \quad \rightarrow \quad S_2 \quad \rightarrow \quad B$$

   (Current Situation)   (Desired Result)   (Benefits)

2. Proposal Logics:
   Construct a Logical Methodology

   O

   A   A

   A   A   A   A

   Objective (the expression of S_2)

   Actions to Achieve the Objective

3. Proposal Psychologics:
   Reconcile Different Perspectives
   Across Multiple Buyers

   | Benefits | Hot Buttons | Proposal Evaluation Criteria | Counters to Competition |

4. Proposal Psychologics:
   Crystallize and Develop
   Key Messages and Themes

   Themes Selection → Themes Development

5. Proposal Preparation:
   Weave in Key Messages and Themes Throughout the Proposal

   | Situation | Objectives | Methods | Goals | Costs | Benefits |

Adapted from Richard C. Freed, Shervin Freed, and Joseph D. Romano, *Writing Winning Business Proposals: Your Guide to Landing the Client, Making the Sale, Persuading the Boss* (New York: McGraw-Hill, Inc., 2003).

Implementer

This is the group or individual who will have to implement the solution from the project. These are the people who have to make it work and must be committed. They must be involved. They must be willing to take whatever steps necessary to make the project a success. The ultimate success of the project solution rests with the implementer.

Champion

Behind almost every project there is a champion, a person who wants this project in the worst way, the person who is eagerly awaiting the outcomes of the project. The champion may be at any level. At lower levels, it may be a person who located the consultant or discovered the process and wants the requester to request a proposal, the decision maker to make the decision, and the implementer to make it work. This is a very important person who can provide much insight into the project and issues surrounding it.

Senior Executive

In almost every setting there is a senior executive who may not necessarily be the decision maker but is responsible for the ultimate budget. This individual needs to be pleased, either directly or indirectly, with the success of the project. It may be the division head, the department head, chief operating officer, chief information officer, chief marketing officer, or even the CEO in smaller firms.

Detractor

For almost every project there is someone who would prefer not to do it, who may even be opposed to it. At best, this person is completely indifferent to it. At worse, this person will try to kill the project before it gets started or even kill it before the contract is awarded. Knowing this individual is critical so that the proper information can be in the proposal to at least render them neutral concerning the project.

Information and Actions

Each of these individuals plays an important part in the project. In simple, small-scale projects, many of these roles would be served by one person, but as the complexity of the project grows, the scope of the project increases, and the size of the budget blossoms, all of these stakeholders may be in separate roles. It's necessary to analyze the stakeholders with as much intelligence as possible. Table 7-2 shows a useful form for collecting information about them. It provides places for the name and the role of the individuals to be identified, which could simply be their title or responsibility.

Table 7-2 Stakeholder Analysis

Stakeholder	Name/Job	Concerns/Perspectives	Action Needed
Requester			
Decision Maker			
Contractor			
Implementer			
Champion			
Senior Executive			
Detractor			

It is important to understand what concerns these individuals will have and what perspective they will bring into the project, including their level of enthusiasm for it. Finally, the most important issue is to see what action is necessary. Is contact needed with each stakeholder? Should something be included in the proposal to address each of these roles? Do some of the roles have to be validated? For example, is the implementer interested in implementing this project and committed to making it work? These may be action items, either conducted formally or informally, to understand more about the proposal process.

Understanding the Situation

The intelligence gathering and the stakeholder analysis lead to more detailed questioning concerning the situation. Table 7-3 provides a checklist for a situation analysis. Ideally, these questions should be addressed in order to thoroughly understand the situation. Each of the questions delves in detail into the reasons for the proposal and the client's experience with this issue. Collectively, these issues, when combined with the stakeholder analysis and other information gathered in the intelligence checklist, provide a wealth of information about the current situation and the viability of the project.

All information collected is used in several important ways. First and foremost, three documents— intelligence, stakeholder analysis, situation analysis—provide information to decide if the proposal should even be developed. Adverse information on several of these issues may mean that it will not be a successful project, may be destined for someone else, or will not be fully supported. In many cases these analyses will provide enough information to continue and contain the detail needed to address the very specific proposal issues discussed in the remainder of the chapter. A clear understanding of all of these issues provides the backdrop for developing an effective and successful proposal.

Table 7-3 Situation Analysis Checklist

What created the need?	☐	Have the funds been secured?	☐
What motivated the client to pursue this now?	☐	Are there underlying assumptions?	☐
		Are there any hidden agendas?	☐
How thoroughly has the need been described?	☐	What deliverables are expected?	☐
		How much detail is expected?	☐
What is the client's experience with this topic?	☐	What are the expected outcomes?	☐
		Is there a specific protocol?	☐
Do all of the stakeholders see the need the same way?	☐	Will the culture support this?	☐
Has the commitment for implementation been secured?	☐	What procedures must be followed?	☐
		Is there a proposal conference?	☐
Is the needs assessment accurate?	☐	What are the proposal evaluation criteria?	☐
Can we shape the client's requirements?	☐	Why is the client interested in us?	☐
What is the scope of the project?	☐	Is there a history of effective consultant-client relationships?	☐

The situational analysis is also used to summarize for the client, in the proposal, a specific understanding of the situation. This is important because many clients want to make sure that the consultant fully understands the issue. A complete description of the situation in a nonchallenging and nonthreatening way can keep the client's interest in the proposal and help ensure that the client reads the rest of the proposal.

Simple Proposals

As briefly mentioned early in the chapter, the proposal can have a wide variety of complexity and length. For the very simplest issues, with one-on-one contracting between the client and consultant, a very simple proposal needs to be utilized. The more formal the process, the more detailed the proposal needs to be, up to and including a comprehensive process presented later.

For the very simple proposal, it's important to convey the basic understanding of the project and present what is planned. A one- or two-page proposal, or perhaps even just a long letter, may suffice. Table 7-4 shows the bare essentials using the logic methodology mentioned earlier.[3] Using this approach has helped consultants and their clients think about the logic flowing from the bottom up, essentially telling the client: Here are the *benefits* you will receive from our project, considering the *costs* that will be involved, given our *qualifications* to complete the project, using our *methods* to achieve the project's *objectives*, and therefore improve your basic *situation*. These are the very bare essentials of telling the client what is expected. It is a good practice to put this in a letter even if it is not requested.

A Comprehensive Proposal Process

Building from the simple process, the proposals become more complex to include more detail, parts, and requirements. Obviously, every proposal must address all the issues in the RFP. However, at a minimum, a comprehensive process should include the topics listed in Table 7-5. This comprehensive approach is a useful framework to think through any proposal, even if the detail is not desired or needed. It helps clarify these important critical issues.

Table 7-4 The Essentials of a Brief Proposal

Issue	Comment
Situation	This is our understanding of your problem or opportunity.
Objectives	Given that problem or opportunity, these are our objectives for solving or realizing it.
Methods	Given those objectives, these are the methods we will use to achieve them.
Qualifications	Given those methods, these are our qualifications for performing them.
Costs	Given those qualifications and methods, this is how much it will cost.
Benefits	Given our efforts and their associated costs, these are the benefits or value that you will receive.

Table 7-5 Outline for a Comprehensive Proposal

1. Title Page	9. Responsibilities
2. Executive Summar	10. Deliverables
3. Situation Analysis	11. Costs
4. Scope	12. Unique Advantages
5. Objectives	13. Results Guarantee
6. Methodology	14. Terms and Conditions
7. Proposed Approach	15. Acceptance
8. Project Schedules	16. References/Exhibits

Situation Analysis

Use all the information described previously to summarize your understanding of the situation. This combines information from the intelligence gathering, stakeholder analysis, and situation analysis. Together, they provide an excellent insight into the current situation. This should not be long, but it should be specific, showing the client that you understand the issues. It should be focused and straightforward, but diplomatic.

Scope

This essentially defines the magnitude of the project. It confines the project to a particular group, task, location, issue, or time frame. The purpose is as much to indicate what is not included as to indicate what is. This description should help you to avoid "scope creep," which we will discuss later.

Objectives

The objectives of the project should be clear and specific, not vague and ambiguous. They come in two categories: (1) the overall project objective, which details specifically what the proposal intended or has requested, and (2) the objectives of the solution provided by the consultant. These objectives are arranged in levels of anticipated reaction, learning, application and implementation, business impact, and ROI (yes, an ROI objective from the perspective of the client may be the biggest hook you can provide). We will discuss these levels of objectives in Chapter 8.

Methodology

Some consultants, if not most of them, use a specific methodology that they have developed. Often this methodology is the basis for the consulting practice. In some cases it is trademarked or copyrighted, and in a few situations, even patented. The important point is to have a methodology and to offer it as your approach. This will involve describing the methodology, its use, and its acceptance in other organizations. A description of its uniqueness, its advantages, and the success obtained in delivering the results needed in similar situations would be very helpful.

Proposed Approach

The proposed approach would use the methodology along with actions and activities to show what approach would be taken in this particular project. Essentially, this shows how things will progress in this setting. Figure 7-2 shows one proposed approach using actions, activities, methodology, and methods. In this example, the actions are defined to achieve the specific objectives, the specific activities that will take place, the unique methodology—along with the rationale for using it—and the particular way the objectives will ultimately be achieved. Regardless of the arrangement of sequencing, the approach section takes the mystery out of how you will accomplish the objectives using your unique methodology.

Project Schedule

The schedule of the project details the events from proposal acceptance to the last step in the process, which is usually delivering the final results after the solution has been implemented. This could be shown on any type of project management tools or perhaps even a Gantt chart. A flow chart could be used to show how steps are sequentially followed, the times with each step, and the timing of the entire process.

Figure 7-2   Proposal Development Approach

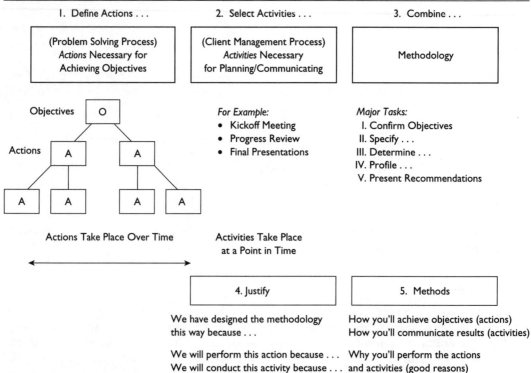

Adapted from Richard C. Freed, Shervin Freed, and Joseph D. Romano, *Writing Winning Business Proposals: Your Guide to Landing the Client, Making the Sale, Persuading the Boss* (New York: McGraw-Hill, Inc., 2003).

Responsibilities

This is an often overlooked part of the process. The consultant obviously has certain responsibilities, but others will have responsibilities for securing data and assisting in the implementation. In complex projects, the responsibilities become quite involved, utilizing different groups as well as individuals in their specific roles. In this section, accountabilities need to be underscored.

Deliverables

The specific items delivered to the client should be listed and detailed. This may include a solution, in whatever form it may take. It may include various reports, job aids, procedures, policies, and, in some cases, even software.

Costs

The most sensitive part of the proposal, and yet the most important part for many clients, is the cost schedule. The detailed costs should be included to indicate the fees of the different consultants involved, the estimated time it would take following the schedule and the costs of those times, the cost of various support staff, and the cost of external resources. All of the costs from analysis, design, development, implementation, and evaluation are often arranged in those categories. The important point is to show enough detail so the client can be comfortable that the pricing is fair and that the fees are in line with expectations. This is a difficult issue since many consultants have a fear of offering this much detail, particularly if there's concern that the timing may be underestimated. But it must be done for credibility to be maintained.

Unique Advantages

It is important to communicate to the client the unique advantages of the proposal and the rationale for using your consulting practice. The advantages may hinge on the proprietary methodology, experience with the type of project, or the qualifications offered to achieve it. Advantages may include the ability to do this quickly, perhaps faster than others, because of the size of the staff, experience of the team, and the priority that will be placed on the project.

Results Guarantee

Consultants should consider providing a guarantee of results. Some consultants are offering complete satisfaction for the project or there is no charge. Others put specific conditions around the guarantee. Still others offer variable pay depending on the success of the project. These options are discussed in Chapter 9.

Terms and Conditions

This would include any condition that has not been set forth under the project schedules, responsibilities, or costs. It may include a summary of these items and place an expiration date on the project proposal. If the client decides to wait until a particular time beyond what is specified in the RFP, then the proposal may no longer be viable. Conditions and terms for addressing disputes, difficulties, and problems—including how they will be resolved—should be addressed here. It could also address issues such as how communication will be two-way and flowing. Essentially, this is a place to clarify conditions for both sides of the parties.

Acceptance

The final piece of information provides the client with an opportunity to agree and return a particular part of the proposal, which is a recognition of acceptance. This makes the acceptance formal, although many clients may prefer to issue an acceptance letter following some predetermined procedure, guideline, or compliance requirement. If that is not in place, the acceptance is there to take care of that. With this, the client is indicating the approval of the project and is in agreement with all parts of it.

Back Matter

Usually, the proposal will have some additional materials. These could be exhibits showing the unique methodology, appendices showing detailed flow charts on the approach, or details on the project schedules. The résumés and/or qualifications of the consulting team would also be outlined in the back matter.

Presentation Strategies

As discussed earlier in the book, written communications is a critical skill for consultants. There are three distinct opportunities to employ written communication skills:

1. The proposal, which may be the most important document for securing business.
2. Final reports on the consulting project.
3. Routine correspondence or communication between clients and prospective clients.

To be sure, communication skills must be at their best when presenting the proposal. From the title page to the appendix, the writing should be clear, specific, professional, and compelling. It must be logical, error-free, engaging, and content rich. This is a challenge for some consultants, who underestimate the importance of the written word. While there are other ways to present the proposal, the written document will be the most significant.

Proposal Presentation

The proposal begins with the cover. It should be uncluttered and direct, usually beginning with the words "proposal from" and then listing the company, the title of the project, followed by "submitted by" the consulting firm, and the date.

The executive summary should be a very brief presentation of the entire proposal, highlighting the key points. It should contain the summary items discussed in the simple proposal, using the same logic. Usually two pages for a comprehensive proposal would be enough.

The writing style throughout should be consistent with headings, formatting, and itemizing, using the same bullets and consistent formats for tables and charts. Very clear writing is important. There should be several "hooks" that quickly get to the point to make this proposal stand out. A hook is a one or two sentence conclusion and compelling reason to accept the proposal. They may even be boxed to make those points clearer. There could be a hook for each section of the proposal.

Delivery of the Proposal

Obviously, the proposal must be delivered by the deadline, but not much earlier than that. An earlier delivery may be too soon to reflect adjustments that might be made in the RFP. Ideally, proposals should be delivered in person. This provides a chance to see who else is delivering or involved in the process. In some cases, e-mail delivery is acceptable, but it's important to follow up to make sure that the proposal has been received. Express package services are quite effective, but they must be traceable and with guaranteed delivery dates.

Electronic Communications

In some settings, the proposal can be discussed electronically. In simple terms, a telephone conversation may be helpful to underscore the important parts (the hooks) and express appreciation for being a part of the process. Beyond telephones, teleconferencing may be allowable. This approach brings decision makers with the consulting team together in a live teleconference, providing an opportunity to discuss highlights, review issues, and clarify key points. In some cases the client may accept a Web cast, which essentially follows the format of a live presentation but is conducted over the Internet.

Face-to-Face Presentation

Although not allowed in every situation, live presentations of proposals are appropriate. Some clients even demand this. A face-to-face meeting is a great opportunity to present the proposal in a professional and compelling way, highlighting the key points and underscoring the hooks. This is the time to have a powerful presentation, though not necessarily a PowerPoint presentation. PowerPoint slides with bullets may not engage the audience, but highlighting certain parts of it, showing examples of work, underscoring the deliverables, and describing the payoff will. Measurable results might hook the decision makers. A compelling story is needed that leads to an obvious action: accepting the proposal.

The live presentation has several distinct advantages and affords several important opportunities for the consultant. For one, it provides an opportunity to develop or refine a relationship on a personal basis. After all, the chemistry and the relationship with the consultant is a critical issue in the decision making. Also, the meeting represents an opportunity to underscore the unique methodology and advantages the consultant offers. You have their attention, and this may be the best time to get them to focus on what you provide and others cannot. Finally, the meeting is an opportunity to present the proposal in quick summary—with details provided in the document—and to clarify any issues. There may be some confusion over parts of it.

Negotiations

In some cases, proposals are not accepted as is, but are brought into a negotiation process. This is particularly useful when they did not address the needs that the client expected. Also, if costs are extremely high, or what is offered exceeds what's needed, the negotiation may be a way to adjust the proposal. To be fair, all individuals are involved in renegotiating their proposal. This process represents both good news and bad news. The good news is that it is an opportunity to clarify, change, and adjust to fit the needs of the client. The bad news is that others get the same opportunity, and that apparently there were some miscommunications that led to the negotiation.

Whatever approach is taken, the presentation is important to proposal success, and planning it is essential. Suggesting that a live presentation be included might be a significant strategy. It might be the best way to make sure that the proposal is accepted.

Grant Proposals

Sometimes proposals respond to grant opportunities for consulting. In some ways, developing a proposal for a grant to provide consulting for a nonprofit or government agency is no different than a proposal made to any type of organization. However, in some ways they are different, and the difference must be considered in the process.

Great Source of Consulting

The amount of money granted to consultants from states, federal governments, nonprofits, and non-government organizations is growing significantly. In some cases governments have been trying to reduce the number of employees, thus creating contracting opportunities for consultants to provide the same or similar services. In fact, using consultants in the government is the norm, as compared to the private sector. After you've mastered the procedures and the process has been fine-tuned, responding to grant requests may be an efficient way to obtain new business. Relationships, of course, are still important, and many of the issues are the same.

The Differences

In the opinion of most consultants, several differences make grant writing more difficult. First, there are more formal requirements. Rarely will an opportunity be provided by handshake agreements. Also, the process is much more structured, following more detailed procedures. Consequently, it is perceived to be more time consuming and difficult for some consultants, requiring a much more detailed proposal. For grants, the qualifications are more critical and the budgets often tighter, which may mean lower fees for the consultants. Also, grants usually require an evaluation of the project—although an evaluation is recommended for all projects.

Major Components

Table 7-6 shows the major components of a proposal to state and federal agencies.[4] The sections are similar to the components presented in the comprehensive approach earlier, but five key differences are often found:

1. A statement of assurance or compliance is required to ensure that the consultant is able to provide the services and that there are no conflicts of interests.
2. An abstract is often presented and is similar to the executive summary.
3. The sustainability is important because there are so many government contracts, with one often immediately following the other. This essentially shows how the consulting solution will be sustained over a period of time.
4. Evaluation indicates how it will be evaluated as well as the types of data that will be collected.
5. The qualifications and credentials of those who are part of the consulting team is emphasized.

Problems and Issues with Proposals

Several problems or issues may surface that deserve additional attention. We will go into some of them here.

Proposal Conference

The client may ask for a conference to discuss the proposal when a live presentation was not required. While this is an excellent opportunity to present the proposal and clarify issues, it's also a signal that the process went astray, something wasn't clear, or in some way the proposal is off base.

A conference should be accepted as a welcome opportunity and scheduled as quickly as possible. Insist that the key decision maker attend, and find out who else will be there. It also may be helpful to specifically ask if there are any concerns about the proposal. This can present an opportunity to explore the issue prior to the meeting. Finding out everything you can about what the concerns are is helpful. It might also be helpful to explore how close they may be to accepting your proposal. Ask bluntly: "If we can work out the differences and adjustments, are you willing to go with us?" This can help you understand how close you may be to actually landing the project.

Ethics

While every attempt is made to uncover information needed for the proposal and gather as much intelligence as possible, this should all be done ethically. Using clandestine ways to determine information, and finding unnamed sources to reveal insiders' viewpoints, may backfire. All information

Table 7-6. Major Components of a Proposal to State and Federal Agencies

Element/Information Usually Provided	Approximate Length
Title Page	1 page

Title of project, name and contact information of the project director, name and address of submitting organization, name of the program and agency to which the proposal is being sent, inclusive dates of the project, total budget and amount requested in this proposal, signatures of persons authorizing submission.

Signed Assurances	Varies

All government sources will describe what assurance or compliance statements are required for their programs.

Abstract	$1/2$ page

A self-contained, ready-for-publication description of the project, covering purpose/outcomes/objectives, need and significance, procedures, evaluation, dissemination. This should stress the end products and benefits of the project if funded. Normally this is 200 to 250 words long. It will be used verbatim by the program manager to describe your effort.

Statement of Purpose	$1 1/2$ pages

Specific description of the expected outcomes, goals, and objectives to be achieved through this project.

Statement of Need	1 page

Well-documented description of the problem to be addressed, the need, and why it is important. Should establish significance, timeliness, generalizability, and contribution to other work. Credible sources should be used for all statistics supporting and explaining the needs.

Procedures	3 pages

A plan of action for how the purposes will be achieved and why this approach is the most effective. Discuss how it is different from or complementary to similar efforts by others. Stress collaborations, if possible. Describe how theresults will be disseminated to others.

Sustainability	$1/2$ page

Government funders want to know how these activities will be supported after this grant ends. Some agencies ask that this be discussed as part of the procedures or in the budget. Others want it to be a separate component. Be specific about your plans for future funding, including other grantors, individual donors, and earned income.

Evaluation	2 pages

Details the means by which the applicant and funding source will know what the project has accomplished. Should describe the questions to be asked, the methods to be used in gathering and analyzing the data, and how the information will be used and reported. Many government sources are now requiring that this section be formatted as outcome-based evaluation.

Qualifications/Personnel	$2 1/2$ pages

Provides an overview of the mission, history, programs, and relevant experience of the sponsoring organization, and documents why it is ideally suited to undertake this work. Describes specific consultants and staff who will work on the project, their qualifications, their duties, and, if not covered by the budget, the percentage of time they will spend on the project. Most government sources want résumés of major project staff and often require a specific format or template. This section should also discuss any cooperating organizations and give evidence of their willingness to participate.

Budget	2 pages

The cost of the project for each year of its operation should be displayed by major line items (government sources usually have detailed budget forms). Itemize what is being provided by the sponsoring organization, what is being requested from the government, and what will be contributed by other sources. There is increased interest among government sources in supporting projects that are also funded by private foundations and/or corporations. A plan of action for any additional fundraising should be provided. You may also want to use footnotes or a budget narrative to explain how various costs were computed.

Attachments	Varies

Nonprofits should attach their 501(c)(3) letter unless told in the guidelines that this is not necessary. All organizations should include the names and affiliations of their boards. The program guidelines will describe what other attachments are desired, such as an audited financial report of the organization. Letters of support or agreements to participate should be provided from any organizations or groups whose involvement is essential to the project's success. In some cases it is useful to get a letter of support from your congressional delegation or, if applying to the state, from key legislators. Ask the program officer if this would be appropriate. Be very careful to follow the funder's guidelines about what can go into attachments.

Adapted from Mary Hall and Susan Howlett, *Getting Funded: The Complete Guide to Writing Grant Proposals*, 4th edition (Portland, Oregon: Portland State University Extended Studies, Continuing Education Press, 2003).

should be collected ethically, using the same sources that would be available to anyone else who could be responding. Chapter 10 addresses ethics in more detail.

Jargon

Unfortunately, a proposal is an opportune time for some business writers to use terms, concepts, and statements that are not known, vague, or represent the latest jargon. The proposal is not a place for this. Perhaps the best prerequisite for writing the proposal is to refer to the book, *Why Business People Speak Like Idiots: A Bullfighter's Guide.*[5] This handy book is a must-have for any consultant's library since it explains how so much miscommunication has seeped into the corporate vernacular. Certainly, jargon should be left out of the proposal.

Vagueness

Several times during this chapter the point was made that vagueness should be replaced with specific statements; objectives should be clear and unambiguous, results clearly defined, and success measures clearly articulated. Nothing is more dysfunctional than vague proposals. Perhaps more dangerous, vague proposals lead to unmet expectations, false assumptions, and misguided actions. A final step in any proposal would be the review of the document for specificity.

Page Limited Proposals

In some cases the client may require a maximum number of pages. This is often because of the time required to read several proposals. Sometimes this is fixed in the proposal procedures or the compliance regulation. When this is the case, it means that the same topics must be covered but in a shorter presentation. Precise, to-the-point presentations would be helpful, with additional references placed on the Web site for more detail.

Overselling

Although the proposal is about convincing the client that your approach is superior, the proposal itself should not be a walking commercial. It should show value, explain value, and promise value. It should do it in a way that is logical yet content rich with information. Claims that cannot be validated, promises that cannot be met, and references that cannot be checked may do more harm than good.

Scope Creep

Scope creep occurs when there are many add-ons suggested by the client, often with the expectation that there will be no additional charge. In the eagerness to secure the contract, the consultant may agree to provide them. Also, add-ons often emerge during the project as issues are uncovered or new issues are raised, and ultimately scope creep—moving the project beyond what was intended—eats away at any profit margin that may have been generated from the consulting project.

To avoid scope creep the consultant must say no, diplomatically of course, or offer to do any additional item for an additional amount. It does not have to be as blunt as asking for more money for everything you may do, but you may suggest that it can be provided quickly through a separate proposal since it was not in the original contract or RFP. This brings the issue to the attention of the client and provides the client with options. In essence, scope creep can become a revenue enhancement.

The Unresponsive Client

When the client does not respond by a particular date, there may be good reasons. It may be a sign that something is not working. A courtesy phone call after the due date would certainly be appropriate. If there is still no answer, a second or even third phone call may be appropriate. Beyond that, it may be helpful to send a letter, an e-mail, or maybe even consider a certified letter.

It might be helpful to find out from colleagues if there is some particular problem. At some point it may be helpful to just let it go after every effort has been made to make contact. Just to be covered, it might be helpful to send a certified letter after several weeks have passed indicating that unless there is some correspondence or communication by a particular date, you would have to consider the proposal null and void. This would prevent the client from asking for the proposal to be implemented a year later, when things have changed and costs might have to be adjusted.

When You Lose

Losing a bid—not having a proposal accepted—provides a unique learning experience and an opportunity to build a relationship. Although you'd like to learn in some other way, failing to have your proposal accepted should compel you to shift into trying to understand why. Most clients will explain why it was rejected, and then how you handle the rejection and work with the client in the future can show much in terms of building that relationship and others.

Understanding the Reasons for Rejection

There can be many reasons for rejection, and many of them are completely out of the hands of the decision maker. Table 7-7 shows some of the more common reasons.

These and other reasons for not obtaining the proposal provide an opportunity to find out why. Most clients will explain, particularly if it's a reason that is completely out of their control. But even if it is their decision, most clients are prepared to tell you your weaknesses or the parts of the proposal that presented the most concern. This is not a time to argue, but a time to listen and understand.

Handling the Loss

Taking the rejection personally is a serious mistake. The best response is to thank the client for the opportunity and ask to be considered again for similar projects as they arise in the future. If you are familiar with any of the winning consultants, sending a note of congratulations can be a nice gesture that reflects positively on your character and professionalism. Attempting to challenge the decision or discredit the winning firm can do nothing but destroy your reputation.

Table 7-7 Common Reasons for Rejection

- The proposal missed the deadline.
- The project was delayed or cancelled.
- The funding or budget went away.
- There is a reorganization that caused the project to be postponed.
- The proposal guidelines were not followed.
- The proposal was not clear and compelling in terms of what was being provided.
- The program was not complete in providing detail.
- A more thorough, compelling, and complete proposal was accepted.
- The proposal costs were unrealistic in terms of the budget for the project.
- The quality of the proposal was unacceptable.
- The proposed approach appeared to be beyond the capability of the consultants.
- The problem went away.

Consider this scenario: The ROI Institute was engaged by a large public broadcasting company in Europe to measure the success of its leadership program. A consultant based in the country where the contract was awarded did not handle the rejection well and complained to the decision maker and ultimately to the publicly controlled company's board of governors. He next attempted to discredit the winning firm, effectively committing professional suicide, since he will not be considered for projects in the future.

A more likely scenario is that the client will closely observe bidders who did not win the project to see how they handle the rejection. Attempting to maintain a cordial, friendly, and productive relationship with the client is a valuable character-building exercise and highly recommended. Doing so sets the stage for you to work on strengthening the relationship with that ongoing prospect and to identify and overcome the shortages and weaknesses in your proposal.

Final Thoughts

In this chapter we explored one of the most crucial processes in a consulting business: creating winning proposals. Describing a compelling solution to a problem or opportunity represents both an art and a science.

It is a science because there are some general principles that should be followed, steps that should be included, and topics that must be addressed in a logical, sequential way.

It is an art in terms of making sure it's crafted in a clear and compelling way so that the proposal addresses all of the issues, captures the imagination of the client, creates a powerful reason to accept the proposal, and clearly communicates the outcome.

We examined the reasons for developing proposals, the roles of proposals, and how to prepare for the proposal development process. The different components of proposals were presented, along with rationale for each part of the process. The various tips and techniques to ensure that the proposal process is on track and on target were presented with examples, checklists, and details. There is a proposal example in Appendix B.

Notes

[1] Edward de Bono, *Six Thinking Hats* (Boston: Little, Brown and Company, 1999).

[2] Richard C. Freed, Shervin Freed, and Joseph D. Romano, *Writing Winning Business Proposals: Your Guide to Landing the Client, Making the Sale, Persuading the Boss* (New York: McGraw-Hill Inc., 2003). Adapted with permission of the author.

[3] Ibid.

[4] Mary Hall and Susan Howlett, *Getting Funded: The Complete Guide to Writing Grant Proposals*, 4th edition (Portland, Oregon: Portland State University Extended Studies, Continuing Education Press, 2003).

[5] Brian Fugere, Chelsea Hardaway, and Jon Warshawsky, *Why Business People Speak Like Idiots: A Bullfighter's Guide* (New York: Free Press, 2005).

THE CONSULTING ENGAGEMENT: ANALYSIS AND OBJECTIVES PLANNING

Few things are more important in a consulting process than the initial analysis and planning, which involve a number of key issues that we will explore in this chapter. The first one is specifying the project in detail. Next, and perhaps more important, is anticipating the success of the project—in advance, in specific detail. We will then examine the process of ensuring that all key measures or groups of measures are identified to reflect the success of the project, focusing on objectives and different levels of analysis. Finally, we will introduce a variety of planning tools that can be helpful in setting up the initial consulting project.

Pinning Down the Details: Project Requirements

When it comes to specifying the requirements of a consulting project, there can never be too much detail. Projects often go astray and fail to attain full success because of misunderstandings and differences in expectations. Several key issues must be addressed before the consulting project actually begins. These are often outlined in the project proposal, in the outline and scope of the project's documentation, or in the planning or implementation document for consulting. Regardless of when it is developed, or for what purpose, each of the areas listed below should be identified in some way. The client and the consultant must reach agreement on these key issues.

Overall Project Objectives

When it comes to consulting projects, two types of objectives are developed. There are the objectives for the consulting project itself, indicating specifically what will be accomplished and delivered in the consulting assignment. And there are a set of objectives called "solution objectives," which focus on the goals of the actual solution that will ultimately add value to the organization. The solution objectives are discussed later; here, our focus will be on the objectives of the project.

Every consulting assignment should have a major project objective, and in some cases multiple objectives. The objectives should be as specific as possible and focused directly on the assignment. Examples of project objectives are presented in Table 8-1. As this table illustrates, the objectives are broad in scope, outlining what is to be accomplished from an overall perspective. The details of timing,

Table 8-1 Examples of Broad Consulting Project Objectives

- Identify the causes of excessive, unplanned absenteeism, and recommend solutions with costs and timetable.
- Evaluate the feasibility of three alternative approaches to new product development and rollout. For each approach, provide data on projected success, resources required, and timing.
- Implement a new accounts payable system that will maximize cash flow and discounts and minimize late-payment penalties.
- Design, develop, and implement an automated sales-tracking system that will provide real-time information on deliveries, customer satisfaction, and sales forecasts.
- Enhance the productivity of the call center staff as measured in calls completed, without sacrificing service quality.
- Build a customer feedback and corrective action system that will meet customer needs and build customer relationships.
- Reorganize the sales and marketing division from a product-based unit to a regionally based, fully integrated structure.
- Collect review, advice, and oversight input during the relocation of the headquarters staff. Input for the project will be gathered via weekly memos and used to address concerns, issues, problems, and delays.
- Explore the feasibility of developing an employee wellness and fitness center.

Table 8-2 Scoping Issues

- Target group for consulting
- Location of target group
- Time frame for project
- Technology used
- Access to stakeholders
- Functional area for coverage
- Product line for coverage
- Type of process or activity
- Category of customers

specifications, and defined deliverables come later. The broad consulting project objectives are critical because they bring focus to the project quickly. They define the basic parameters of the project.

Scope

The scope of the project must to be clearly defined, pinpointing key parameters addressed by the project. Table 8-2 shows typical scoping issues that should be defined in the project. Perhaps the project is limited to certain employee groups, a functional area of the business, a specific location, a unique type of system, or a precise time frame. Sometimes there is a constraint on the type of data collected or access to certain individuals, such as customers. Whatever the scope involves, it needs to be clearly defined in this section.

Timing

Timing is critical in showing specifically when activities will occur. This includes the timing of the delivery of the final project report and the timing of particular steps and events—including when data

Table 8-3 Typical Timing Events

• Start of project	• Preliminary results available
• Data collection design complete	• Solutions developed
• Evaluation design complete	• Implementation started
• Data collection begins	• Implementation complete
• Data collection complete	• Phases complete
• Specific data collection issues (e.g., pilot testing, executive interviews)	• Report developed
	• Presentation to management
• Data analysis complete	

are needed, analyzed, and reported, and when presentations are made. Table 8-3 shows typical events needing specific time frames.

Deliverables from the Project

This section will describe exactly what the client will receive when the project is completed: terms of reports, documents, systems, processes, manuals, forms, flow charts, or rights to new technology; whatever the specific deliverables, they are clearly defined here. While most projects will have a final report, most go much further, delivering process tools, software, and sometimes even hardware.

Methodology

If a specific methodology is planned for the consulting project, it should be defined up front. Sometimes a reference should be made to the appropriateness of the methodology as well as its reliability, validity, previous success, and how the methodology will accomplish what is needed in this consulting intervention.

Steps

The specific steps that will occur should be defined, showing key milestones. This provides the client with a step-by-step understanding and tracking of the intervention so that at any given time the client can see not only where progress is made, but where the project is going next.

Required Resources

This section will define the specific resources required for the project, if applicable. This could include access to individuals, vendors, technology, equipment, facilities, competitors, or customers. All resources that may be needed should be listed, along with amounts and timing.

Cost

The cost section details the specific cost for different parts of the project, tied to the different steps of the process. Sometimes consulting firms are reluctant to detail costs because it exposes the actual consulting hourly charges and uncovers some of the mystery in the process. These firms prefer to present the bottom-line cost and leave it up to the client to figure out how it was reached. A better approach is to be open with the fees, showing the different steps and issues relative to costs. In general, clients will appreciate this transparency, and it will set the stage for a trusting relationship between consultant and client.

Guarantees

Satisfaction guarantees, made in a final section, are now commonplace in consulting assignments. With some firms, a complete satisfaction guarantee is provided, stating that if the client is not satisfied with the project, then there is no charge for the consulting intervention. This may be too much for some firms—particularly for long-term engagements. However, the mere presence of this feature helps keep the consulting team focused and ensures that the client is satisfied throughout the project and never asks for a refund. This is discussed further in a later chapter.

Objectives for Consulting Solutions

In most cases, a consulting project leads to a solution; that relationship is shown in Figure 8-1. The solutions could range from a new system or procedure to new technology. Objectives are needed for the project and the solution. In some situations, the consulting project is aimed at implementing a solution to a particular problem or to address an opportunity. In other situations, the initial consulting project is designed to develop a range of feasible solutions, or one desired solution, prior to implementation.

Whatever the case, solutions should have multiple levels of objectives. These levels, ranging from qualitative to quantitative, define precisely what will occur as a particular solution is implemented in the organization. Table 8-4 shows the different levels of objectives. They are so critical that their development and use need special attention.

Satisfaction and Reaction

For any project solution to be successful, various stakeholders must react favorably, or at least not negatively. The stakeholders are those directly involved in implementing or utilizing the solution developed. These can be the employees who are involved in implementing the work (usually called the users) or the

Figure 8-1   Relationship Between Consulting Project and
Consulting Solution

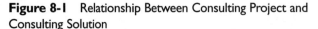

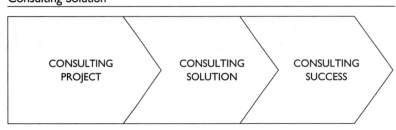

CONSULTING PROJECT   CONSULTING SOLUTION   CONSULTING SUCCESS

Table 8-4. Multiple Levels of Objectives

Levels of Objectives	Focus of Objectives
Level 1 Reaction and Satisfaction	Defines a specific level of satisfaction and reaction to the consulting solution as it is revealed and communicated to the users
Level 2 Learning	Defines specific skills and knowledge requirements as the users process information about the consulting solution
Level 3 Implementation	Defines key issues around the implementation of the solution in the workplace
Level 4 Business Impact	Defines the specific business measures that will change or improve as a result of implementing the solution
Level 5 ROI	Defines the specific return on investment from the implementation of the solution, comparing costs against benefits

supervisors or team leaders responsible for the redesigned or changed process. Stakeholders could also be managers who must support or assist the process in some way. Finally, the stakeholders could involve the teams and task forces involved in project solutions.

Ideally, the stakeholders should be satisfied with the solution since the best solutions offer win-win relationships. Table 8-5 shows some of the typical areas for specific satisfaction objectives. It's important to obtain this type of information routinely through a consulting project so that feedback can be used to make adjustments, keep the project on track, and perhaps even redesign certain parts of the solution. One problem with many consulting projects is that specific objectives at this level are not developed and data collection mechanisms are not put in place to ensure appropriate feedback for making the necessary adjustments.

Learning Objectives

Almost every consulting solution will involve a learning objective. For example, if a consulting project leads to a new procedure being installed (the solution), the learning objectives focus on understanding how to use the new procedure. In some cases involving major change projects, the learning component is quite significant. To ensure that the various stakeholders have learned what they need to learn to make the solution effective, learning objectives are developed.

Learning objectives are critical to measuring learning because they communicate expected outcomes from the solution and define the desired competence or performance necessary to make the

Table 8-5 Typical Areas for Satisfaction Objectives

• Usefulness of the consulting solution	• Difficulty in maintaining the consulting solution
• Relevance of the consulting solution	• Perceived support for the consulting solution
• Economics of the consulting solution	• Perceived value of the consulting solution
• Difficulty of the consulting solution	• Overall satisfaction with the consulting solution
• Importance of the consulting solution	
• Usability of the consulting solution	

Table 8-6 Typical Areas for Learning

- Awareness: familiarity with terms, concepts, and processes in the consulting solution
- Knowledge: general understanding of concepts, processes, or procedures for the consulting solution
- Skills: ability to demonstrate skills needed to use the consulting solution at least on a basic level
- Perception: changes in attitudes, perceptions, or points of view on the consulting solution
- Networking: new contacts who can help with the consulting solution

consulting solution successful. These objectives provide a basis for evaluating the learning, since they often reflect the type of measurement process. Perhaps, more important, learning objectives provide a focus for participants to clearly indicate what they must learn—sometimes with precision.

The best learning objectives describe behaviors that are observable and measurable, which are necessary for success with the consulting solutions. They are often outcome-based, clearly worded, and specific. They specify what the particular stakeholder must do as a result of implementing the learning solutions.

Learning objectives often have three components:

1. Performance: what the user will be able to do at the end of the consulting project.
2. Conditions: circumstances under which the user will perform the various tasks and processes.
3. Criteria: the degree or level of proficiency necessary to perform a new task, process, or procedure that is part of the solution.

The typical areas for learning objectives are presented in Table 8-6.

Implementation and Application Objectives

As a solution is actually implemented in the workplace, the implementation and application objectives clearly define what is expected and often to what level of performance. Application levels are similar to learning-level objectives, but they reflect the actual use on the job. They also involve particular milestones, specifically indicating when parts of the process or the entire process is implemented.

Application objectives are critical because they describe the expected outcomes in the intermediate area, that is, between the actual learning of new tasks and procedures and the actual impact that will be improved. Application or implementation objectives describe how things should be performed in the workplace after the solution is implemented. They provide a basis for the evaluation of on-the-job changes and performance. The emphasis is on what has occurred on the job as a result of the learning objectives.

The best application objectives identify behaviors that are observable and measurable, or action steps in a process that can easily be observed or measured. They specify what the various stakeholders will change or have changed as a result of the consulting solution. As with learning objectives, application or implementation objectives may have three components:

1. Performance describes what the users have changed or accomplished in a specific time frame after the implementation of the learning solution.
2. Condition specifies the circumstances under which the stakeholders have performed or are performing the tasks or implementing the solution.
3. Criteria indicates the degree or level of proficiency under which the solution is implemented, the task is being performed, or the steps are completed.

There are two types of basic application objectives. They are knowledge-based—when the general use of concepts, processes, and procedures is important—and behavior-based, when the participant is able to demonstrate the actual use of skills, accomplishment of particular tasks, or completion of particular milestones. Table 8-7 shows typical key questions asked to develop application and implementation objectives.

Application objectives have almost always been included in consulting projects, but they have not been as specific as they could be or need to be. To be effective, they must clearly define the environment at the work site when the solution is successfully implemented.

Table 8-7 Typical Questions for Application and Implementation Objectives

Regarding the consulting solution:

1. What new or improved knowledge will be applied on the job?
2. What is the frequency of skills required?
3. What specific new task will be performed?
4. What new steps will be implemented?
5. What action items will be implemented?
6. What new procedures will be implemented or changed?
7. What new guidelines will be implemented?
8. What new processes will be implemented?
9. Which meetings need to be held?
10. Which tasks, steps, or procedures will be discontinued?

Impact Objectives

Every consulting solution should improve one or more business measures. Business impact represents the key business measures that should be improved as the application or implementation objectives are achieved. The impact objectives are critical to measuring business performance because they define the ultimate expected outcome from consulting. They describe business-unit performance that should be connected to consulting. Above all, they place emphasis on achieving bottom-line results that key client groups expect and demand.

Objectives contain measures that are linked to the solution from the consulting. They describe measures that are easily collected and are well-known to the client group. They are results-based, clearly worded, and specify what the stakeholders have ultimately accomplished in the business unit as a result of the consulting intervention.

The four major categories of hard data objectives are output, quality, cost, and time. The major categories of soft data objectives are customer service, work climate, and work habits. Examples of the measures that frame the objectives are presented in another chapter.

Return on Investment

A fifth level of objectives for consulting solutions is the expected return on investment (ROI). These objectives define the expected monetary benefits from the solution in relation to the cost of the consulting project. Typically, it is expressed as a desired ROI percentage that compares the annual monetary benefits minus the cost, divided by the actual cost, and multiplied by 100. A zero percent ROI indicates a break-even consulting solution. A 50 percent ROI indicates that the cost of the consulting project is recaptured and an additional 50 percent in "earnings" are achieved.

For many consulting projects, the ROI objective is larger than what might be expected from the ROI on other expenditures, such as the purchase of a new company, a new building, or major equipment, but the two are related. In many organizations, the consulting ROI objective is set slightly higher than the ROI expected from other interventions because of the relative infancy of applying the ROI concept to consulting. For example, if the expected ROI from the purchase of a new company is 20 percent, the ROI from consulting might be in the 25 percent range. The important point is that the ROI objective should be established up front and through discussions with the client.

Importance of Specific Objectives

Developing specific objectives at different levels for consulting solutions provides important benefits. First, they provide direction to the consultants directly involved in the process to help keep them on track. Objectives define exactly what is expected at different time frames, from different individuals, and involving different types of data. They give guidance to the support staff and the client so that they fully understand the ultimate goal and impact of the consulting project. Also, they provide important information and motivation for the stakeholders.

In most consulting projects, key stakeholders are actively involved and will influence the results of the solution. Specific objectives provide goals and motivation for the stakeholders so that they will clearly see the gains that should be achieved. More important, objectives provide valuable information to help the key client groups understand how the landscape will change after the consulting solution is implemented.

Finally, from an evaluation perspective, the objectives offer a basis for measuring success.

Linking Evaluation with Client Needs

There is a distinct linkage between the evaluation of a project and the original needs driving a consulting project. The five levels of evaluation, described above, show how they are critical to providing an overall assessment of the impact of a consulting solution—particularly when a solution is implemented as part of the consulting project. The objectives define the specific improvements sought.

In this section, we will make a further connection to the original needs assessment. Figure 8-2 shows the connection between evaluation and the initial needs assessment. It demonstrates the important linkage

Figure 8-2   Connection Between Evaluation and the Initial Needs Assessment

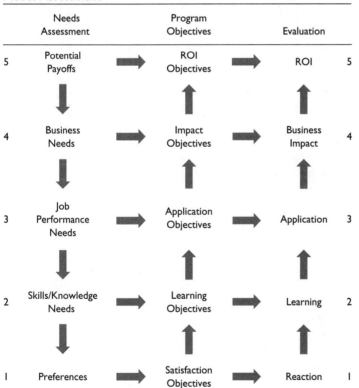

Needs Assessment	Program Objectives	Evaluation	
5	Potential Payoffs	ROI Objectives	ROI	5
4	Business Needs	Impact Objectives	Business Impact	4
3	Job Performance Needs	Application Objectives	Application	3
2	Skills/Knowledge Needs	Learning Objectives	Learning	2
1	Preferences	Satisfaction Objectives	Reaction	1

between the initial problem or opportunity that created the need for consulting and the evaluation and measurement showing the success of the project.

Level 5 defines the potential payoff for solving the problem and examines the possibility for a return on investment before the project is even pursued. This may be an intuitive analysis (it is too serious not to solve), a simple analysis (our ROI estimates suggest a positive ROI), or a detailed analysis (we forecast a positive ROI).

Level 4 analysis focuses on the business needs that precipitated the consulting project. Specific business measures are derived at this level.

At level 3 the specific needs in the workplace are examined. This describes what users must change (on the job) to improve the business measures.

At level 2 the specific knowledge, skill, or attitude needs are uncovered. This defines what the users must know to change job performance.

Finally, at level 1 the preferences for the structure of the solution determine the preference needs. Essentially, the users and stakeholders define the preferred solution format (design, duration, timing, substance, etc.).

The linkage at all levels is critical to understanding all of the elements that comprise an effective consulting project.

An example will help illustrate this linkage. Figure 8-3 shows an example of linking needs with the outcomes of a consulting project involving a reduction in absenteeism. The first step (at level 5) is to determine if the problem is serious enough to address. A review of the operator problems associated with excessive absenteeism leads to a positive response here. If necessary, a potential payoff can be calculated by estimating both the cost of absenteeism and the actual potential reduction that the consulting solution could produce. This develops a profile of the potential payoff to decide if the problem is worth solving.

At level 4 the business measure is defined and the problem is validated. As noted in the figure, four benchmarks are used to compare the current rate for unplanned absenteeism. In fact, they are:

1. Absenteeism is higher than it has been historically.
2. Absenteeism is higher than at other locations within the organization.
3. Absenteeism is higher than at comparable businesses in the local area.
4. Absenteeism is higher than the general manager desires.

At level 3 the causes of excessive absenteeism are explored using a variety of techniques. One issue that is uncovered is that a positive counseling procedure is not currently available to team leaders for responding to an unexpected absence. A learning need (level 2) is also uncovered, since the team leaders need to understand how and when to administer the counseling procedure. Finally, at level 1 the specific way in which the solution should be implemented is explored in terms of preferences. In this case, supervisors preferred to attend a half-day meeting to learn the procedure and leave the session with a job aid that further helps them understand the process and how to apply it effectively.

These five levels provide a method for aligning the project with key measures and developing the data necessary to formulate project objectives. The consulting solution objectives for each level are also shown in the figure, as is the data collection method (called "Evaluation" in the figure) needed to verify that the appropriate change did occur. This process is important to the development and implementation of a consulting solution. Many consulting projects involve developing the actual solution

Figure 8-3 Linking Needs with the Outcomes of a Consulting Project Aimed at Reducing Absenteeism

Needs Assessment	Consulting Solution Objectives	Evaluation
5 Problem is creating serious costs	→ ROI of 25% →	Calculate the ROI **5**
↓		↑
4 An absenteeism problem exists when compared to four benchmarks	→ Weekly absenteeism rate will reduce →	Monitor absenteeism data for 6 months **4**
↓		↑
3 Counseling procedure is not currently available to team leaders	→ Counseling procedure must be used in 95% of situations when an unexpected absence occurs →	Follow-up questionnaire to team leaders in 3 months (frequency of use) **3**
↓		↑
2 Need to understand how to administer the positive discipline procedure	→ Learn how and when to use positive discipline procedure →	Self-assessment checklist on key items **2**
↓		↑
I Supervisors prefer to attend half-day meeting and have a job aid	→ New procedure receives favorable rating of 4 out of 5 →	Reaction questionnaire at the end of the meeting **I**

and then implementing it, as in this particular example. When this is the case, the above linkage connects the needs to actual objectives and then to evaluation.

The solution to the problem or opportunity is an important element of this linkage. Some consulting projects may involve uncovering needs with the initial analysis to determine the causes of the problem and then recommend solutions. It's up to the client to implement the solution, or implementation might be the objective of a subsequent consulting effort. In either case, the solutions are ultimately developed for a complete consulting project. If this has not been accomplished, multiple levels of analysis may be necessary for the project. While there are many other references that focus more specifically on the performance analysis for uncovering different levels of needs, a brief summary is presented here.

Payoff Needs

The first step in the process is to determine whether the problem is worth solving or if the opportunity is promising enough to warrant serious consideration. In some cases this need is obvious, as when there are serious problems clearly affecting an organization's operations and strategy. Other issues may not be so obvious. At level 5 it is important not only to identify business measures at level 4 that need improvement, but also to convert them into monetary values so the actual improvement can be converted to financial measures.

The second part of the process is to develop an approximate cost for the entire consulting project. This could be based on a detailed proposal, or it may simply be a rough estimate. At this stage it is only an estimate, though, as the projected cost of the effort is compared to the potential benefits to roughly determine if there will be a payoff in pursuing a solution. This step may be omitted in situations where the problem must be solved regardless of cost or if it is glaringly obvious that the effort will produce a high payoff. Still, other projects may be undertaken knowing up front that there is no expectation the potential payoff will be developed. For example, an organization may be striving to evolve into a technology leader, but it may be difficult to ascribe a value to such a goal.

Business Needs

In conjunction with level 5, actual business data are examined to determine which measures need to improve. This includes an examination of organizational records and involves examining all types of hard and soft data. It is usually one of the data items and its current performance level that triggers the need for the consulting assignment.

For example, market share is not as much as it should be, costs are excessive, quality is deteriorating, or productivity is not as high as should be. These are the key issues that come directly from the data in the organization and are often found in the operating reports or records. The supporting data may also come from annual reports, marketing data, industry data, major planning documents, or other important information sources that clearly indicate operating performance in terms of operation or strategy.

Workplace Needs

The level 3 analysis involves individual job performance at the workplace. The task is to determine the cause of the problem as seen at level 4 (i.e., what is causing the business measure not to be at the desired level, or to be inhibited in some way). The different types of needs can vary considerably and may include, among others:

- Ineffective or inappropriate behavior
- Ineffective systems
- Improper process flow
- Ineffective procedures
- Inappropriate technology

These and other types of needs will have to be uncovered using a variety of problem-solving or analysis techniques. This may involve the use of data collection techniques such as surveys, questionnaires, focus groups, or interviews. It may involve a variety of problem-solving or analysis techniques such as root-cause analysis, fishbone diagrams, and others. Whatever is used, the key is to determine all of the causes of the problem so that solutions can be developed. Often, multiple solutions are appropriate.

Learning Needs

Most problem analysis from level 3 uncovers specific learning needs. Perhaps deficiencies in knowledge and skills may be contributing to the problem, or might be the major cause of it. In other situations, the solution recommended may need a specific learning component as users learn how to implement a new process, procedure, or system. The extent of learning required will determine whether formalized training is needed or if more informal, on-the-job methods can be utilized to build the necessary skills and knowledge. The learning would typically involve acquisition of knowledge or the development of skills necessary to improve the situation. In some cases, perceptions or attitudes may need to be altered to make the process successful in the future.

Preference Needs

The final level is to consider the preference for the solution. This involves determining the way in which those involved in the process (users) prefer to have it changed or implemented. It may involve implementation preferences and/or learning preferences. Learning preferences may involve decisions such as when learning is expected and in what amounts, how it is presented, and the overall time frame. Implementation preferences may involve issues such as timing, support, expectation, and other key factors. The important point is to try to determine the specific preferences to the extent possible so that the complete profile of the solution can be adjusted accordingly.

Planning for Project Evaluation

An important ingredient in measuring the success of the consulting ROI process is to properly plan for project evaluation early in the consulting cycle. Appropriate up-front attention will save much time later when data are actually collected and analyzed, thus improving accuracy and reducing the cost of the process. It also avoids any confusion surrounding what will be accomplished, by whom, and at what time. Two planning documents—the data collection plan and the ROI analysis plan—are important and should be completed before the consulting is designed or developed.

Data Collection Plan

Table 8-8 shows a completed data collection plan for the sexual harassment prevention consulting project. The project was initiated to reduce sexual harassment complaints and the employee turnover associated with them. An ROI calculation was planned to show the value of the preventive project.

   This document provides a place for the major elements and issues regarding collecting data for the five evaluation levels. You will find, respectively:

- *The broad objectives for the solution.* More detailed objectives are developed later, before the consulting solution is finalized. In the second column, the specific measures or data descriptors are indicated when they are necessary to explain the measures linked to the objectives.

Table 8-8 Example of Completed Data Collection Plan

Project: Preventing Sexual Harassment   **Responsibility:** _____   **Date:** _____

Level	Broad Objectives	Measures/Data	Data Collection Method	Data Sources	Timing	Responsibilities
			Data Collection Plan			
1. Reaction, Satisfaction, and Planned Actions	• Obtain a positive reaction to project and materials • Obtain input for suggestions for improvement • Identify planned actions		• Questionnaire	• Supervisors	• End of Implementation	• Project coordinator
2. Learning	• Knowledge of policy on sexual harassment • Knowledge of inappropriate and illegal behavior • Skills to investigate and discuss sexual harassment	• True/False statements • Skill practices	• Pre- and Posttest • Observation	• Supervisors	• Beginning of project and end of implementation • During Session	• Meeting facilitator
3. Application Using Implementations	• Administer policy • Conduct meeting with employees to explain policy and issues • Ensure that the workplace is free of sexual harassment	• Completed meeting records	• Questionnaire • Company records • Employee survey (25% sample)	• Supervisors • New supervisors and employees	• 6 months after program • 1 month after program • 6 months after program	• Project evaluator • HRIS staff • Employee communications
4. Business Impact	• Reduce internal complaints • Reduce external complaints • Reduce employee turnover	• Formal complaints filed with HR VP • Charges filed with EEOC • Monthly voluntary termination	• Performance monitoring • Questionairre	• Company records • Supervisors	• Monthly for 1 year before and after program • 6 months after program	• Project evaluator
5. ROI	• BCR 1.25 • ROI 25%	• Benefits/Cost Ratio • Financial ROI (Earnings/Investment)	• Comments: Positive ROI not required for project continuation. Level 3 and 4 data are very important.			

- *The specific data collection method, briefly described, using standard terminology.* A variety of different data collection methods are available, ranging from very subjective low-cost methods such as questionnaires to more expensive and accurate methods such as observation and performance monitoring. (The data collection methods are described in more detail in another chapter.)
- *The source of the data.* These data sources will vary considerably, but usually include users, team leaders, company records, and the client.
- *The time frame to collect data.* This is usually referenced from the beginning of the project.
- *The responsibility for data collection.* In most cases, team members in the client operation will collect the data.

There are five levels:

Level 1. The objectives for reaction and satisfaction usually include positive reactions to the consulting projects and suggested improvements. Planned actions may be included in the input. Reaction and satisfaction data may be collected at different intervals; questionnaires, interviews, and focus groups are the usual methods. In this example, feedback is taken only at one time—at the end of implementation of the solution using a questionnaire.

Level 2. Because evaluation at this level focuses on the measures of learning, specific objectives include those areas where users are expected to learn new tasks, knowledge, skills, or perceptions. Data collection methods usually include tests, questionnaires, interviews, and focus groups. In this case, it's a test and observation of skill practice by the facilitator of the meeting. The timing for level 2 evaluation is at the end of the implementation.

Level 3. For application and implementation evaluation, the objectives represent broad areas of application, including significant on-the-job activities and implementation steps. Data collection methods include questionnaires, interviews, focus groups, observations, and records monitoring. In this example, the methods include questionnaires, surveys, and monitoring company records. This information is usually collected a matter of months after the implementation. Because responsibilities are often shared among several groups, including the consultants, it is important to clarify this issue early in the process. In this example, four groups share the responsibilities.

Level 4. For impact evaluation, objectives focus on business impact measures influenced by the consulting project. The measures/data column includes the way in which each item is measured. For example, if one of the objectives is to improve quality, a specific measure would indicate how that quality is actually measured, such as defects per 1,000 units produced. In the example, two types of complaints are defined and are very different. The third measure, turnover, is also defined. While the preferred data collection method is performance records monitoring, other methods, such as questionnaires, interviews, and focus groups, may be appropriate. Here, two sources of data are utilized: company records and questionnaires. The timing depends on how quickly the solution can generate a sustained impact on the three measures. It is usually a matter of months after the consulting intervention is completed. In this example, data were collected at six-month intervals. A project evaluator is responsible for data collection at this level.

Level 5. If appropriate, an ROI objective is included. This is usually stated as benefit/cost ratio (BCR), a percentage (financial ROI), or a specific time (payback period). Both BCR and ROI were considered appropriate for this example.

The data collection plan is an important part of the evaluation strategy and should be completed prior to moving forward with the project; the plan is completed before pursuing the project. The plan provides a clear direction of what types of data will be collected; how, where, and when they will be collected; and who will collect them.

ROI Analysis Plan

Table 8-9 shows a completed ROI analysis plan for the same sexual harassment prevention project. This planning document is the continuation of the data collection plan presented in Table 8-8 and captures information on several key items that are necessary to develop the actual ROI calculation. (Additional detail on ROI analysis is presented in the next chapter.)

- In the first column significant data items are listed, usually business impact measures (level 4 data items), but in some cases they can include level 3 data. These items will be used in the ROI analysis.
- The second column lists the methods for isolating the effects of consulting next to each data item. For most projects, the method will be the same for each data item, but there can be variations. For example, if no historical data are available for one data item, then trend line analysis is not possible for that item; although it may be appropriate for other items. In this example, a control group arrangement was not feasible, but a trend line analysis was. Participant estimates were used as a backup. (These methods are described in Chapter 10.)
- The method for converting data to monetary values is in the third column. In this example, complaints are converted to monetary values with two approaches: using costs from company records, and collecting expert input directly from the staff involved in the process.
- The cost categories planned for capture are outlined in the fourth column. Notations about costs that should be prorated are listed. Usually, the cost categories will be consistent from one project to another. However, a specific cost that is unique to this project is also noted.
- Anticipated intangible benefits expected from this solution are outlined in the fifth column. This list is generated from discussions about the solution with sponsors and subject matter experts.
- Communication targets are outlined in the sixth column. Although there could be many groups that should receive the information, four target groups are always recommended: senior management, solution users, managers of users, and the consultants. Each of these four groups needs to know about the results of the consulting ROI analysis.
- Finally, other issues or events that might influence implementation are highlighted in the seventh column. Typical items include the capability of participants, the degree of access to data sources, and unique data analysis issues.

The ROI analysis plan, when combined with the data collection plan, provides detailed information on calculating the ROI, illustrating how the process will develop from beginning to end. When completed, these two plans should provide the direction necessary for a consulting ROI evaluation and should integrate with the overall project plan.

Table 8-9 Example of Completed ROI Analysis Plan

Project: Preventing Sexual Harassment   **Responsibility:** _____   **Date:** _____

ROI Analysis Plan

Data Items	Methods for Isolating the Effects of the Intervention	Methods of Converting Data	Cost Categories	Intangible Benefits	Communication Targets	Other Influences/Issues
Formal internal complaints of sexual harassment	• Trend-line analysis • Participant estimation (as a backup)	• Historical costs with estimation form EEO/AA staff (internal expert)	• Initial analysis and assessment • Solution development • Coordination/ facilitation • Client time for project • Materials • Food/refreshments • Salaries and benefits for participants • Evaluation and reporting	• Job satisfaction • Absenteeism • Stress reduction • Public image • Recruiting	• All employees (condensed info.) • Senior executives (summary report with detailed backup) • All supervisors and managers (brief report) • HR/Consulting staff (full report)	• Several initiatives to reduce turnover were implemented during this time period • Must not duplicate benefits from both internal and external complaints
External complaints of sexual harassment	• Trend-line analysis • Participant estimation (as a backup)	• Historical costs with estimation form EEO/AA staff (internal expert)				
Employee voluntary turnover	• Forecasting using percentage of turnover related to sexual harassment	• External studies within industry				

163

Shortcut to Plan for the Evaluation

In this chapter we have presented an approach to planning the evaluation of consulting projects. The process is comprehensive and thorough, which is often needed in most major consulting projects. When a project involves hundreds of thousands or even millions of dollars of investment, it is important to allocate the appropriate time and budgets for developing the actual consulting ROI. For smaller-scale projects, a more simplified process is appropriate.

There are four key issues to address when taking a shortcut approach to planning for the evaluation:

Define Expectations and Requirements

Even in small-scale, simple projects, it is important to detail the specific requirements needed for the consulting project to be successful and to clearly define the expectations. Here, the client should be as specific as possible in terms of the desired conduct and expectations from the consulting solution. As much detail as can be developed is recommended. This can be included in the proposal or a brief working document, but it should highlight the very key issues that can cause the process to go astray.

Define Workforce Changes

It is important to define the anticipated changes at the work site—changes that will be driven by the consulting solution and, more specifically, the solutions from the consulting project. Thinking through the changes will often help identify potential barriers and enablers to the process. It will define what the employees (users of the solutions) and other stakeholders will experience or be expected to do to make the consulting project successful. Perhaps a checklist of things to be concerned about would be appropriate to ensure that both client and consultant agree on anticipated changes and the work flow, work process, working conditions, and workplace environment.

Define Expected Outcomes

The various levels of objectives are helpful for the simplest projects. It is recommended that consideration be given to developing these multiple level objectives. More important, the ultimate impact expected should be clearly defined in terms of the measures that should change or improve if the project is successful. Along with this definition would be the parameters for collecting data and methods to isolate the effects of the process. The more specificity there is about these outcomes, the more successful the project will be in terms of focusing on results and having a clear understanding of what is necessary for success.

Develop a Plan

While the two documents presented in Tables 8-7 and 8-8 may include too much detail for a simple project, there is no substitute for detailing these issues. Even a $50,000 project is worth the few hours of planning to make sure that the key issues are covered in some way. Shortcut ways to develop some of those processes are possible and are described later in the book. The important point here is to develop some type of simplified plan, although it may be less detailed than the two formal planning documents presented. Overall, this step is critical and cannot be ignored because the key issues must be addressed.

Final Thoughts

This chapter presented the initial analysis and planning for the evaluation of a consulting project. We explored the rationale for thorough initial analysis and detailed objectives, as well as the linkage of levels of evaluation, objectives, and initial needs. This connection greatly simplifies the consulting accountability process. Next, evaluation planning tools were introduced. When the consulting ROI process is thoroughly planned, taking into consideration all potential strategies and techniques, it becomes manageable and achievable.

CHAPTER 9

MEASURING THE SUCCESS OF CONSULTING

This chapter explores the rationale for measuring the success of consulting. To begin understanding this rationale, consultants must first answer several important accountability questions, among them:

- How should I approach evaluation?
- Is a credible process available?
- Can it be implemented using the resources available to me?
- What is involved in the process?
- What is my role in the process?
- What would happen if I do nothing?

These and other related issues are detailed thoroughly in this chapter as the case is presented for consultants to embrace a more comprehensive measurement and evaluation process—one that includes developing the consulting return on investment (ROI). To that end, this chapter presents a rational, credible approach for undertaking measurement and evaluation efforts, explains how the process can be applied within the resources of a consulting firm, and examines the various elements and issues necessary to build credibility with the process.

Why Measure Consulting Success?

Developing a balanced set of measures, including those designed to measure ROI, is among the most critical issues surrounding the consulting field. The topic routinely appears on conference agendas and at professional meetings. Journals and newsletters embrace the concept with increasing print space. Several consulting experts are recommending ROI calculations. Even top executives have increased their appetite for ROI information.

Although interest in the topic has grown and progress has been made, consulting ROI remains an issue that challenges even the most sophisticated and progressive consulting firms. Some consultants argue that it is not possible to calculate the impact of consulting, while others quietly and deliberately go about developing such measures, including ROI calculations. Regardless of differing opinions on the issue, the reasons for measuring the consulting ROI are valid. Most consultants share a concern that they must eventually show the value of their work; otherwise, consulting budgets may be reduced or the consulting practice becomes unable to maintain or enhance its present status with clients.

Although the rationale for focusing on the ROI may be obvious, it is helpful to examine the various reasons why now is the time to develop it. The consulting industry has been established for many years, and consulting projects have earned an important spot in the internal business activities of most large and mid-size organizations. So why begin measuring the success in more detail than in the past? Here are a few reasons:

Client Demands

Today, clients are increasingly requesting more comprehensive evaluation data on consulting projects up to and including measurement of the actual ROI. It is now common for clients to ask the irritating question at the outset of many consulting projects: "How do I know if this will pay off for me?"

Although accountability issues have always been considered, they've never been studied at the levels they are today. When a client demands that accountability be examined, new processes must be implemented, and those processes must be credible enough to produce results that satisfy clients. Client questions concerning accountability must be addressed in a straightforward, rational manner. Simply avoiding the issue will only serve to foster client distrust of consultants and the consulting process, and it will ultimately damage the credibility of both the particular practice and the consulting industry.

Competitive Advantage

Meeting or beating the competition is one important reason for implementing more comprehensive measurement and evaluation methods, including ROI development. Some consulting firms are beginning to make it standard operating procedure to calculate the value of their consulting as a value-adding service rather than in response to client request—to sharpen their competitive edge or to stay a step ahead of others developing similar processes. The issue must be addressed in a proactive way using a comprehensive approach to measuring consulting success, since it may be the foremost way to distinguish your practice in a sea of competition.

Increased Revenues and Profits

When a consulting firm can quantify the contribution of its consulting engagements in monetary terms, it helps make an excellent case for additional fees—or at least additional projects. Some firms are emphasizing the process to the point of using it to drive additional revenue.

For example, the practice might discount its standard fees for a consulting project by a specified amount and then place an amount at risk by linking it to the achievement of a target ROI that is mutually agreed upon at the outset of the project. The contingent compensation could be a set amount, or it may defined as any savings generated beyond the target. This option is an excellent way to increase overall revenues and possibly expand the profit margin on a particular project while strengthening credibility, proactively addressing accountability concerns, and building client satisfaction and loyalty. This concept is described later in the chapter.

Enhanced Marketing Database

Developing a history of consulting success lays the groundwork for building a valuable database that highlights for clients the goals and outcomes from previous engagements. Over time, it can also identify important trends and patterns in projects completed for various clients. A substantial database of project evaluation data generated using a credible, undisputed process can become a powerful competitive advantage—and a persuasive selling point.

Self-Satisfaction

Individuals engaged in professional work want to know that their efforts make a positive difference. Likewise, consultants need to see that they are making contributions that managers respect and appreciate. Therefore, communicating a positive consulting ROI from a project can be one of the most self-satisfying steps for the consultant. To be sure, consultants can realize a great deal of self-worth through assignments that proceed smoothly in terms of schedule, budget, and client feedback. However, communicating the value added in monetary terms with an impressive ROI analysis puts a crowning touch on a major project—and offers reinforcing evidence that what we do makes a difference.

The Dilemma of ROI Accountability

The dilemma surrounding consulting ROI is a major source of frustration—albeit unwarranted in most cases if the measure is properly developed—for many clients, consultants, and even within the profession itself. Most business leaders realize that consulting engagements are a basic necessity for organizations challenged by generally negative changes such as increased competition, increased operating cost, excessive turnover, demanding new external regulations, and greater workload pressures on key employees. Consulting is perhaps equally important, though, for helping organizations manage positive changes, or "good problems," including rapid growth, new technology, integrating acquired businesses, unmet product demand, and international expansions.

In either case, consultants bring objective insight and diverse experience to the table in preparing the organization and its employees to meet a wide range of business challenges.

Many clients intuitively understand the need for consulting and readily acknowledge the value it adds. They can logically conclude that consulting pays off in important bottom-line measures such as productivity improvements, quality enhancements, cost reductions, and time savings. Many also believe that consulting projects can strengthen customer satisfaction, improve morale, and build teamwork. The frustration that does exist, however, often stems from a lack of evidence showing that the process really works. While the payoffs are assumed to exist and the consulting project appears to be necessary, additional evidence is needed if the allocation of consulting funds is to grow or even continue in the future. The logical, rational approach to measuring the consulting ROI is the most promising way to bring accountability to the process and thus justify its existence and future in an organization.

Why this Concern for Accountability?

Another important consideration is the impetus behind increased accountability. What exactly is generating this emphasis, including consulting ROI? What follows is a discussion of several powerful forces that began converging in recent years and created the tremendous pressure to pursue consulting ROI that now permeates the profession.

Failure of Consulting

As mentioned in Chapter 1, many consulting projects have not lived up to their promises and have not delivered the results clients and consulting firms sought or expected, at least not in terms that management understands—primarily bottom-line contributions. Although more and more consulting projects are being commissioned today, increasingly consuming precious resources in an organization, the results being sought have simply not materialized for many projects. And when the results *are* reported, they are often met with skepticism and concern about the credibility and objectivity of the data and the thoroughness of the analysis. This has prompted many clients to rethink the role and value of consulting and to impose more restraints and demands on consultants.

Economic Pressures on Clients

As businesses strive for success in today's global economy, they are increasingly burdened with mandates for efficiency and cost savings. Companies must squeeze every possible dollar out of each process, activity, and resource—or, if possible, avoid spending that dollar in the first place. They must account for every expenditure and project, and in some cases it's a sheer matter of survival. This escalating competition for resources has prompted many organizations to examine the payoff from consulting to ensure that they are getting the most out of the associated expenditures.

Budget Growth

With the increased use of consultants comes increased spending on consulting activities, and those expenses are easy and obvious targets for critics of the process. It is one thing to spend $50,000 on a small consulting project, but spending $10 million on a consulting assignment that doesn't produce hard results that are easily understood is likely to enrage consulting critics. Consulting accounts for a growing percentage of the operating budgets of many companies, and most predict that those expenditures will continue to grow—not only in sheer dollars, but also as a percentage of operating costs. Thus, to satisfy critics, if for no other reason, consulting will likely remain a prominent target for increased accountability.

Accountability Trends

The focus on accountability is not a new issue, and in fact has been building for years, but only recently has it been growing in intensity throughout modern organizations. Today, it is sweeping across organizations, which demand accountability not only for consulting activities, but for almost every type of business process. Quality initiatives, technology implementation, human resources programs, and major change initiatives are all being subjected to increased scrutiny. Consequently, any new process implemented must address accountability.

Balanced Measures

Debate over which results should or should not be measured, and how, has been going on for years. Some prefer soft data directly from clients or customers. Others prefer hard data focused on key issues of output, quality, cost, and time. Still others argue for a balance of measures, and this camp seems to be winning. There is a critical need to examine data from a variety of groups at different time frames and for different purposes. This mixture of data, often referred to as "a balanced approach," is driving additional demand for the process described in this chapter.

Executive Interest

After enduring years of skepticism and resistance at the top of the corporate ladder, consulting ROI methods today enjoy keen interest from the executive suite. Organizational leaders grew increasingly frustrated watching their consulting budgets grow without the supporting ROI justification from accountability measures that they now demand be applied to consulting efforts.

The business press was partly responsible for the consulting ROI interest now common among top executives, as revealing articles on accountability and measuring the payoff of consulting began appearing regularly in the *Wall Street Journal*, the *Financial Times, Fortune, BusinessWeek*, and *Forbes*. As measuring the consulting ROI has become a global topic of interest among all top executives intent on requiring accountability in consulting, this interest is increasingly mirrored in organizations throughout the world. Whether an economy is mature or developing, the economic pressures of running a global enterprise have focused new emphasis on accountability in consulting.

Passing Fads

Finally, ROI application has flourished in tandem with the wide variety of organizational improvement and change interventions offered by many consulting firms, particularly in North America, where at least some organizations are quick to embrace nearly any business trend that appears on the horizon. However well-intentioned, though, many of these change efforts fail and are dismissed as passing fads almost as quickly as they were adopted.

Consulting firms are often caught in the middle of this issue, either by supporting the fad with consulting or actually coordinating the fad in client organizations. Unfortunately, the consulting ROI process was not used to measure the accountability of these projects. An implementation of the complete process requires thorough assessment and significant planning before the ROI is attempted. If these two elements are in place, unnecessary passing fads doomed for failure can be avoided. With the ROI process in place, a new change program that does not produce results will be exposed. Management will be fully aware of it early, so that adjustments can quickly be made.

Figure 9-1 shows the five reasons for measuring the success of consulting in today's environment and the seven forces that are driving the need for ROI. Together they form the rationale for consulting ROI today.

Figure 9-1   Rationale for ROI

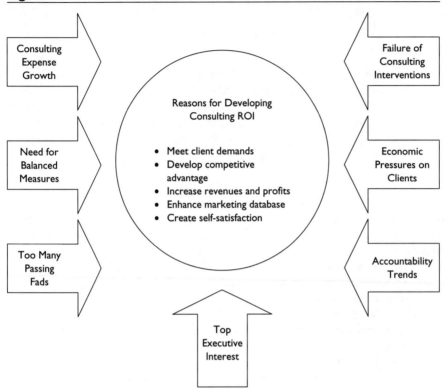

Finally, a Credible Approach

To develop a credible approach for measuring the success of consulting, several pieces of an important puzzle must be developed. Figure 9-2 shows the five major elements of this puzzle.

1. There should be an evaluation framework defining the various types of data, which must be captured at different times from different sources to develop a comprehensive set of measures.
2. A process model must be developed that shows a step-by-step procedure for collecting and analyzing data. Inherent in this process is a technique to isolate the effects of consulting from other factors and to actually calculate the monetary payoff compared to the cost of the consulting assignment. A process model with many options and sequential steps helps ensure that the process can be replicated.
3. There should be a set of operating standards, "guiding principles" that illustrate the philosophy behind the process and are designed to keep it on track. A standard process increases the likelihood of replication (i.e., if two individuals conducted the same study, the same results would be obtained). Also, an operating standard builds credibility in the process by taking a conservative approach.

4. There should be ample applications that build experience with a process to show how it actually works in real-world settings. This is particularly important for larger firms.
5. Finally, appropriate resources should be devoted to implementation issues, addressing responsibilities, procedures, goals, and skill-building.

Together, these five pieces of the puzzle are necessary to develop an evaluation system that contains a balanced set of measures, enjoys credibility with the various stakeholders involved, and can be replicated from one group to another.

For a measurement process to be feasible, it must balance many issues, including feasibility, simplicity, credibility, and soundness. More specifically, two major target audiences must be satisfied.

First, consultants who use a process must have a simple approach. Unfortunately, many consultants who attempt to measure success are overwhelmed by long formulas, complicated equations, and complex models that prompt many consultants to give up in a fit of frustration. They conclude that measuring impact by ROI cannot be developed or that it would be too expensive for most applications. Because of these concerns, many consultants seek a process that is simple and easy to understand so they can implement the steps and strategies. Also, they need a process that will not require excessive time to implement and will not consume too much precious consulting time. Finally, the consultants need a process that is not too expensive. Given the fierce competition for financial resources, the process should not command a significant portion of the consulting budget.

Second, the measurement process must meet the unique requirements of clients. The client who requests consulting and approves consulting projects needs a process that will provide both quantitative and qualitative results. If necessary, they need a process that will develop a calculation similar to the ROI formula applied to other types of investments. And as with consultants, they want a process that is simple, easy to understand, and that reflects their point of reference, background, and level of understanding. They neither want nor need a string of formulas, charts, or complicated models.

Figure 9-2   ROI Methodology Elements

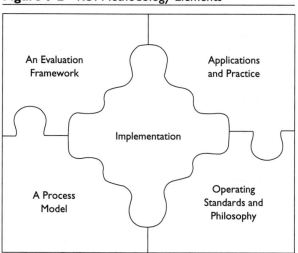

Instead, they need a process they can explain to others if necessary. More important, they need a process with which they can identify—one that is sound and realistic enough to earn their confidence.

Not only does the ROI process outlined in this chapter meet the critical challenges of the two important groups, but it also provides consultants with a useful, helpful tool that can be a routine and integral part of consulting. The next five sections describe the five critical parts of the puzzle that come together to create a viable measurement process.

The Framework: Evaluation Levels

Consulting success can be measured on five levels, as described in the previous chapter. The concept of different levels of evaluation is both helpful and instructive in understanding how consulting can add value. Table 9-1 shows the five-level framework.

- At level 1, "Reaction and Satisfaction," reaction to the consulting project is measured using input from a variety of stakeholders. Almost all consulting firms evaluate at this level, usually with generic questionnaires and client surveys. While this evaluation is important as a client satisfaction measure, a favorable reaction does not ensure that users of a consulting solution will know how to implement the improvements.
- At level 2, "Learning," measurements focus on what users have learned about the consulting solution. A learning check is helpful to ensure that users have absorbed new skills and knowledge and know how to use it to make the consulting solution successful. However, a positive measure at this level is no guarantee that the solution will be successfully implemented.
- At level 3, "Application and Implementation," a variety of follow-up methods are used to determine if users applied on the job what is needed to make the project successful. The progress made on action plans is an important measure at this level. In addition, this measure includes all the steps, tasks, and processes involved in the implementation of the solution. While level 3 evaluation is important to gauge the success of the solution implementation, it still does not guarantee that it will produce a positive impact on the organization.
- At level 4, "Business Impact," the measurement focuses on the actual results achieved by the consulting solution. Typical level 4 measures include output, quality, cost, time, employee satisfaction, and customer satisfaction. Although the consulting may produce a measurable business impact, there is still a concern that the solution may have cost too much.
- At level 5, "Return on Investment," the measurement compares the solution's monetary benefits with the consulting costs. Although ROI can be expressed in several ways, it is usually presented as a percentage or a benefit-cost ratio. If the ultimate level of evaluation is needed, the cycle is not complete until the level 5 evaluation is conducted.

While almost all consulting firms conduct evaluations to measure satisfaction, very few actually conduct evaluations at the ROI level. Perhaps the best explanation for this is that ROI evaluation is often characterized as a difficult and expensive process. Although business results and ROI are desired, it is very important to evaluate the other levels. A chain of impact should occur through the levels as the reaction, skills, knowledge, and actions are captured (levels 1 and 2) as the consulting solution is

Table 9-1 Characteristics of Evaluation Levels

Level	Brief Descriptions
1. Reaction and Satisfaction	Measures stakeholders' reaction to the consulting and stakeholder satisfaction with the consulting solution, along with planned implementation.
2. Learning	Measures skills, knowledge, or attitude changes related to consulting and the consulting solution.
3. Application and Implementation	Measures changes in behavior on the job and specific application and implementation of the consulting solution.
4. Business Impact	Measures business impact changes related to consulting.
5. Return on Investment	Compares the monetary value of the business impact with costs for consulting, usually expressed as a percentage.

applied on the job (level 3) to produce business impact (level 4). If measurements are not taken at each level, it is difficult to conclude that the results achieved were actually produced by the consulting project. Because of this, it is recommended that evaluation be conducted at all levels when an ROI evaluation is planned.

As an example to help illustrate the different levels of evaluation, consider a project that was designed to streamline the accounts receivable process in a manufacturing company. The consulting project analyzed the current process that was used and recommended changes, including new software. In the context of the levels, the project and its solution can be evaluated in the following ways:

- At level 1, the users of the solution (i.e., the employees in the accounts receivable section) were asked about their reaction to the new process. This involved collecting information regarding the relevance, importance, appropriateness, and usefulness of the new procedure and software.
- At level 2, the users (employees) were taught how to use the new procedure and use the new software. The measure of learning was a self-assessment scale on each of the tasks and processes in the software.
- At level 3, a profile of user performance with the procedure and software was generated. The success of use was detailed, including the steps in the procedures and the processes, features, and options of the software. These were all examined through both questionnaires for self-input and checking the routines in the actual use of the software. This was essentially an invisible observation.
- At level 4, the consequences were captured. Invoice processing in accounts receivable analysis took less time, with fewer errors and improved customer satisfaction. These three measures, time reduction, quality improvement, and client satisfaction represent business impact level 4 measures.
- At level 5, the monetary values of two measures (time and quality) were compared to the actual consulting costs to yield an ROI of 23 percent.
- Customer satisfaction could not be converted to money credibly with minimum resources. It was reported as an intangible.

The Process: Consulting ROI

The consulting ROI process, presented briefly in this chapter, had its beginnings several years ago as the process was applied to a variety of business processes. Since then the process has been refined and modified to represent what is presented in Figure 9-3.

As the figure illustrates, the process is comprehensive, as data are developed and collected at different times from different sources to develop the six types of measures that are the focal point of this chapter (i.e., the five levels of data plus intangibles). To date, there have been more than 100 case studies published utilizing the ROI process, and the number is growing. The process meets all of the criteria for success and use outlined in this chapter, and we touch upon each part of the process. More detail is provided in other books.[1]

Evaluation Planning

To measure the success of consulting, two planning steps must be addressed. The first is to develop appropriate objectives for the consulting solution. These range from developing objectives for reaction, to developing an objective for the ROI; they are defined in more detail in Chapter 8.

With the objectives in hand, the next step is to develop a detailed evaluation plan. This involves two important documents. A data collection plan indicates the type of data collected, the method for data collection, data sources, the timing of collection, and the various responsibilities. The ROI analysis plan details how the consulting solution is isolated from other influences, how data is converted to monetary values, the appropriate cost categories, the expected intangible measures, and the anticipated target audience for communication. These planning documents are necessary for the process to be implemented appropriately.

Collecting Data

Data collected during the implementation of the consulting solution measure reaction and satisfaction at level 1 and learning at level 2. Collecting data during the implementation ensures that adjustments are made and the process is altered as necessary to make sure the assignment is on track. The reaction, satisfaction, and learning data are critical for immediate feedback and necessary to the project's success. Data collection is central to the calculation of the ROI.

Postconsulting data are collected and compared to preconsulting situations, control group differences, and expectations. Both hard data—representing output, quality, cost, and time—and soft data, including work habits, work climate, and attitudes, are collected. Data are collected using a variety of methods outlined in Table 9-2.

The important challenge in data collection is selecting the method or methods appropriate for the setting and the specific consulting project, within the time and budget constraints. Data collection methods are covered in more detail in other books.[2]

Isolating the Effects of Consulting

An often overlooked issue in most evaluations is the process of isolating the effects of consulting. In this step of the process, specific techniques are explored that determine the amount of performance improvement directly related to the consulting. This is essential because many factors influence performance data

Figure 9-3 The ROI Model

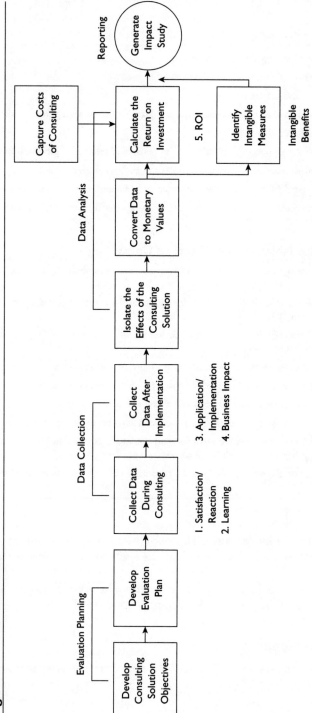

177

Table 9-2. Methods of Data Collection

- Surveys measure reaction learning and application.
- Questionnaires measure reaction learning application and impact.
- On-the-job observation captures actual application.
- Tests and assessments are used to measure the extent of learning (knowledge gained or skills enhanced).
- Interviews measure reaction and application.
- Focus groups determine the degree of application of the consulting solution in job situations.
- Action plans show progress with implementation on the job and the impact obtained.
- Performance contracts detail specific outcomes expected or obtained from the consulting solution.
- Business performance monitoring shows improvement in various performance records and operational data.

Table 9-3 Methods for Isolating the Effects of Consulting

- A pilot group with consulting is compared to a control group without consulting to isolate consulting intervention impact.
- Trend lines are used to project the values of specific output variables, and projections are compared to the actual data after consulting.
- A forecasting model is used to isolate the effects of consulting when mathematical relationships between input and output variables are known.
- Participants/stakeholders estimate the amount of improvement related to a consulting solution.
- Supervisors and managers estimate the impact of consulting on the output measures.
- External studies provide input on the impact of a consulting solution.
- Independent experts provide estimates of the impact of consulting on the performance variable.
- When feasible, other influencing factors are identified and the impact is estimated or calculated, leaving the remaining, unexplained improvement attributable to consulting.
- Customers provide input on the extent to which the consulting solution has influenced their decision to use a product or service.

after a consulting solution is implemented. The specific technique in this step will pinpoint the amount of improvement directly related to the consulting. The result is increased accuracy and credibility of the ROI calculation.

The techniques shown in Table 9-3 have been utilized by organizations to tackle this important issue. Collectively, these strategies provide a comprehensive set of tools.

Converting Data to Monetary Values

To calculate the return on investment, business impact data are converted to monetary values and are compared to consulting costs. This requires that a value be placed on each unit of data connected with the consulting. Table 9-4 shows most of the key techniques available to convert data to monetary values. The specific strategy selected usually depends on the type of data and the situation. This step in the consulting ROI model is very important and absolutely necessary for determining the monetary

Table 9-4 Methods for Converting Data to Money

- Output data are converted to profit contribution or cost savings and reported as a standard value.
- The cost of a quality measure, such as a reject, is calculated and reported as a standard value.
- Employee time saved is converted to wages and benefits.
- Historical costs of preventing a measure, such as a customer complaint, are used when they are available.
- Internal and external experts estimate a value of a measure.
- External databases, search engines, and Web sites contain an approximate value or cost of a data item.
- Participants estimate the cost or value of the data item.
- Supervisors or managers provide estimates of costs or value when they are both willing to and capable of assigning values.
- The consulting staff estimates value of a data item.
- The measure is linked to other measures for which the costs are easily developed.

Table 9-5 Recommended Consulting Costs

- The cost of initial analysis and assessment, possibly prorated over the expected life of the consulting solution
- The cost to design/develop solutions
- The cost to acquire technology and equipment
- The cost of launching the consulting solution
- The cost for application and implementation of the consulting solution
- The cost of maintaining and monitoring the solution
- The cost of evaluation and reporting
- The costs of client administration and overhead for the consulting solution, allocated in some convenient way

benefits from consulting. The process is challenging, particularly with soft data, but can be methodically accomplished using one or more of these strategies.

Tabulating the Consulting Cost

The other part of the equation in a benefit-cost analysis is the consulting cost. Tabulating it involves monitoring or developing the cost related to the consulting project. A fully loaded approach is recommended where all direct and indirect costs are tabulated. The cost components that should be included are outlined in Table 9-5. The conservative approach is to include all of these costs so the total is fully loaded.

Calculating the Return on Investment

The return on investment is calculated using benefits and costs. The benefits/cost ratio is the benefits of consulting divided by cost. The formula is:

$$BCR = \frac{\text{Consulting Benefits}}{\text{Consulting Costs}}$$

Sometimes this ratio is stated as a cost/benefit ratio, although the formula is the same as BCR.

The ROI uses the net benefits divided by consulting costs. The net benefits are the consulting benefits minus the costs. In formula form, the ROI becomes:

$$\text{ROI\%} = \frac{\text{Net Consulting Benefits}}{\text{Consulting Costs}} \times 100$$

This is the same basic formula used in evaluating other investments where the ROI is traditionally reported as earnings divided by investment.

The BCR and the ROI present the same general information, but with a slightly different perspective. The following example will illustrate the use of these formulas.

A consulting project produced benefits of $581,000, with a cost of $229,000. Therefore, the benefits/costs ratio is:

$$\text{BCR} = \frac{\$581,000}{\$229,000} = 2.54 \ (\text{or } 2.5:1)$$

As this calculation shows, for every $1.00 invested, $2.50 in benefits are returned. In this example, net benefits are $581,000 – $229,000 = $352,000. Thus, the ROI is:

$$\text{ROI\%} = \frac{\$352,000}{\$229,000} \times 100 = 154\%$$

This means that for each $1.00 invested in the consulting project, there is a return of $1.54 in net benefits, after costs are covered.

The benefits are usually expressed as annual benefits for short-term consulting projects, representing the amount saved or gained for a complete year after the consulting solution has been implemented. While the benefits may continue after the first year, the impact usually diminishes and is omitted from calculations in short-term situations. For long-term projects, the benefits are spread over several years. This conservative approach is used throughout the application of the ROI process.

Identifying Intangible Benefits

In addition to tangible, monetary benefits, most consulting projects will generate intangible, nonmonetary benefits. During data analysis, every attempt is made to convert all data to monetary values. All hard data such as output, quality, and time are converted to monetary values. The conversion of soft data is attempted for each data item. However, if the process used for conversion is too subjective or inaccurate, and the resulting values lose credibility, then the data are listed as intangible benefits with the appropriate explanation.

For some consulting projects, intangible, nonmonetary benefits are extremely valuable, often commanding as much influence as the hard data items. Intangible benefits include such positive changes as:

- Improved public image
- Increased job satisfaction
- Increased organizational commitment

- Enhanced technology leadership
- Reduced stress
- Improved teamwork
- Improved customer service
- Reduced customer-response time

Reporting with an Impact Study

A final operational step of the consulting ROI process is to generate an impact study that is used to document the results achieved by consulting and to communicate these results to various target audiences. The impact study shows the basic process used to generate the six measures of data. The methodology, assumptions, key concepts, and guiding principles are all outlined before the actual results are presented.

Next, the six categories of data, beginning with reaction and satisfaction, and moving through ROI and intangible measures, are presented in a rational, logical process, showing the building blocks to success for the study. This becomes the official document that presents the complete assessment of the success of the consulting. Its length ranges from 20 to 30 pages for a small project, to 200 to 300 pages for a substantial, long-term consulting impact study.

Because there are a variety of target audiences, different reports may need to be generated. All of the stakeholders involved will need some communication regarding the success of the consulting, including key clients who are not interested in knowing the full details. A stakeholder report may be appropriate for stakeholders who are involved but not directly responsible for the project. Still other reports may be necessary for different target audiences. The key issue in this step of the consulting ROI process is to analyze the target audiences (detailed in the evaluation planning) and develop the appropriate report to meet their specific needs. Chapter 10 provides more detail on this topic.

Operating Standards: Guiding Principles

To ensure that each study takes the same conservative philosophy, and to increase the likelihood of replication, a set of guiding principles have been developed for the consulting ROI process. They are listed in Table 9-6.

Principle 1 focuses on the need for an initial analysis to ensure that the proper solutions are identified for the problem or opportunity creating the need for consulting. In other words, it's important that the right problem is addressed and the proper implementation planned.

Principle 2 focuses on the levels of objectives described in more detail in Chapter 8. Although in theory the ROI can be developed for consulting projects even if there were no objectives, the process is much more efficient and effective—and the evaluation more accurate—if there are detailed objectives all the way through to business impact and ROI.

Principle 3 represents a way to conserve important resources. Shortcuts can perhaps be taken on lower-level evaluations, whereas more emphasis is regularly placed on higher levels. This is important when the client wants to see the business impact. In those cases, shortcuts can be taken perhaps at levels 2 and 3 (Measuring Learning and Application/Implementation).

Table 9-6 Guiding Principles

1. If a consulting intervention is not needed, the economic benefits will be negligible.
2. An evaluation can be taken to the highest level of the consulting solution's objectives.
3. When an evaluation is planned for a higher level, the previous level does not have to be comprehensive.
4. When a higher-level evaluation is conducted, data must be collected at lower levels.
5. At least one method must be used to isolate the effects of consulting.
6. If no improvement data are available for a consulting participant, it is assumed that little or no improvement has occurred.
7. Estimates of improvement should be adjusted for the potential error of the estimate.
8. Extreme data items and unsupported claims should not be used in ROI calculations.
9. The first year of benefits (annual) should be used in the ROI analysis of short-term consulting interventions.
10. Consulting costs should be fully loaded for ROI analysis.
11. Intangible measures are defined as measures that are purposely not converted to monetary values.
12. The results from the ROI methodology must be communicated to all key stakeholders.

Principle 5 adds to the credibility of the process. Without some method to isolate the effects of consulting, the studies are considered highly inaccurate and their results overstated.

Principle 6 addresses missing data from individuals involved in consulting projects. If the participants are no longer on the job or no longer performing the work, it is assumed that little or no improvement has occurred. This is an ultraconservative approach.

Principles 7 and 8 build on the conservative approach to data analysis.

Principle 9 focuses on the issue of timing of the actual stream of benefits from a consulting assignment. A conservative approach is recommended, usually dictating one year of benefits for short-term assignments, but multiple years for a more extensive consulting project.

Principle 10 focuses on the issue of fully loaded costs, ensuring that all direct and indirect costs of the consulting project are included.

Principle 11 provides the definition for intangibles. Along with this are some rules for deciding when not to convert the data to monetary value. In other words, if data cannot be credibly converted to money with minimum resources, they are left as intangibles.

And finally, principle 12 concerns the individuals who will receive the data. Four key stakeholders are always recommended for communications:

1. The client who requested the consulting.
2. The users who are actively involved in making the consulting solution work.
3. The supervisors and managers of the users who must see the success of consulting, and support it in the future.
4. Other consultants in the same firm. This provides an opportunity to learn much from others.

Collectively, these principles will ensure that the proper conservative approach is taken and that the impact study can be replicated and compared to others.

Case Applications: The Progress

Although a significant number of case applications have been developed, the consulting status of ROI among consultants in the field is difficult if not impossible to pinpoint. Top consulting firms and senior consultants are reluctant to disclose internal practices and, even in the most progressive consulting firms, confess that too little progress has been made. It's difficult to find cases in the literature that show how a consulting firm has attempted to measure the ROI in a consulting project. Recognizing this void, the American Society for Training and Development (ASTD) undertook an ambitious project to develop a collection of cases that illustrate real-world examples of measuring ROI in a variety of consulting and training projects. To date, five casebooks have been published by the ASTD.

One of the most interesting signs of progress with consulting measurement and evaluation comes from industry newsletters designed for and distributed to consultants, consulting managers, and specialists in the consulting field. These newsletters routinely report about consulting successes, often using qualitative data mixed with some quantitative data. They occasionally express the need for more data and accountability in the profession. The editors believe that many consultants are finding innovative ways to measure their success.

While examples of the progress of consulting ROI are available, it has become a critical topic that is constantly haunting the consulting field. The need is clear. The interest in ROI will be persistent as long as consulting budgets continue to increase and consulting holds the promise of helping organizations improve. Much progress must be made to meet this important need. More progress is needed.

Implementation of the Process

The best tool, technique, or model will not be successful unless it is properly utilized and becomes a routine part of the consulting process. As a new process, it will be resisted by both the consultants and clients, just as with any other significant change. Some of the resistance is based on realistic barriers, while some will be based on misunderstandings and perceived problems that may not exist. In either case, specific steps must be taken to overcome the resistance by carefully and methodically implementing the ROI process.

Implementation involves many issues, including assigning responsibilities, building the necessary skills, and developing the plans and goals around the process. It will also involve preparing the environment, individuals, and support teams for this type of comprehensive analysis. The firms with the most success with this process are those that have devoted adequate resources to implementation and deliberately planned for the transition from the current state to where they want the organization to be in terms of accountability.

Barriers to Consulting ROI

Although some progress has been made in the implementation of ROI, barriers can inhibit implementation of the concept. Some of these barriers are realistic, while others are actually myths based on false perceptions. Each barrier is briefly described in this section.

Costs and Time

Measuring the success of consulting will add some additional costs and time to the consulting project, although the added amount should not be excessive. As described earlier, a comprehensive ROI process will probably not add more than 3 to 5 percent to the consulting project budget. The additional investment in ROI would perhaps be offset by the additional results achieved from these consulting projects and the elimination or prevention of unproductive or unprofitable consulting. This barrier alone stops many ROI implementations early in the process.

Lack of Skills and Mind-set for Consultants

Many consultants do not understand how to measure the success of consulting, nor do they have the basic skills necessary to apply the process within their scope of responsibilities. Also, the typical consulting project does not focus on results, but on qualitative data. Consequently, a tremendous barrier to implementation is the change needed for the overall orientation, attitude, and skills of consultants. As Pogo, the cartoon character, once said, "We have met the enemy, and he is us." This certainly applies to consulting ROI implementation.

Faulty Initial Analysis

Many consulting projects do not have an adequate initial analysis and assessment. Some may have been implemented for the wrong reasons and are based on management requests or efforts to chase a popular fad or trend in the industry. If consulting is not needed, the project probably will not produce enough benefits to overcome the costs. An ROI calculation for unnecessary consulting will likely yield a negative value. This is a realistic barrier for many consulting projects.

The Fear Factor

Some consultants do not pursue ROI due to fear of failure or fear of the unknown. Fear of failure manifests itself in many ways. There may be a concern about the consequences of a negative ROI. Also, a comprehensive measurement process will stir up the traditional fear of change. This fear, often based on unrealistic assumptions and a lack of knowledge of the process, is so strong that it becomes a real barrier to many ROI implementations.

Discipline and Planning

Measuring the success of consulting requires a great deal of planning and a disciplined approach to keep the process on track. Implementation schedules, evaluation targets, analysis plans, and follow-up schedules are required. The consultant, however, may not have enough discipline and determination to stay on course, which becomes a barrier—particularly when there are no immediate pressures to measure the return. If the client is not requiring ROI, the consultant may not allocate time for planning and coordination. Also, other pressures and priorities will often eat into the time necessary for ROI implementation. Only carefully planned implementations will succeed.

False Assumptions

Many consultants have false assumptions about the ROI process that discourage them from attempting it, such as:

- ROI can be applied to only a few, narrowly focused projects.
- Senior managers do not want to see the results of consulting projects expressed in monetary values.
- If the client does not ask for ROI, it should not be pursued.
- Our consultants are professional and competent! Therefore, we do not have to justify the effectiveness of our consulting.
- Consulting is a complex but necessary activity. It should not be subjected to a quantitative evaluation process.

These false assumptions form realistic barriers that impede the progress of measuring the success of ROI.

Benefits of Consulting ROI

Although the benefits of adopting a comprehensive measurement and evaluation process (including ROI) may be obvious, several important benefits can be derived from the routine use of this process.

Showing the Contribution of Selected Consulting Projects

With the consulting ROI process, the consultant and the client will know the specific contribution of the consulting project in terms that were not previously developed or explained in a way that was understood by the client group. The ROI will show the actual benefits versus the cost, elevating the evaluation data to the ultimate level of analysis. This process presents indisputable evidence to convince the client that the project was successful.

Earning the Respect of Senior Management

Measuring the ROI of a consulting project is one of the best ways to earn the respect and support of the senior management team—not only for a particular consulting project, but for overall consulting as well. Senior managers will respect processes that add bottom-line value presented in terms they understand. The result of this analysis is comprehensive and, when applied consistently and comprehensively in several projects, it can convince the management group that consulting is an important investment and not just an expense. Mid-level managers will see that consulting is making a viable contribution to their immediate objectives. This is a critical step toward building an appropriate partnership with the senior management team.

Gaining the Confidence of Clients

The client, who requests and authorizes a consulting project, will now have a complete set of data to show the overall success of the process. Not hampered by a lack of qualitative or quantitative data, this provides a complete profile from different sources, at different time frames, and with different types of data. This reveals the process that has occurred and validates the client's initial decision to move forward with the consulting.

Improve the Consulting Processes

Because there is a variety of feedback data collected during the consulting project, a comprehensive analysis (including consulting ROI) provides data to drive changes in consulting processes and make adjustments during a project. It also provides data that helps improve consulting in the future when it is realized that certain processes are nonproductive while others add value. Thus, the consulting ROI is an important process-improvement tool.

Developing a Results-Based Approach

The communication of data at different time frames and with the detailed planning that is involved with the consulting ROI focuses the entire team, including stakeholders, on bottom-line results. This focus often enhances the results that can be achieved because the ultimate goals are clearly in mind. In essence, the process begins with the end in mind. All of the processes, activities, and steps are clearly focused on the ultimate outcomes. As the project shows success, confidence is built by using the process, which enhances the results of future projects.

Altering or Enhancing Consulting Projects

This benefit is twofold. First, if a project is not proceeding properly and the results are not materializing, the consulting evaluation will prompt changes or modifications to move it back on track. In rare occasions the project may have to be halted if it is not adding the appropriate value. While that will take courage, if it's evident that the project will not produce results, it will not reap important benefits with the client. The other part of this issue is that if the consulting project is very successful, perhaps the same type of project can be applied to other areas. It makes a convincing argument that if one division has a successful consulting project and another division has the same needs, the project may add the same value and enhance the overall success.

Guaranteeing Results for Consulting

While most consultants approach engagements with the intent to deliver value, clients need some assurance that a consulting project will add value to the organization. Typical consulting engagements begin with great promise, only to result in some instances in disappointment. Clients misunderstand the value of the project, and consultants are disappointed by the lack of support from the client. Thus, both parties are concerned about the value attached to consulting and are interested in exploring ways to improve consulting value.

The challenge is to offer a consulting project that guarantees results. With this approach, the project must focus on—and deliver—results and have some or all of the payment at risk for the assignment. For this to be successful, the project must be clearly established, adequately supported, and all parties must understand their respective roles. When applied appropriately, this is a tremendous win-win for all parties.

Approach

The first step with this approach is to ensure that the engagement is clearly connected to impact measures at the onset. Part, or all, of the project is placed at risk until the results have been achieved. Part of the cost may be charged, and a sharing arrangement is used for the results. In some cases there are no initial charges, with a larger sharing of success when the project has delivered the results.

Pricing Options

Three basic pricing options are available:

1. Charge nothing for the project initially; if the desired results are not delivered, there is no charge. Only the consultant is at risk, which is undesirable from some perspectives.
2. Half of the cost of the project is paid by the client up front, with the other half paid after the threshold target of results is achieved. Additional bonus is provided—on some type of sharing basis—when the results exceed the target.
3. The client is responsible only for direct costs—excluding overhead or profit anticipated with the project—covering just the bare essentials. A bonus is calculated based on sharing the results when they exceed the recovery of the initial costs.

Bonus

There are three basic approaches for the bonus:

1. The bonus can be based on a percent of the actual savings or profit generated. For projects connected to revenue, the bonus may be a percentage of the profits over a specified period of time. For projects that focus on productivity improvement, quality enhancement, time savings, cost reduction, retention, absenteeism, and other impact variables, the cost savings would be developed and the percent applied to the direct cost savings amount over a specified period of time.
2. The bonus is paid as a percent of the actual return on investment. This allows the client to recoup the cost and share a percentage of the ROI. For example, the payoff may be one-fourth of the return on investment, after costs are recovered.
3. A spread of the savings generated after the investment has been recouped. Essentially, this splits the ROI in half. An example will illustrate. Suppose a project costs $50,000 and delivers a 125 percent ROI.

$$\text{ROI} = \frac{\text{Net Benefits}}{\text{Costs}} \times 100$$

$$\text{Net Benefits} = \frac{\text{ROI} \times \text{Cost}}{100}$$

$$= \frac{125\% \times 50,000}{100} = \$62,500$$

Half of the ROI bonus would be $31,250.

Success Factors

Engagement

For this process to be successful, the consulting project must be connected to business impact measures. An appropriate analysis must be conducted to ensure that the anticipated measures are linked directly to the proposed consulting project. These measures become the impact objectives of the project.

In addition, given the importance of creating change in the organization, application objectives should be developed to show what specifically must be accomplished in the organization to drive the desired impact.

Finally, ROI objectives should be developed, stating the minimum acceptable level of return on investment. This is best described by examining the linkage between the initial analysis, the objectives, and evaluation. This relationship is shown in Figure 9-4 and was described in Chapter 8.[3]

Conditions for Success

The consultant must take the steps necessary to ensure project success. The client's role in achieving the results is defined at the very beginning. Projects can easily go astray if the client did not support or implement the consulting project as needed. The following items must be clearly established prior to entering into this type of guarantee:

1. Determine the specific objectives, particularly at the application and impact levels. This clearly defines what is planned for the implementation and how it would be monitored and measured. At the impact level, the objectives indicate which specific groups of measures should be changing or improving as a consequence of this project.
2. Define the method of data collection. While some methods are more accurate and expensive, others are less accurate and less expensive. The method of data collection must be defined along with responsibilities in as much detail as possible.
3. Choose the sources of data. Some sources are more credible than others; some are inaccessible, while others are readily accessible.
4. Set the timing of data collection. Often, multiple data collections are needed at different time frames. Time frames should be identified within parameters of when the data will actually be collected for the project.
5. To ensure that the project is evaluated fairly, the data should be collected by an independent party. If there is an opportunity to influence data, it is usually in this phase of the process, where the consultant can alter, add to, or delete data from the database. External collection alleviates most concerns about potential bias. A low-cost data collector could be used to capture, tabulate, and summarize the data for both the client and the consultant; another consulting firm, a graduate student, or a professor will usually suffice. If the data are collected electronically, it can be sent to an external server to be organized, tabulated, and the results sent to both client and consultant. This is inexpensive and would be appropriate when data collection is automated.
6. Determine the method of isolation of the project. Although the project is usually implemented with other complementary processes, it's important to isolate the impact of consulting from other interventions. This may be the most important issue. The specific technique used to determine these will range from the comparison group analysis to estimates from the most credible sources.

Figure 9-4   Linking Evaluation with Needs Assessment

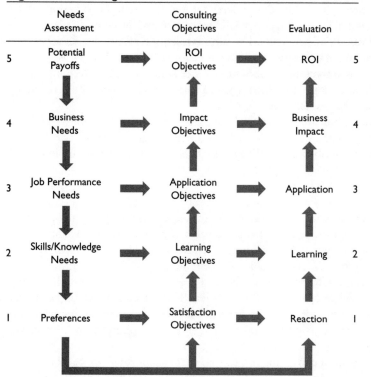

7. Decide which method to use for converting data. Since this process yields a monetary value, it's important to indicate the specific measures used to convert data to a money value. Some methods are more credible than others. Fortunately, many standard values are available for these data items.

8. Agree on the appropriate time frame for placing a value on the project. Ideally, a short time frame is preferred, using one year of data. Long-term projects may involve additional years, but a conservative approach should be pursued. More important, this time frame must be established before the project begins. It may mean that data are collected in three months and extrapolated for an entire year. In many projects the data would be collected for the full year, so extrapolation is not needed.

9. Ensure that the project is implemented by the organization. Failure to do this would mean that the results guarantee is void and that the client would pay the alternative (normal) pricing for the services.

10. Provide alternative pricing for services. If the conditions for the guarantee are not adhered to by the client, then the full price is charged. The full price is determined up front as an alternative pricing schedule.

11. Define project implementation. This definition depends upon the type of project and may involve listing the deliverables and what must be accomplished with each deliverable.

12. Require clients to secure support from various stakeholders within the client organization. Stakeholder support is necessary to ensure the project's success. Failure to provide the required level of support will make the guarantee void and alternative pricing will apply.

13. Define support required from the stakeholders. The various roles of each stakeholder are defined to include a description of the support required for success. This needs to be as specific as possible so there is no dispute about the level of support needed. If possible, determine how support would be assessed, for example, whether through a questionnaire (someone's perception) or verifying specific actions that are taken or not taken.

14. Establish the consequences of noncompliance for both parties. The consultant must meet specific deadlines and complete the deliverables that are acceptable to the client. The client must support the process as described above. The consequences for both parties are itemized.

Advantages

Several advantages emerge with these guaranteed results. For one, it develops a unique and powerful marketing strategy. Clients often get excited about the prospects of guaranteed results and will be attracted to consultants offering this approach. A willingness to take risks and define value in specific ways is an excellent way to strengthen the relationship between the client and consultant.

Eventually, a database of projects can be developed to be used as a strategic marketing tool, showing how consulting assignments have delivered value to the customers. The implementation of the project will often be enhanced. When the client realizes the consequences of not implementing what was provided in the consulting, there is more concern about implementation. Support for the project will be enhanced.

One of the most serious problems of consulting projects is lack of support by key stakeholders in the organization. While there may be many reasons for nonsupport, one of them is that various stakeholders fail to recognize the value of the consulting project. With this approach, stakeholders are encouraged, required, and sometimes motivated to support the project to achieve results or, more specifically, to avoid the consequences of not supporting the project. This approach will avoid frivolous, unnecessary projects that ultimately can tarnish the reputation of a consulting firm and add little value for the client. And finally, it also keeps projects on track, raising the satisfaction level of the participants from both the consulting firm and the client.

Summary

This is a win-win approach for consulting projects. While it takes a bit of courage, it can be managed properly if the consultant is convinced that projects and services provided add value to the organization. While this is not a common approach, it is logical, feasible, and clients find it desirable. Maybe it should be on the agenda for every consulting firm in the future.

Shortcuts to Develop Consulting ROI

The process described in this chapter is comprehensive and represents an approach recommended for major consulting projects. The more complex the project, the more comprehensive the evaluation process must be. However, there are a variety of shortcuts that may help reduce the time and resources necessary to develop consulting ROI. The following techniques or approaches are helpful for conserving resources while taking advantage of the key issues involved in the consulting ROI process.

Plan Early for the Evaluation

Planning early for the evaluation is critical to a successful process in terms of accuracy, credibility, and completeness. In addition, it can conserve resources, since planning can take advantage of the most efficient and resourceful way to capture data, analyze data, and report results.

Build Evaluation into the Consulting Process

When data collection and other evaluation steps are built into consulting, the time requirements are reduced significantly. Participants directly involved in the project solution can provide important data, thus preventing some of the data collection. Other key stakeholders may be able to provide some of the initial analysis, such as isolating the effects of the consulting or converting data to monetary values. All of these key issues can be built into the process, thereby reducing the amount of time and cost for the process.

Share Responsibilities for the Evaluation

While the consultant or consulting project leader may have the ultimate responsibility for driving the evaluation, it may be helpful to share the responsibilities with others, including the client team within the organization. This is not only a way to reduce the amount of resources required for the evaluation, but it also helps maintain the objectivity that is often needed. Key individuals within the client organization will take on important responsibilities for the measurement and evaluation, including data collection and analysis. In addition, other stakeholders may have important responsibilities for the evaluation.

Use Shortcut Methods for Major Steps

Throughout this book, several shortcut methods are provided to collect data, isolate the effects of consulting, convert data to monetary values, and capture costs. Shortcuts are available for every step of the process. While the accuracy may be somewhat inhibited by shortcut methods, the trade-off is savings in money and time.

Select Appropriate Projects for Detailed Analysis

The comprehensive, detailed analysis should be reserved only for those consulting projects that are long-term, complex, and expensive. A shortened analysis and reduced process is appropriate for simpler projects and involves less cost and shorter time frames. The important message here is to match the analysis with the complexity of the project, reserving a comprehensive ROI analysis for those critical, important, and more involved consulting projects.

Use Estimates in Collection and Analysis of Data

The process of estimating values, factors, or even improvement data represents a useful tool in this analysis. Estimates are simple, easy to obtain, and keep the cost and time to a minimum. The accuracy and reliability of estimates can be improved significantly if the proper steps are taken to ensure that data are provided within the proper framework and environment and appropriate adjustments are made in the analysis.

Develop Internal Capability to Implement the Process

It may be helpful to transfer skills to build the ROI process internally to the client so the client can use the process to show the value of other consulting assignments. This places the client in the position of fully evaluating consulting processes. Also, it significantly reduces the time and resources needed to measure the success of consulting. Sometimes, just offering the process, and the willingness to develop the process internally, will satisfy clients' accountability needs.

Streamline the Reporting Process

One of the most time-consuming steps in the process is developing detailed reports in the form of an impact study. This important process can be streamlined significantly by having a standard reporting process or even a shortcut method to present the data. In one organization, the result of the consulting project is reported on a single sheet, showing the six types of measures.

Utilize Web-based Software to Reduce Time

Fortunately, as with many complex processes, software can save time. Internet-based software tools are available that will cut in half the amount of time needed to conduct an impact study.

Application of the Consulting ROI Process: A Case Example

To illustrate how the data collected in the consulting ROI are reported, consider the following example.

The problem addressed by the consulting firm focuses directly on sexual harassment. In this hospital chain, the actual number of sexual harassment complaints, internally and externally, has steadily increased and is considered excessive by the senior management group. In addition, there appears to be a linkage to turnover, since the turnover rate exceeds industry averages. The consultants were asked to analyze the causes of the problem, develop solutions, and implement those solutions to bring harassment complaints and turnover down. The complete analysis is presented elsewhere but is included here in tabular form as Figure 9-5.

As the project profile illustrates, the project involved virtually all employees and was comprehensive, requiring an analysis to develop solutions and implement the solutions. The solution objectives were developed at levels 1 through 5. The remainder of the table presents the methods selected for data collection during the intervention as well as after the implementation of the solution. In addition,

Figure 9-5   A Case Study: Healthcare, Inc.

Project Profile

Title:	Preventing Sexual Harassment
Target Audience:	First & Second Supervisors and Administrators (655) and Nonsupervisory Employees (6,844)
Duration:	Six months—from initial analysis and assessment, solution development, and implementation
Program Objective:	Determine the cause of excessive sexual harassment complaints, the potential linkage to employee turnover, and recommended solutions. The project also includes the implementation of solutions.
Origination:	Management directive with needs analysis and assessment
Facilitation and Coordination:	HR Coordinators/Managers

Solution Objectives

After implementing this project:

- All employees should react favorably to the new emphasis on sexual harassment and this project.
- All supervisors and administrators should be able to understand and administer the company's policy on sexual harassment.
- All employees should be able to identify inappropriate and illegal behavior related to sexual harassment.
- All supervisors should be able to investigate and discuss sexual harassment issues.
- All supervisors should conduct a meeting with all employees to discuss policy and expected behavior.
- The workplace should be free from sexual harassment actions, activities, and behavior.
- The number of sexual harassment complaints should reduce by 20%.
- Employee turnover should reduce to 20%.

Data Collection During Intervention

- Interview
- Questions
- Tests

Data Collection After Implementation

- Surveys
- Questionnaires
- Business Performance Monitoring

Isolating the Effects of Consulting

- Complaints—trend analysis and estimates as a backup
- Turnover—trend analysis, forecasting, and estimates as a backup

Converting Data to Monetary Values: Techniques

- Complaints—historical costs of complaints and expert input
- Turnover—external studies, same industry

Monetary Benefits from Complaint Reduction

- Value of one internal complaint = $24,343
- Annual improvement related to program = 14.8 complaints
- $24, 343 × 14.8 = $360,276

(Continued)

Figure 9-5   *(Continued)*

Monetary Benefits from Turnover Reduction

- Value of one turnover statistic = $20,887
- Annual improvement related to program = 136 turnovers (prevented)
- $20, 887 × 136 = $2,840,632

Consulting Intervention

• Initial Analysis and Assessment (Fees)	$ 9,000
• Solution Development	15,000
• Coordination/Facilitation Fees	9,600
• Travel & Lodging for Facilitators & Coordinators	1,520
• Materials (655 @ $12)	7,860
• Food/Refreshments (655 @ $30)	19,650
• Facilities (17 meetings @ $150)	2,550
• Client Salaries Plus Benefits ($130,797 × 1.39)	181,807
• Evaluation and Reporting	31,000
Total	**$277,987**

Level 1 Results: From Supervisors and Administrators

- Overall satisfaction rating of 4.11 out of a possible five
- 93% of supervisors and managers provided list of action items

Level 2 Results: From Supervisors and Administrators

- Pretest scores average 51
- Posttest scores average 84 (Improvement 65%)
- Successful skill practice demonstration

Level 3 Results: Key Issues

- 96% of supervisors and administrators conducted meetings with employees and completed meeting record
- On a survey of nonsupervisory employees, significant behavior change was noted—4.1 out of a 5 scale
- 68% of supervisors and administrators report that all action items were completed
- 92% of supervisors and administrators reported that some action items were completed

the methods used to isolate the effects of consulting and the methods to convert data to monetary values are shown.

The results are presented beginning with level 1, ranging through level 5, and on to the intangibles. Collectively, the monetary benefits achieved in a one-year time frame from reducing complaints and turnover amounted to $3,200,908. The cost of the consulting program, as shown, is a fully loaded cost profile of $277,987. A summary is included to show how the report is developed.

This brief example shows the richness of this approach in terms of presenting a comprehensive profile of success, ranging from reaction to ROI to the intangible benefits.

Figure 9-5   *(Continued)*

Level 4 Results

Sexual Harassment Business Performance	One Year Prior to Intervention	One Year After Intervention	Factor for Isolating the Effects of Consulting
Internal Complaints	55	35	74%
External Charges	24	14	62%
Litigated Complaints	10	6	51%
Legal Fees and Expenses	$632,000	$481,000	
Settlement/Losses	$450,000	$125,000	
Total Cost of Sexual Harassment Prevention, Investigation, and Defense	$1,655,000	$852,000	
Turnover* (*Nonsupervisory Annualized)	24.2%	19.9%	

ROI Calculation

$$\text{BCR} = \frac{\text{Consulting Benefits}}{\text{Consulting Costs}} = \frac{\$2,840,632 + \$360,276}{\$277,987} = \frac{3,200,908}{277,987} = 11.5:1$$

$$\text{ROI} = \frac{\text{Net Consulting Benefits}}{\text{Consulting Costs}} = \frac{\$3,200,908 - \$277,987}{\$277,987} \times 100 = 1051\%$$

Intangible Benefits

- Job satisfaction improvement
- Absenteeism reduction
- Stress reduction
- Community image enhancement
- Recruiting image

Final Thoughts

In this chapter we provided a brief overview of a comprehensive measurement system. We clearly underscored the urgency of the challenge; now is the time to develop a comprehensive measurement and evaluation process including the ROI. We also showed how various forces created this important need for a comprehensive evaluation process. Finally, the process presented in the chapter was defined by four important elements: evaluation framework, consulting ROI process model, implementation, and guiding principles.

When combined with experience in case application, a reliable, credible process is developed that can be replicated from one project to another. This process is not without its concerns and barriers, but many of them can be overcome with simplified, economical methods.

Finally, the chapter presented a radically new approach to measuring success—guaranteed results. This is a win-win approach for consultants and clients.

Notes

[1] Jack J. Phillips, *The Consultant's Scorecard: Tracking Results and Bottom-Line Impact of Consulting Projects* (New York: McGraw-Hill, 2000).

[2] Patricia P. Phillips and Associates, *ROI Field Book* (Boston: Butterworth-Heinemann, 2006).

[3] Jack J. Phillips, Patricia P. Phillips, and Ron D. Stone, *The Human Resources Scorecard: Measuring Return on Investment*, 2nd edition (Boston: Butterworth-Heinemann, 2006).

CHAPTER 10

DELIVERING THE SERVICE

This final chapter explores the issues of making the process work to deliver the consulting service. It begins with the issue of developing a specific methodology—something that many consultants have accomplished. It is often a part of the unique service. Next, the issues involved in managing the project are explored: How to keep the project on schedule and on task, and how to maintain project communications. Much of the chapter is focused on communicating results. If the results are not properly communicated to the appropriate target audiences, the project will fall short of its value to the client. We also discuss ethical issues that may arise while delivering the service. Such issues are critical in light of the current tarnished image of consulting.

Developing Your Methodology

There are two issues connected to having a unique methodology. The first is the expertise you bring to the project. This is often the rationale for starting the consulting practice and growing it into a successful business. Your methodology must be used and protected throughout the process. The second issue is the approach to consulting—showing that there is a systematic way in which the project is to be conducted and delivered. The systematic process ensures consistency and replication and shows the client exactly what will be done and what steps will be taken to ensure success. All of this is contained in the proposal process, and now must be delivered according to the proposal's terms.

Systematic Process

Apart from the unique advantage offered by a consulting process, and the expertise of the consultant(s), is the method in which the consulting is delivered. A systematic, step-by-step process should be developed that defines the approach outlined in the proposal. Figure 10-1 shows one approach, a five-phase consulting model offered by Mooney.[1]

Phase 1: The first phase of the process is the initial involvement that leads to firming up the objectives. As indicated in Chapter 8, the project objectives are broad and the solution objectives may be developed in more detail after the initial project has begun. This is an output of Phase 1.

Figure 10-1   The Five-Phase Consulting Model

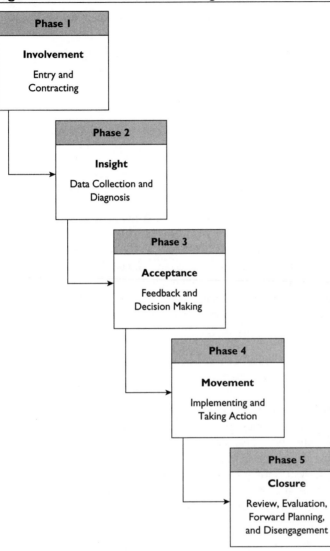

Adapted from Paul Mooney, *The Effective Consultant: How to Develop the High Performance Organisation* (Dublin: Oak Tree Press, 1999).

Phase 2: Data collection begins in this phase, along with the diagnosis of the situation. This is the heart of the consulting process.

Phase 3: This involves communicating the data to the appropriate individuals to secure acceptance and to drive the decision making for the consulting solution.

Phase 4: This is the implementation of the consulting solution.

Phase 5: The final phase includes the evaluation described in Chapter 9, along with recommendations and communication of the data described in this chapter.

The important issue is to have a systematic approach to solving the problem or pursuing the project. This approach may be separate from the unique methodology and know-how provided.

Protecting the Methodology

Sometimes it's necessary to protect the unique methodology, expertise, or know-how that is brought to the consulting process. This may include specific analytical tools, the structure of the entire project as it relates to how the data are collected, or how decisions are made and conclusions are drawn. Whatever the specific methodology, it is important to ensure that it is protected from unauthorized use.

The first decision to be made is based on the public use of the methodology. Some consultants prefer their approach to be proprietary with little discussion or disclosure of the process in the consulting reports. They may require the client to sign a confidentiality agreement with a commitment not to disclose proprietary methods. While this may work for some consultants, it can create frustration and anxiety for clients—leaving them with the impression that the consultant does not trust them to be discreet. Other consultants are very open with their process and will make presentations about it, write about it, discuss it, and display it on their Web sites. This is a personal decision.

The recommended approach is to be as open as possible about the process, while protecting any unauthorized use through obtaining a trademark, sales mark, copyright, or, in some cases, a patent. Part of the protection is to ensure that materials are presented with the appropriate notations and markings. Attempts to protect the methodology should be based in common sense. Copyrights, trademarks, and sales marks can be overused. It should be mentioned early in the report that the process is protected by law, but mentioning it in every instance or on every page is unnecessary. Being aware of what competitors are using and writing about will let you know if others are using the process.

Managing the Project

To ensure the success of the project and client satisfaction, everything must be delivered on a timely basis according to the initial proposal. Keeping the project on track and the client happy will require excellent project management skills.

Creating a Service Agreement

Some consultants avoid disappointments and surprises by developing a service agreement. This agreement details expectations throughout the project. It builds on the concept of guaranteed results described in Chapter 9 and provides details about how the project will be accomplished, as well as the expected outcomes. It complements the proposal process as it addresses the major items in the proposal, but often provides more details. Table 10-1 shows the topics contained in a typical service agreement.[2]

While this may appear to be excessive detail for proposals and guaranteed results, some consultants think the detailing is absolutely essential to avoid surprises and to keep the client informed throughout the process. Service quality agreements and service level agreements are typical in many service organizations; maybe they should be a necessary part of all major consulting projects.

Table 10-1 Typical Topics in a Service Agreement

- Precisely what you will do for the client
- Precisely what benefits the client can expect from your work
- When you will start to work for the client
- When you will stop working for the client
- How much time in aggregate you will spend on the client's behalf
- How much money you will be charging as expenses
- The basis for a cost qualifying as a rechargeable expense
- When you will be sending invoices
- The amount of the invoice
- When you expect your invoices to be paid
- When the client can expect a written report
- The length of the report
- Other deliverables the client might expect
- Any other key issues relating to your work for the client
- The resources the client needs to make available to you, including access to people, systems, and premises
- How success will be measured

Adapted from Alex Dembitz and James Essinger, *Breakthrough Consulting: So You Want to Be a Consultant? Turn Your Expertise into a Successful Consulting Business* (London: Prentice Hall, 2000).

Project Plan

As discussed earlier, a project plan is a valuable tool to show how and when the data will be collected, along with the sequencing of events and particular decisions. There are many types of project management software available that can be used to keep a consulting project on track. One of the most popular is offered by Microsoft under the name of Microsoft Project. The important point is to have a systematic way to keep the project on schedule and ensure timely reports to the client. This leads to the next issue.

Project Communications

Several chapters in this book have focused on the importance of maintaining communication between the consultant and the client. This is particularly critical during delivery of the service. Routine feedback and debriefings are necessary to show the progress of the project as well as the issues that are being confronted. These debriefings not only keep the client aware of what is occurring, but facilitates client involvement in the process. More on this later in the chapter.

Deliverables

The consulting project proposal and promised deliverables must be developed and delivered on time and with the appropriate quality. Tracking the progress of the deliverables, ensuring that they are in place and approved when promised, is absolutely critical to the integrity of project management and the ultimate success of the project.

Communicating Results

With data in hand, what's next? Should the data be used to modify the consulting project, show the contribution, justify new projects, gain additional support, or build goodwill? How should the data be presented? Who should present the data? When should the data be communicated? The worst course of action is to do nothing. Communicating results is as important as achieving them.

There are at least five key reasons for being concerned about communicating results:

- Measurement and evaluation mean nothing without communication.
- Communication is necessary to make improvements.
- Communication is necessary for explaining contributions.
- Communication is a sensitive issue.
- A variety of target audiences need different information.

Several methods, both oral and written, are available to communicate consulting success to the various audiences.[3]

The skills required to communicate results effectively are almost as delicate and sophisticated as those needed to obtain results. The style is as important as the substance. Regardless of the message, audience, or medium, a few general principles apply and are presented in Table 10-2. These principles provide guidance for effective, timely communication and offer a checklist for communicating results.

Planning the Communication

Any successful activity must be carefully planned for it to produce the maximum results. This is a critical part of communicating the results of major projects. The actual planning of the communications is important to ensure that each audience receives the proper information at the right time and that appropriate actions are taken.

Seven questions will need some attention when results are communicated. These are listed in Table 10-3.

Table 10-2 Communication Principles

Communication must be timely

Communication should be targeted to specific audiences

Media should be carefully selected

Communication should be unbiased and modest

Communication must be consistent

Testimonials are more effective coming from individuals the audience respects

The audience's opinion of consulting and the consultant will influence the communication strategy

Table 10-3 Questions to Address in Communication

1. What will be communicated?
2. When will the data be communicated?
3. How will the information be communicated?
4. Where will it be communicated?
5. Who will communicate the information?
6. What is the target audience?
7. What specific actions are required or desired?

When a major project is approved, a communication plan is usually developed. This details how specific information is generated and communicated to various groups, and the expected actions. In addition, this plan details how the overall results will be communicated, the time frames for communication, and the appropriate groups to receive information. The consulting team and the client need to agree on the extent of detail in the plan.

Another planning issue is aimed at presenting the results of an impact study. This occurs when a major project is completed and the detailed results are known. One of the major issues is who should receive the results and in what form. This is more specialized than the plan for the entire project because it involves the final study from the project. Table 10-4 shows the communication plan for a major stress management consulting project. Teams were experiencing high levels of stress. Through a variety of consulting activities and behavior changes, the teams experienced lower levels of stress.[4]

Table 10-4 Communication Plan for Project Results

Communication Document	Communication Target	Distribution Method
Complete report with appendices (75 pages)	• Project sponsor • Consulting firm • Team manager	Distribute and discuss in a special meeting
Executive summary (8 pages)	• Senior management in the business units • Senior corporate management	Distribute and discuss in routine meeting
General interest overview and summary without the actual ROI calculation (10 pages)	• Participants	Mail with letter
General interest article (1 page)	• All employees	Publish in company publication
Brochure highlighting program, objectives, and specific results	• Team leaders with an interest in the project • Prospective sponsors	Include with other marketing materials

Five different communication pieces were developed for different audiences. The complete report was an ROI impact study, a 75-page report that served as the historical document for the project. It went to the client, the consulting staff, and the manager of each of the teams involved in the stress reduction (users). An executive summary, a much smaller document, went to some of the higher-level executives. A general interest overview and summary without the ROI calculation went to the participants. A general-interest article was developed for company publications, and a brochure was produced to show the success of the project. The brochure was used in marketing the same project internally to other teams and served as additional marketing material for the consultants.

Selecting the Audience for Communications

When approaching particular audiences, the following questions should be asked about each group:

- Are they interested in the project?
- Do they actually want to receive the information?
- Has someone already made a commitment to them regarding communication?
- Is the timing right for this audience?
- Are they familiar with the project?
- How do they prefer to have results communicated?
- Do they know the team members?
- Are they likely to find the results threatening?
- Which medium will be most convincing to this group?

For each target audience, three actions are needed:

1. To the extent possible, the consultant should know and understand the target audience.
2. The consultant should find out, for each group, what information is needed and why. The nature of the information will range from brief and concise to extensive and detailed. Relying on input from others, the consultant should determine for each group what information is needed.
3. The consultant should understand audience bias, knowing that different audiences will bring different perspectives and varying expectations. Some will quickly support the results, while others may be against them or be neutral. The consultant should be empathetic and try to understand differing views. With this understanding, communications can be tailored to each audience. This is especially critical when the potential exists for the audience to react negatively to the results.

The potential target audiences to receive information on results may vary in terms of job levels and responsibilities. A sound basis for audience selection is to analyze the reason for communication. Table 10-5 shows common target audiences and the basis for selecting the audience.

Perhaps the most important audience is the client for the consulting project. This group (or individual) initiates the project, reviews data, and weighs the final assessment of the effectiveness of the project solution. Another important target audience is top management. This group is responsible for allocating resources to the project and needs information to help justify expenditures and gauge the effectiveness of the consulting effort.

Table 10-5 Common Target Audiences

Reason for Communication	Potential Target Audiences
To secure approval for the project	Client, Top Executives
To gain support for the project	Immediate Managers, Team Leaders
To secure agreement with the issues	Users, Team Leaders
To build credibility for the consultant	Top Executives
To enhance reinforcement of the processes	Immediate Managers
To drive action for improvement	Client, Users
To prepare users for the project solution	Team Leaders
To enhance results and quality of future feedback	Users
To show the complete results of the project	Client
To underscore the importance of measuring results	Client, Consultant
To explain techniques used to measure results	Client, Support Staff
To create desire for a participant to be involved	Team Leaders
To stimulate interest in the consulting	Top Executives
To demonstrate accountability for expenditures	All Employees
To market future projects	Prospective Clients

Selected groups of managers (or all managers) are also important target audiences. Management's support and involvement in the consulting process and the consultant's credibility are important to success. Effectively communicating project results to management can increase both support and credibility.

Communicating with the users' team leaders or immediate managers is essential. In many cases they must encourage participants to implement the project solution. Also, they often support and reinforce the objectives of the project solution. An appropriate return on investment improves the commitment to consulting and provides credibility for the consultant.

Users of the consulting solution need feedback on the overall success of the effort. Some may not have been as successful as others in achieving the desired results. Communicating the results increases the likelihood of effective implementation of future consulting solutions. For those achieving excellent results, the communication will reinforce the need for consulting. Communicating results to users is often overlooked, with the assumption that since the project is complete, they do not need to be informed of its success.

All consultants on the project must receive information about results. For small projects with a single consultant, this is not an issue. For larger projects, where a team is involved, all team members must be given information on the project's effectiveness. Evaluation information is necessary so that adjustments can be made if the project was not as effective as it could have been. All other consultants in the firm should receive results, even if they are not directly involved in the project. They need to understand how the measures were taken and how the analysis was conducted. These studies become excellent teaching tools for the entire team.

Company employees and stockholders may be less likely targets. General interest news stories may increase employee respect for consulting, but only if the process and the information are credible. Goodwill and positive attitudes toward the organization may also be by-products of communicating results. Stockholders, on the other hand, are more interested in the return on their investment.

While Table 10-5 shows the most common target audiences, there can be others. The number of audiences can be large in a complex organization. At a minimum, four target audiences are always recommended: the client (individual or group), the users' immediate manager or team leader, the users themselves, and the consultant.

Developing the Information: The Impact Study

The type of formal evaluation report depends on the extent of detailed information presented to the various target audiences. Brief summaries of results with appropriate charts may be sufficient for some communication efforts. In other situations, particularly with significant projects requiring extensive funding, the amount of detail in the evaluation report is more crucial. A complete and comprehensive impact study report may be necessary.

For example, a three-day consulting project to provide advice on a proposed software purchase required only a summary of the project, including the recommendation. No evaluation data was included. In contrast, in a three-year consulting project to implement a major transition process for a large electric utility, a 200-page impact study was produced showing the value of the project, including the ROI. This report was used as the basis of information for specific audiences and various media.

The report may contain the following sections:

Executive summary. A brief overview of the entire report, explaining the basis for the evaluation and the significant conclusions and recommendations. Designed for individuals who are too busy to read a detailed report. Usually written last but appears first in the report for easy access.

Background information. Provides a general description of the project. If applicable, summarizes the needs assessment that led to the implementation of the project. The project is fully described, including the events that led to the consulting project. Other specific items necessary to provide a full description of the project are included. The detail depends on the amount of information the audience requires.

Objectives. Outlines goals for both the consulting project and solution. Sometimes they are the same, but they may be different. The particular objectives of the project help the reader understand its rationale. In addition, specific objectives of the consulting project are listed in detail, since these are the objectives from which the different types or levels of data will be collected.

Evaluation strategy/methodology. Outlines all the components that make up the total evaluation process. Several components of the ROI methodology presented in Chapter 9 are discussed in this section of the report. Specific purposes of evaluation are outlined, and the evaluation design and methodology are explained. Instruments used in data collection are described and presented as exhibits, and any unusual issues in the evaluation design are discussed. Includes other useful information related to the design, timing, and execution of the evaluation.

Data collection and analysis. Explains the methods used to collect data and presents the data in summary form. The methods used to analyze data are presented with interpretations.

Reaction data. Describes the data collected from key stakeholders to measure reactions to the consulting project. Input from the client is a critical part of this presentation.

Learning data. Presents a brief summary of data and explains how users of the consulting solution have learned new processes, skills, tasks, procedures, and practices necessary to make the consulting solution successful.

Application and implementation data. Shows how the consulting solution was implemented and the success with the application of new skills and knowledge. Key implementation issues are addressed.

Barriers and enablers. The various problems and obstacles influencing the success of the project are detailed and presented as barriers to implementation. Also, those factors or influences that had a positive effect on the project are included as enablers. Together, they provide insight into what can hinder or enhance projects in the future.

Business impact data. Shows the actual business impact measures representing the business needs that initially drove the project. Also shows the extent to which these performance measures have changed during the implementation of the project.

Project costs. A summary of the consulting costs, by category. For example, analysis, development, implementation, and evaluation costs are recommended categories for cost presentation. The assumptions used in developing and classifying costs are discussed here.

Return on investment. Shows the ROI calculation along with the benefits/cost ratio. Compares the value to what was expected, and provides an interpretation of the actual calculation.

Intangible measures. Shows the various intangible measures directly linked to the consulting solution. Intangibles are those measures not converted to monetary values or included in the actual ROI calculation.

Conclusions and recommendations. Presents conclusions based on all of the results. If appropriate, briefly explains how each conclusion was reached. A list of recommendations or changes in the solution, also if appropriate, is provided, with brief explanations for each recommendation. It's important that the conclusions and recommendations are consistent with one another and with the findings described in the previous section.

Developing the Report

While this report is an effective, professional way to present ROI data, several cautions need to be followed. Since this document reports the success of a group of employees who implemented the consulting solution, complete credit for the success must go to these users and their immediate leaders. Their performance generated the success. Another important caution is to avoid boasting about results. Although the methodology may be accurate and credible, it may still have some subjective issues. Huge claims of success can quickly turn off an audience and interfere with the delivery of the desired message.

A final caution concerns the structure of the report. The evaluation methodology should be clearly explained, along with assumptions made in the analysis. The reader should readily see how the data were developed and how the specific steps were followed to make the process more conservative, credible, and accurate. Detailed statistical analyses should be placed in the appendix.

Table 10-6 shows the table of contents from a typical evaluation report for an ROI evaluation.

Table 10-6 Format of an Impact Study Report

- Executive Summary
- General Information
  - Background
  - Objectives of Study
- Methodology for Impact Study
  - Levels of Evaluation
  - ROI Process
  - Collecting Data
  - Isolating the Effects of Consulting
  - Converting Data to Monetary Values
  - Assumptions

  > Builds credibility for the process

- Data Analysis Issues
- Project Costs
- Results: General Information
  - Response Profile
  - Success with Objectives
- Results: Reaction and Satisfaction
  - Data Sources
  - Data Summary
  - Key Issues
- Results: Learning
  - Data Sources
  - Data Summary
  - Key Issues
- Results: Application and Implementation
  - Data Sources
  - Data Summary
  - Key Issues
- Results: Business Impact
  - General Comments
  - Linkage with Business Measures
  - Key Issues
- Results: ROI and Its Meaning
- Results: Intangible Measures

  > The results with six measures: levels 1, 2, 3, 4, 5, and intangibles

- Barriers and Enablers
  - Barriers
  - Enablers
- Conclusions and Recommendations
  - Conclusions
  - Recommendations
- Exhibits

Selecting the Communication Media

There are many options available to communicate project results. In addition to the impact study report, the most frequently used media are meetings, interim and progress reports, the organization's publications, e-mail, Web site, brochures, and case studies.

Meetings

In addition to meeting with the client to discuss results, other meetings are fertile opportunities for communicating results. All organizations have a variety of meetings, and the proper context and consulting results are an important part in each.

Some organizations have best practices meetings or videoconferences to discuss recent successes and best practices. This is an excellent opportunity to learn and share methodologies and results. In other organizations, business update meetings for all members of management may be an opportunity. A few highlights of major project results can be integrated into the presentations, showing top executive interest, commitment, and support. Results are mentioned, along with operating profit, new facilities and equipment, new company acquisitions, and next year's sales forecast.

Interim and Progress Reports

Although usually limited to large projects, a highly visible way to communicate results is through interim and routine memos and reports. Published or disseminated periodically via the intranet, they usually have several purposes:

- To inform management about the status of the project
- To communicate the interim results achieved in the project
- To recommend needed changes and improvements

A more subtle reason for the report is to gain additional support and commitment from the management group and to keep the project intact. This report is produced by the consulting team and distributed to a select group of managers in the organization. Format and scope vary considerably. Typical topics are schedules, initial reaction, interim results, issues, and recognition of team members.

The Organization's Publications

To reach a wide audience, the consultant may use in-house publications. Whether a newsletter, magazine, or newspaper, these types of media usually reach all employees. The information can be quite effective if communicated appropriately. The scope should be limited to general interest articles, announcements, and interviews.

E-Mail and Electronic Media

Internal and external Web pages on the Internet, companywide intranets, and e-mail are excellent vehicles for releasing results, promoting ideas, and informing employees and other target groups about results. E-mail, in particular, provides a virtually instantaneous means with which to communicate and solicit response from large numbers of people.

Case Studies

Because case studies represent an effective way to communicate the results of a successful consulting solution, it is recommended that a few projects be developed in a case format. A typical case study describes the situation, provides appropriate background information (including the events that led to the solution), presents the techniques and strategies used to develop the study, and highlights the key issues in the project. Case studies tell an interesting story of how the consulting project was developed and the problems and concerns that were identified along the way.

Case studies, whether published internally or externally, have many useful applications in an organization:

- They can be used in group discussions, where interested individuals can react to the material, offer different perspectives, and draw conclusions about approaches or techniques.
- The case study can serve as a self-teaching guide for individuals trying to understand how consulting solutions are developed and evaluated.
- They provide appropriate recognition for those involved in the actual case. More important, they recognize the users who achieved the results, as well as the managers who supported the project.
- A published case study has become one of the most effective ways to strengthen the client relationship.

Communicating the Information

One of the greatest challenges of communication is delivering the message. This can be accomplished in a variety of ways and settings, based on the target audience and the media selected for the message. Three approaches deserve additional coverage. The first is providing insight into how to give feedback throughout the project to make sure information flows so changes can be made. The second is presenting an impact study to a senior management team, which may be one of the most challenging tasks for the consultant. The third is communicating regularly and routinely with the executive management group.

Let's explore these three approaches in more detail.

Providing Feedback

One of the most important reasons for collecting reaction, satisfaction, and learning data is to provide feedback so adjustments or changes can be made throughout the project. In most consulting solutions, data are routinely collected and quickly communicated to a variety of groups. Table 10-7 shows a feedback action plan designed to provide information to several audiences using a variety of media.

As the plan shows, data are collected during the project at four specific time intervals and communicated to at least three audiences—sometimes as many as five. Some of these feedback sessions result in identifying specific actions that need to be taken. This process becomes comprehensive and needs to be managed proactively. The following steps are recommended for providing feedback and managing the feedback process.[5]

- *Communicate quickly.* Whether the news is good or bad, it's important to let individuals involved in the project have the information as soon as possible. The recommended time for providing feedback is usually a matter of days—certainly no longer than a week or two after the results are known.
- *Simplify the data.* Condense data into an understandable, concise presentation. This is not the format for detailed explanations and analysis.

Table 10-7 Feedback Action Plan

Data Collection Item	Timing	Feedback Audience	Media	Timing of Feedback	Action Required
1. Pre-Project Survey	Beginning of the Project	Users	Meeting	One Week	None
• Climate/Environment		Team Leaders	Survey Summary	Two Weeks	None
• Issue Identification		Consultants	Survey Summary	Two Weeks	Communicate Feedback
			Meeting	One Week	Adjust Approach
2. Implementation Survey	Beginning of Actual Implementation	Participants	Meeting	One Week	None
• Reaction to Plans		Team Leaders	Survey Summary	Two Weeks	None
• Issue Identification		HRD Staff	Survey Summary	Two Weeks	Communicate Feedback
			Meeting	One Week	Adjust Approach
3. Implementation Reaction Survey/Interviews	One Month into Implementation	Users	Meeting	One Week	Comments
		Support Staff	Study Summary	Two Weeks	None
• Reaction to Solution		Team Leaders	Study Summary	Two Weeks	None
• Suggested Changes		Immediate Managers	Study Summary	Two Weeks	Support Changes
		Consultants	Study Summary	Three Weeks	Support Changes
			Meeting	Three Weeks	Adjust Approach
4. Implementation Feedback Questionnaire	End of Implementation	Users	Meeting	One Week	Comments
		Support Staff	Study Summary	Two Weeks	None
• Reaction (Satisfaction)		Team Leaders	Study Summary	Two Weeks	None
• Barriers		Immediate Managers	Study Summary	Two Weeks	Support Changes
• Projected Success		Consultants	Study Summary	Three Weeks	Support Changes
			Meeting	Three Days	Adjust Approach

- *Examine the role of the consulting staff and the client in the feedback situation.* Sometimes the consultant is the judge, and sometimes jury, prosecutor, defendant, or witness. On the other hand, sometimes the sponsor is the judge, jury, prosecutor, defendant, or witness. It is important to examine the respective roles in terms of reactions to the data and the actions that need to be taken.
- *Use negative data in a constructive way.* Some of the data will show that things are not going so well and the fault may rest with the consultant or the client. In either case, the story basically changes from, "Let's look at the success we've made," to "Now we know which areas to change."
- *Use positive data in a cautious way.* Positive data can be misleading, and if communicated too enthusiastically, may create expectations beyond what may materialize later. Positive data should be presented in a cautious way—almost in a discounting mode.
- *Choose the language of the meeting and communication very carefully.* Use language that is descriptive, focused, specific, short, and simple. Avoid language that is too judgmental, macro, stereotypical, lengthy, or complex.
- *Ask the client for reactions to the data.* After all, the client's reaction is critical.
- *Ask the client for recommendations.* The client may have some good recommendations about what needs to be changed to keep a project on track or put it back on track if it derails.
- *Use support and confrontation carefully.* These two approaches are not mutually exclusive. There may be times when support and confrontation are needed for the same group. The sponsor may need support and yet need to be confronted for lack of improvement or sponsorship. The consultant may be confronted on problem areas that have developed but may need support as well.
- *React and act on the data.* Weigh the various alternatives and possibilities to arrive at the necessary adjustments and changes.
- *Secure agreement from all key stakeholders.* This is essential to make sure everyone is willing to make adjustments and changes that seem necessary.
- *Keep the feedback process short.* Do not let it become bogged down in long, drawn-out meetings or lengthy documents. If this occurs, stakeholders will avoid the process instead of being willing to participate in the future.

Following these steps will help move the project forward and provide important feedback, often ensuring that adjustments are supported and made.

Presenting Data to Senior Management

Perhaps one of the most challenging and stressful company communications is presenting a consulting impact study to the senior management team, which also serves as the client for a project. The challenge is convincing this highly skeptical and critical group that outstanding results have been achieved (assuming they have), in a reasonable time frame, addressing the salient points, and making sure that the managers understand the project success.

Two particular issues can create challenges. If the results are very impressive, it may be difficult to make the managers believe the data. At the other extreme, if the data are negative, it will be a challenge to make sure managers do not overreact to the negative results and look for someone to blame. Improving communications with this group requires developing an overall strategy, which may include all or part of the actions outlined below.

Strengthen the relationship with executives. An informal and productive relationship should be established between the consultant (responsible for the project evaluation) and the top executive at the location where the project is taking place. Each should feel comfortable discussing needs and project results. One approach is to establish frequent, informal meetings with the executive to review problems with current projects and discuss other performance problems or opportunities in the organization. Frank and open discussion can provide the executive with insight not available from any other source.

Show how consulting has helped solve major problems. While hard results from recent projects are comforting to an executive, solutions to immediate problems may be more convincing. This is an excellent opportunity to discuss possible future projects.

Distribute memos on project results. When a consulting solution has achieved significant results, the appropriate top executives should be made aware of them. This can easily be accomplished with a brief memo or summary outlining what the project was intended to accomplish, when it was implemented, who was involved, and the results achieved. This should be presented in a for-your-information format that consists of facts rather than opinions. A full report may be presented later.

Managing Tough Issues

Several issues surface during the consulting project that deserve attention. They can affect the approach taken to the project as well as the success. More important, they can affect the client's satisfaction along the way.

Transferring Knowledge

Because the consultant may be providing a unique methodology, transferring the knowledge gained in a consulting process and the knowledge of the methodology itself are important issues. Some consultants (though a minority) protect their knowledge by shielding much of the methods that are used and the information obtained. This can create distrust and frustration with clients. A more open approach is to transfer the knowledge gained in the project as well as the knowledge surrounding the methodology to the client, letting the client use it—perhaps on a limited basis. This often provides more value to the client, and it certainly increases their satisfaction with the project.

Transferring Capability

An extension of transferring knowledge is transferring capability. Many consultants are reluctant to build internal capability with the issues addressed in the consulting project just completed. They think that if the client knows how to conduct these types of projects, there would be no need for the consultant. In reality, building capability can be helpful to the consultant. Teaching others to achieve the same results as the consultant may:

- Strengthen the consulting relationship
- Enable the consultant to be more involved
- Extend the process to others, taking it to a higher level
- Address future implementation and application issues

This is a tough issue because many consultants are afraid that they may be working themselves out of an opportunity. On the other hand, it is simply "teaching them how to fish instead of giving them a fish."

Being an Equal Partner

Throughout the process, the consultant should treat the client as an equal partner. Although the consultant is delivering a service, working in harmony enables problems to be corrected or opportunities addressed. The communications, the dialogue, and the relationship should reflect this balance.

Delivering Value

Value is defined in many ways, as described in Chapters 8 and 9. It is important that the consultant know what value systems exist in the organization. Different stakeholders have different value systems and, thus, want to see different types of data. Making constant adjustments to ensure that value propositions are met and stakeholders have what they perceive as value brings a constant focus on delivering value throughout the project.

Knowing When to Walk Away

There are times when a project should not be pursued in the first place; this is described in more detail in the next section, on ethics. Sometimes a project gets more involved than the consultant realized, or the issues are not as they first appeared, presenting huge problems.

In these cases, instead of continuing with the project, it may be wise to confront the situation and be prepared to abandon the project. Knowing when and how to do this is very important. "When" would be as early as possible—as soon it appears to be the most advisable option. "How" is to treat the matter openly and honestly, presenting the facts as they appear. This can strengthen a relationship instead of destroying it, which is often the fear in this type of situation.

Making Peace with a Project's Enemies

Almost every consulting project will have individuals who are not in favor of the project. They may oppose it publicly or try to destroy it privately. These are the enemies of the success of the project, and every attempt should be made to understand and address their issues and concerns.

Essentially, work on the hot buttons of these detractors, ensuring that they are addressed to the extent possible. In the best case, attempt to turn the enemy into a friend; in the worst case, make them neutral in the process. These and other issues can get in the way of a project being successful and are often not anticipated or addressed as precisely and thoughtfully as they can or should be.

Consulting Ethics

Practicing acceptable ethics is one of the consulting success factors. Ethics involves the behavior of the consultant, the rules followed throughout the consulting process, communications with stakeholders, expectations created with stakeholders, and relationships developed throughout the project. Stakeholders must understand the role of ethics and their role in ethical behavior. Acceptable ethics is not a threat; it is a desired way of operating that should not create conflicts for the client. Most clients want an ethical project, and client satisfaction can be achieved with ethical behavior.

The consultant should be aware of ethical problems that emerge in their potential projects and know the steps to avoid them. This approach does not suggest that being ethical is just a matter of doing the right thing; rather, it is a matter of adopting behavior using integrity, establishing trust, and being fair and honest throughout the project.

Ethical Problems

Ethical issues may frequently appear throughout a project. They can sometimes derail the entire project, destroying the relationships between the consultant and the clients. Sometimes lack of ethics results in formal complaints or litigation. Serious ethical dilemmas faced by consultants can be prevented or avoided by following strict guidelines and by openly communicating expectations, roles, and responsibilities. Typical issues are:

- The consultant changes the evaluation questions to match the data, in order to make the project more positive.
- The consultant promises confidentiality when it cannot be guaranteed.
- The consultant makes decisions without consulting with the client when consultation has been agreed to.
- The consultant conducts an evaluation when he or she lacks sufficient skills or experience.
- Final reports are written in a biased way—either positive or negative.

The problems vary, as do the opportunities for danger. The key is to build the correct approach into the project from the beginning. In the rest of this chapter we will focus on some of the prescriptive processes to help focus on this critical issue.

Preventing Personal Ethical Issues

The first area for consideration is the personal conduct of the consultant—issues the consultant should address in every project. The following issues transcend ethical behavior and define good client relationships:

Provide quality work. Providing value-added work to the client is the key responsibility of the consultant. Providing work that is accurate, timely, and consistent helps the consultant avoid ethical issues created by errors, omissions, inconsistencies, and other quality-related problems.

Ensure qualifications for the project. Consultants must have the skills and expertise to conduct the evaluation study. Pretending to have skills or competencies that the consultant does not possess is a serious problem. Sometimes it is best to admit to the sponsor or client that the capability is not there, avoiding many problems associated with substandard work.

Learn to say no or "I don't know." Consultants need to be honest with clients and let them know when they do not have the information needed or if they're unsure as to what is needed. One of the most refreshing comments to the client is for the consultant to admit that he or she does not have all the answers.

Avoid a conflict of interest. Conflicts of interest can surface if the consultant has a particular interest, ownership, or connection to the project being evaluated. If there is a relationship to individuals involved in the project, a conflict of interest may exist. These situations can be avoided with an up-front assessment of this issue before beginning a project. If the conflict turns out to be a surprise, acknowledge it as quickly as possible and rectify it.

Invoice appropriately. An important issue in any type of transaction, proper invoicing (or appropriate charging) is a fundamental business requirement. Only the time used on the project should be charged. All expenses must be legitimate and related to the project. Double charges for expenses (when two clients are involved) must be avoided. These are essential actions that must be tackled in order to gain trust.

Adhere to proposals. Problems can occur when there are deviations with what was planned and what was delivered. The proposal often outlines the scope of the work and the plan of the project. It is important to follow through with the plan and not make adjustments unless the client asks for or approves the changes. Changes should be documented. This approach keeps a clear understanding of expectations and deliverables for the project.

Underpromise and overdeliver. Creating unrealistic expectations can cause tremendous problems with a project. The consultant should not promise something that cannot be delivered. Promising specific response rates, for example, or even predicting the outcome of the project, are serious issues that should be avoided. Also, while low expectations may be created in terms of how the project may unfold, every attempt should be made to overdeliver, capturing all of the data and presenting the results in the most effective way.

Respect the confidentiality and anonymity of data sources. Data may be collected anonymously or with the understanding that the input will be treated with confidentiality. These issues need to be defined and communicated to the stakeholders and strictly followed.

Appropriate personal ethics should become a routine mode of operation as consultants assist clients and sponsors with projects. These actions establish productive relationships and build trust.

Ken Blanchard, an international management consultant, says that his company's ethical policy is defined by asking three simple questions. First, "Is it legal?" Ken Blanchard Companies wants to make sure that everything it does is in compliance and follows regulations and laws, particularly as it relates to billing a client. Second, "Is it fair for all parties?" The organization wants its efforts to be a win-win for both the client and consultant. Third, "How would we feel if the issue were printed in the newspaper and made public? Is it something we would be proud of or embarrassed about?" These principles provide guidance in resolving what could be potential ethical dilemmas and issues.[6]

Remaining Independent/Objective

One of the most important challenges for consultants is to operate independently. This may be difficult for consultants who have a longstanding relationship with a client or for consultants who are eager to land another contract with the client. If feasible, evaluation of the project should be independent.

This approach is possible where the individual conducting the evaluation is independent of the design, development, delivery, coordination, and ownership of the project. This is the ideal opportunity, and provides a natural situation to be independent. Some organizations outsource evaluation, relying on other independent consultants to conduct evaluation studies. External providers are available to collect, summarize, and return data in a raw, summarized form. Consultants, professors, and graduate students are available to provide this service. This approach has the advantage of providing objective data collection and tabulation, preventing data from being omitted, changed, or enhanced. In this situation it is important to include all the raw data in the report so stakeholders can see what was provided.

In some situations, the consultant must acknowledge a potential conflict of interest. The stakeholders must understand that the consultant is evaluating his or her own project. The up-front acknowledgment helps build trust. Then the consultant can show all of the data that were returned. Ideally, the data are sent to an assistant who enters it into the database; the appendix contains the raw data. Although this is not optimum, it acknowledges to stakeholders—particularly those who fund the consulting project—that there is some independence from the ownership, and an attempt to avoid a potential conflict of interest.

Typical Ethical Issues in Consulting Projects

Several opportunities for unethical behavior surface when launching a consulting project. A few possibilities are outlined in Table 10-8.

Addressing Ethics During a Project

Several guidelines can help ensure that ethical issues are avoided during project implementation. The following operating guidelines keep the project focused and free of mistrust and errors:

1. *Communicate expectations.* Make sure that all stakeholders (especially the project sponsors) clearly understand what is expected from the project—the deliverables, the timing, and other important issues.
2. *Clarify roles.* Ensuring that every stakeholder involved knows his or her role in the project is critical. Unclear roles can lead to omissions or unnecessary and excessive involvement of a particular stakeholder.
3. *Show how results are used.* From an ethical perspective, it is important for individuals to understand how the data will be used. Most projects lead to conclusions and recommendations . . . and actions on the recommendations.
4. *Remain independent.* As discussed earlier, it is important to remain independent from data sources, the project itself, and other relationships that might call into question the objectiveness of the project evaluation.
5. *Emphasize process improvement.* All individuals need to understand that project evaluation is designed to improve processes.

In summation, guidance is necessary to keep relationships and projects on track. The consultant must judge situations and make decisions regarding ethical issues. To ensure the highest ethical behaviors, the consultant must anticipate and prevent ethical problems and issues.

Table 10-8 Potential Ethical Problems Encountered During Consulting Projects

Ethical Dilemma	Description	Possible Solution
Project Selection	Selecting consulting projects where there is either conflict or the consultant's capability is in question.	Ensuring that there is appropriate competence to conduct the project.
Team Participation	Purposely omitting certain groups or individuals can generate ethical issues.	Deciding who will be on the consulting implementation team and making sure that all stakeholders are represented and are involved in some way.
Data Collection	Improper sampling; skewed questions on questionnaires, surveys, or for focus groups; and consultant bias are all serious problems that can occur during data collection.	Collect data from all appropriate individuals, ensuring representation of the entire group. An appropriate degree of statistical rigor can help ensure that the data collected is representative and consultant bias is avoided.
Data Omission	Selective omission of data by those involved in data collection. Involves the overt action of purposely leaving data out of the analysis, destroying data, using selective follow-up in certain areas where data are desired, omitting specific types of comments.	All data should be made available for review. Consider using third-party data collectors and/or third-party data analysis.
Data Analysis, Interpretation, and Conclusions	Data interpretation is distorted or biased.	Including and itemizing all of the data. Selecting analytical techniques that are fair, consistent, and methodical. Using logical, rational approaches to reach conclusions, and interpreting data in a way to minimize the possibility of bias, error, and misjudgment.
Identity Protection	Participant responses are tied to their identity.	While it may be important to know the job group and some job characteristics of the individual, in most situations it is not necessary to reveal the source of the data by individual. This should occur only when it is essential to understand the data.
Communication	Selectively emphasizing parts of the report or deemphasizing other parts.	Present the information in a uniform, objective, and consistent manner.
Recommendations	Recommendations are based on subjective considerations; recognizing deficiencies or weaknesses as changes or improvements are explored.	Recommendations must be based on conclusions drawn from factual data analysis rather than opinions or biases.
Client Involvement	Client is involved in interpreting and understanding the data and drawing particular conclusions.	The client needs to help set expectations, approve the consulting solution, and review the data. Sometimes input is helpful but the client should not be able to influence the conclusions and recommendations.

Final Thoughts

This chapter is at the heart of the consulting project—delivering the service that has been promised, communicating the results, and providing the opportunity to have a satisfied client. It stresses issues such as having a consistent methodology, protecting intellectual property throughout the process, and managing the project to be on time, on schedule, and meeting expectations. More important, it involves communicating results in a variety of ways to a variety of audiences. Communicating results is a critical and necessary part of the process. Next, managing issues that surface is a sensitive thing: problems not dealt with can create bigger problems and result in a dissatisfied client. These issues must be addressed early and diplomatically.

Finally, the chapter concludes appropriately with the discussion of ethics. Ethical issues can destroy consulting projects and a consultant's reputation. Unethical practices have tarnished the industry, and ethical issues must be addressed by every consultant early and often throughout the process.

Notes

[1] Paul Mooney, *The Effective Consultant: How to Develop the High Performance Organisation* (Dublin: Oak Tree Press, 1999).

[2] Alex Dembitz and James Essinger, *Breakthrough Consulting: So You Want to Be a Consultant? Turn Your Expertise into a Successful Consulting Business* (London: Prentice Hall, 2000).

[3] Patricia P. Phillips and Jack J. Phillips, *ROI Basics* (Alexandria, Virginia: ASTD, 2006).

[4] Jack J. Phillips, Patricia P. Phillips, and Ron D. Stone, *The Human Resources Scorecard: Measuring Return on Investment*, 2nd edition (Boston: Butterworth-Heinemann, 2006).

[5] Peter Block, *Flawless Consulting: A Guide to Getting Your Expertise Used*, 2nd edition (San Francisco: Jossey-Bass/Pfeiffer, 2000).

[6] Ken Blanchard, ASTD Global Forum (October 2002), Berlin, Germany.

DO YOUR CONSULTING PROJECTS FOCUS ON RESULTS?

A SELF-ASSESSMENT

A Survey for Clients

Instructions. For each of the following statements, please circle the response that best matches the consulting activities and philosophy in your organization. If none of the answers describe the situation, select the one that best fits. Please be candid with your responses.

Select the most correct response:

1. The direction and goals of the consulting process at your organization:
   a. Shifts with trends, fads, and industry issues.
   b. Is determined by individual consultants and adjusted as needed.
   c. Is based on a mission and a strategic plan for the practice.

2. The primary mode of operation of the consulting is:
   a. To respond to any requests by managers and other employees to deliver solutions.
   b. To help management react to crisis situations and reach solutions.
   c. To implement solutions in collaboration with management to prevent problems and crisis situations.

3. Consulting solutions usually focus on:
   a. Changing perceptions and opinions.
   b. Enhancing skills and job performance.
   c. Driving business measures and enhancing job performance.

4. Most new consulting solutions are initiated:
   a. When a solution appears to be successful in another organization.
   b. By request of the client.
   c. After analysis has indicated that the solution is needed.

5. To determine solutions:
   a. Clients are asked to choose from a list of existing packaged solutions.
   b. Employees and unit managers are asked about needs.
   c. Solutions are systematically derived from a thorough analysis of performance problems and issues.

6. If a consulting project is unsuccessful and the client is dissatisfied:
   a. There are no actions or consequences.
   b. Efforts are taken to correct the situation for future projects.
   c. The client does not have to pay until he or she is satisfied.

7. The responsibility for results from consulting:
   a. Rests primarily with the consultants.
   b. Is shared with consultants and managers, who jointly ensure that results are obtained.
   c. Rests with consultants, users, managers, and clients—all working together to ensure accountability.

8. Systematic objective evaluation, designed to ensure that the consulting solution is successful and adds value:
   a. Is never accomplished. Evaluations are conducted during the project, and they focus on how much the users are satisfied with the project.
   b. Is occasionally accomplished. Users are asked if the consulting project was effective on the job.
   c. Is frequently and systematically pursued. Performance is evaluated after the project is completed.

9. Consulting projects are staffed:
   a. Primarily with inexperienced consultants.
   b. With a combination of inexperienced and experienced consultants.
   c. With a variety of experienced consultants, including a senior consultant.

10. The objectives for consulting solutions are:
    a. Nonspecific and based on subjective input.
    b. Based on learning, application, and implementation.
    c. Based on business impact, application, implementation, and satisfaction.

11. Costs for consulting are accumulated:
    a. On a total aggregate basis only.
    b. On a project-by-project basis.
    c. By specific process components such as initial analysis and implementation, in addition to a specific project.

12. Management involvement in consulting is:
    a. Very low, with only occasional input.
    b. Moderate—usually by request, or on an as-needed basis.
    c. Deliberately planned for all major consulting projects to ensure a partnership arrangement.

13. To ensure that consulting projects are translated into performance on the job, we:
    a. Encourage users to apply what they have learned and report results.
    b. Ask managers to support and reinforce consulting project results.
    c. Utilize a variety of transfer strategies appropriate for each situation.

14. The consultant interaction with management is:
    a. Rare; consultants almost never discuss issues with them.
    b. Occasional—during activities such as those that need analysis or project coordination.
    c. Regular—to build relationships, as well as to develop and deliver solutions.

15. The payoff of consulting projects is measured primarily by:
  a. Subjective opinions.
  b. Observations by management or reactions from consulting solution users.
  c. Monetary return through improved productivity, costs, quality, or customer service.

16. New consulting projects, with no formal method of evaluation, are implemented:
  a. Regularly.
  b. Seldom.
  c. Never.

17. The results of consulting projects are communicated:
  a. When requested, to those who have a need to know.
  b. Occasionally, to members of management only.
  c. Routinely, to a variety of selected target audiences.

18. Management responsibilities for consulting:
  a. Are minor, with no specific responsibilities.
  b. Consist of informal responsibilities for selected consulting projects.
  c. Are very specific. Managers have some responsibilities for projects in their business units.

19. During a business decline at client organizations, consulting will:
  a. Be the first to have its budget reduced.
  b. Be retained at the same budget level.
  c. Go untouched in reductions and possibly be increased.

20. Budgeting for consulting is based on:
  a. Last year's budget.
  b. Whatever the consultant can "sell."
  c. A zero-based system based on the need for each project.

21. The principal group that must justify consulting expenditures is:
  a. The consultants.
  b. The consultants and managers of the unit where the project is initiated.
  c. Senior management over the area where the consulting project is implemented.

22. Over the past two years, the consulting budget in your client organizations as a percent of operating expenses has
  a. Decreased.
  b. Remained stable.
  c. Increased.

23. Senior management's involvement in consulting projects:
  a. Is limited to introductions, announcements, and extending congratulations.
  b. Includes reviewing status, opening and closing meetings, discussions of status, presentation on the outlook of the organization, etc.
  c. Includes participation in the project, monitoring progress, requiring key managers to be involved, etc.

24. When an employee is directly involved in a consulting solution, he or she is required to:
   a. Do nothing unless instructed.
   b. Ask questions about the project and use the project's materials and learning.
   c. Implement the project successfully, encourage others to implement, and report success.

25. Most managers in your client organizations view consulting as:
   a. A questionable activity that wastes too much time of employees.
   b. A necessary function that probably cannot be eliminated.
   c. An important resource that can be used to improve the organization.

Score the assessment instrument as follows. Allow:

1 point for each (a) response

3 points for each (b) response

5 points for each (c) response

The total will be between 25 and 125 points.

The interpretation of scoring is provided below. The explanation is based on the input from dozens of organizations.

Score Range	Analysis of Score
99 to 125	Outstanding environment for achieving results with consulting. Great management support. A truly successful example of results-based consulting.
76 to 98	Above average in achieving results with consulting. Good management support. A solid and methodical approach to results-based consulting projects.
51 to 75	Needs improvement to achieve desired results with consulting. Management support is ineffective. Consulting projects do not usually focus on results.
25 to 50	Serious problems with the success and status of consulting. Management support is nonexistent. Consulting projects are not producing results.

PROPOSAL EXAMPLE

PROPOSAL FOR THE NATIONAL SOCIETY FOR PERFORMANCE AND DEVELOPMENT TO CONDUCT ROI STUDIES ON THE ANNUAL CONFERENCE AND EXPOSITION

SUBMITTED BY:
ROI INSTITUTE™

Background Information

The National Society for Performance & Development (NSPD) is the world's largest association dedicated to workplace learning and performance professionals. NSPD's 70,000 members and associates come from more than 100 countries and thousands of organizations—multinational corporations, medium-sized and small businesses, government, academia, consulting firms, and product and service suppliers.

NSPD marks its beginning in 1954, when the organization held its first annual conference. In recent years NSPD has widened the industry's focus to connect learning and performance to a measurable result, and is a sought-after voice on critical public policy issues.

The Situation

NSPD's most prominent meeting is the Annual Conference and Exposition (ACE) held in rotation in major cities in the United States. ACE usually attracts in the range of 8,000 to 12,000 members or prospective members. The meeting is regarded as the most important professional development event for the learning and development professional in the world. Literally hundreds of sessions, workshops, keynotes, panel discussions, breakouts, and other learning opportunities are offered. Since 9/11, attendance has fallen to levels much lower than the association executives would prefer.

As a general rule, the participant costs are paid by the individual's employer. Recently, employers have expressed a concern over the high cost for participating in this conference, particularly when there are many other programs available. NSPD members have several other annual conferences from which to choose—most notably, those offered by the Society for Human Resource Management, *Training* magazine, *CLO* magazine, and the International Society for Performance Improvement. As a target, NSPD attempts to have at least 30 percent of the participants attending from countries outside the United States and, for these participants, the cost can be very high. Roughly one-third of the participants register as consultants, and many of these individuals must bear the cost of attending. Now, they are beginning to weigh the value of participating in this meeting.

Representing an important income segment of the conference, exhibitors provide participants with an impressive amount of new information on products and services. Recently, exhibitors have also been expressing concern about the value of the meeting. Many other learning and development conferences are held each year, and exhibitors must decide which event is worth the money. Consequently, there has been a drop in the number of exhibitors in the past two years. Some exhibitors complain that conference attendees are not the decision makers for purchases.

While NSPD knows its ROI for the meeting (i.e., the revenue generated from participants, exhibitors, and sponsors, minus the total expenses, divided by the total cost), it does not know the ROI from the perspective of either the participant or the exhibitor. To better serve both of these customer groups, NSPD would like to have detailed information about the ROI for both an individual attending and an exhibitor participating in this conference. This information would be extremely valuable in marketing and promotion efforts for future conferences. For the NSPD members and prospective participants, this information would be highlighted along with the conference description and other statistics. From the perspective of exhibitors, the ROI would be useful in determining whether they should participate in this conference.

The Scope

NSPD needs an ROI study conducted on the next Annual Conference and Exposition, developed from the perspective of both the participant and the exhibitor. The leadership of NSPD would like to conduct this study with as little cost as possible. Consequently, sampling must be used to keep costs at a minimum. The individuals in the sample must be committed to provide useful application and impact data. This is a particularly challenging issue because the value derived from this conference may be difficult to track, measure, and convert to monetary value. The data must be credible and collected from an objective viewpoint.

Project Objectives

This project has four key objectives:

1. Show the executive leadership of NSPD the power of the ROI methodology in measuring the consequences of the Annual Conference and Exposition.

2. Provide a detailed study of the success of the meeting from the participant perspective.
3. Provide a detailed study of the success of the meeting from the exhibitor perspective.
4. Improve the structure, content, and marketing for ACE based on the recommendations from these studies.

Objectives of Participant ROI Study

The study will be conducted based on the following objectives from the attendee perspective:

Reaction/Satisfaction

After participating in this conference, participants will find the conference:

- Relevant to current job
- Useful in their work
- Important to job success

After participating in this conference, participants should:

- Intend to make changes as a result of the meeting
- Recommend the conference to others

Learning

After participating in this conference, participants should:

- Obtain new knowledge about the L&D field
- Learn the techniques to solve a problem
- Obtain the skills to address an issue
- Have additional information on resources
- Have confidence to change practices
- Accumulate ideas for presentations
- Develop networking contacts for follow-up
- Gain insights into the latest technology

Application/Implementation

When returning to work after the conference, participants should:

- Apply the knowledge and skills gained
- Use the resources
- Use the contacts
- Complete action plans
- Remove or minimize barriers to application

Business Impact

Conference participation should have a business impact on productivity, efficiency, time savings, cost savings, quality, or client satisfaction.

Return on Investment

Conference participation should achieve an ROI of at least 20 percent.

Exhibit Impact Objectives

The study will be conducted based on the following objectives from the exhibitor's perspective:

Reaction/Satisfaction

At the close of the conference, exhibitors should:

- Perceive the participants to be responsive
- See the value in the conference
- Perceive the NSPD staff to be helpful
- Intend to follow up with prospects
- Experience adequate booth activity
- Recommend the conference to others

Learning

At the close of the conference, exhibitors should have:

- Knowledge about the conference
- Knowledge about the exhibiting process
- Information about resolving issues
- Information on resources
- Ideas for future exhibits
- Contacts for future follow-up
- Insights into competition

Application/Implementation

At the close of the conference, exhibitors should:

- Receive a follow-up from NSPD
- Make improvements in the exhibiting process
- Follow up with contacts
- Receive requests for information about products and services

- Send additional information to hot prospects
- Identify barriers to success

Business Impact

After exhibiting at this meeting, improvements in the following should occur:

- Closed sales
- New awareness
- Revenue
- Brand awareness

Return on Investment

Achieve an ROI of at least 20 percent.

Methodology

The ROI Process

The calculations of the return on investment in meetings, events, trade shows, and sponsorships begins with the basic model shown in Figure 1, where a potentially complicated process can be simplified with sequential steps. The ROI process model provides a systematic approach to ROI calculations. A step-by-step approach helps to keep the process manageable so users can tackle one issue at a time. The model also emphasizes the fact that this is a logical, systematic process that flows from one step to another. Applying the model provides consistency from one ROI calculation to another.

Each step of the model is briefly described in Figure 2.

Meetings and events can be evaluated at five different levels. Data should be collected at levels 1, 2, 3, and 4, if an ROI analysis is planned. This helps ensure that the chain of impact occurs as participants learn new information and skills, apply them on the job, and obtain business results.

Collecting Data

Data collection is central to the ROI process. Both hard data (representing output, quality, cost, and time) and soft data (including work habits, work climate, and attitudes) are collected. Data are collected using a variety of methods including the following:

- Follow-up *surveys* are taken to determine the degree to which participants have utilized various aspects of the meeting or event. Survey responses are often developed on a sliding scale and usually represent attitudinal data. Surveys are useful for level 3 data.
- Follow-up *questionnaires* are administered to uncover specific applications of the meeting. Participants provide responses to a variety of types of open-ended and forced response questions. Questionnaires can be used to capture both level 3 and 4 data.

Figure 1 The ROI Process Model

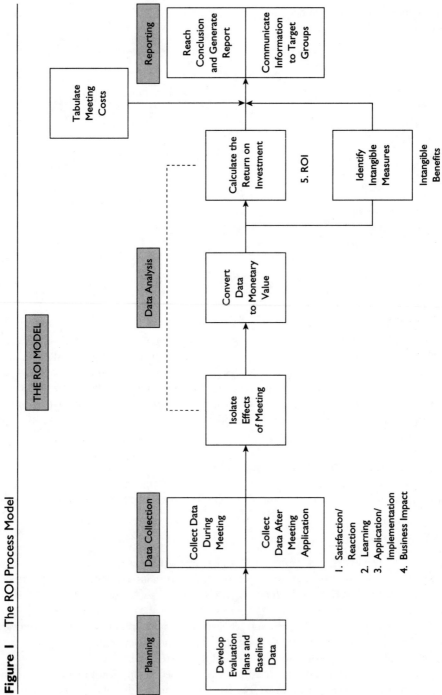

THE ROI MODEL

Planning
Develop Evaluation Plans and Baseline Data

Data Collection
Collect Data During Meeting
Collect Data After Meeting Application

1. Satisfaction/Reaction
2. Learning
3. Application/Implementation
4. Business Impact

Data Analysis
Isolate Effects of Meeting
Convert Data to Monetary Value
Calculate the Return on Investment

5. ROI

Identify Intangible Measures

Intangible Benefits

Tabulate Meeting Costs

Reporting
Reach Conclusion and Generate Report
Communicate Information to Target Groups

Figure 2   Five Levels of Evaluation

Level	Measurement Focus
Reaction & Planned Action	Measures participant satisfaction with the meeting and captures planned action.
Learning	Measures changes in knowledge, skills, attitudes, and professional contacts due to the meeting.
Job Applications	Measures changes in on-the-job behavior related to the meeting and progress with planned actions.
Business Results	Measures changes in business-impact variables.
Return on Investment	Compares meeting benefits to the meeting costs.

- Post program *interviews* are conducted with participants to determine the extent to which learning has been utilized on the job. Interviews allow for probing to uncover specific applications and are appropriate with level 3 data.
- *Focus groups* are conducted to determine the degree to which a group of participants have applied the information, skills, and/or messages of the meeting to job situations. Focus groups are appropriate with level 3 data.
- *Action plans* are developed in meetings and are implemented on the job after the meeting is completed. A follow-up of the plans provides evidence of meeting success. Level 3 and 4 data can be collected with action plans.
- Meetings are designed with a *follow-up session* that is utilized to capture evaluation data as well as present additional information and messages. In the follow-up session, participants discuss their successes with the meeting. Follow-up sessions are appropriate for both level 3 and 4 data.
- *Performance records monitoring* is useful where various performance records and operational data are examined for improvement. This method is particularly useful for level 4 data, such as sales or employee turnover.

Although other methods are available, these are the most likely methods for evaluating meetings and events. The important challenge in this step is to select the data collection method or methods appropriate for the setting and the specific meeting, within the time and budget constraints of the organization.

Isolating the Effects of the Meeting

An often overlooked issue in most evaluations is the process to isolate the effects of meetings and events. In this step of the process, specific strategies are explored that determine the amount of output performance directly related to the meeting. This step is essential because there are many factors that will influence performance data after meetings and events have been conducted. The specific strategies at this step will pinpoint the amount of improvement directly related to the meeting. The result is increased accuracy and credibility of the ROI calculation.

The following strategies have been utilized by organizations to tackle this important issue:

- A *control group* arrangement may be used to isolate impact. With this strategy, one group participates in the meeting while another similar group does not. The difference in the performance of the two groups is attributed to the meeting. When properly set up and implemented, the control group management is the most effective way to isolate the effects of meetings and events.

- *Trend lines* are used to project the value of specific output measures, such as sales, as if the meeting had not been undertaken. The projection is compared to the actual data after the meeting, and the difference represents the estimate of the impact. Under certain conditions this strategy can be an accurate way to isolate the impact of meetings and events. A typical situation where this could be appropriate is in sales meetings and business development conferences.

- *Participants estimate* the amount of improvement related to meetings and events. With this approach, participants are provided with the total amount of improvement, on a pre- and postmeeting basis, and are asked to indicate the percent of the improvement that is actually related to the meeting.

- *Managers estimate* the impact of meetings and events. In these cases, managers of participants provide an estimate or "adjustment" to reflect the portion of the improvement related to the meeting. While perhaps inaccurate, there are some advantages of having management involved in this process, such as management ownership.

- *Experts provide estimates* of the impact of meetings and events on the performance variable. Because the estimates are based on previous experience, the experts must be familiar with the type of meeting and the specific situation.

While other strategies are available, these strategies provide a feasible, comprehensive set of tools to tackle the important and critical issue of isolating the effects of meetings and events.

Converting Data to Monetary Values

To calculate the return on investment, data collected at the impact level are converted to monetary values to compare to meeting costs. This requires a value to be placed on each unit of impact data connected with the meeting. Several strategies are available to convert data to monetary values where the specific strategy selected usually depends on the type of data and the situation.

- *Output data are converted to profit contribution or cost savings.* With this strategy, output increases are converted to monetary value based on their unit contribution to profit or the unit of cost reduction. These values are readily available in most organizations.

- The *cost of quality is calculated,* and quality improvements are directly converted to cost savings. These values are available in many organizations.

- For programs where employee time is saved, the participant *wages and benefits are used for the value of time.* Because a variety of meetings focus on reducing the time required to complete projects, processes, or daily activities, the value of time becomes an important and necessary issue.

- *Historical costs and current records* are used when they are available for a specific variable. In this case, organizational cost data are utilized to establish the specific value of an improvement.

- When available, *internal and external experts* may be used to estimate a value for an improvement. In this situation, the credibility of the estimate hinges on the expertise and reputation of the individual.

- *External databases* are sometimes available to estimate the value or cost of data items. Research, government, and industry databases can provide important information for these values. The difficulty lies in finding a specific database related to the situation.

- *Participants estimate* the value of the data item. For this approach to be effective, participants must be capable of providing a value for the improvement.
- *Supervisors of participants* provide estimates when they are both willing and capable of assigning values to the improvement. This approach is especially useful when participants are not fully capable of providing this input or in situations where supervisors need to confirm or adjust the participant's estimate.
- *Senior management provides estimates* on the value of an improvement when they are willing to offer estimates. This approach is particularly helpful to establish values for performance measures that are important to senior management.
- *Meeting staff estimates* may be used to determine a value of an output data item. In these cases it is essential for the estimates to be provided on an unbiased basis.

This step in the ROI model is very important and is absolutely necessary to determine the monetary benefits from meetings and events. The process is challenging, particularly with soft data, but can be methodically accomplished using one or more of the above strategies.

Tabulating Meeting/Event Costs

The other part of the equation on a benefit/cost analysis is the cost of the meeting or event. Tabulating the costs involves monitoring or developing all of the related costs of the meeting targeted for the ROI calculation. The cost components that may be included depending upon the ROI perspective are:

- The cost to design and develop the meeting/event, possibly prorated over the expected life of the meeting or event
- The cost of all meeting materials—such as participant handouts, signage, decoration, etc.
- The cost of the speakers, instructors, and/or facilitators, including preparation time as well as delivery time
- The cost of the facilities for the meeting
- Travel, housing, and food/beverage costs for the participants
- Salaries plus employee benefits of the participants and staff to attend the meeting
- Administrative and overhead costs of the meeting planning function, allocated in some convenient way to the meeting or event
- The cost of the ROI evaluation

The conservative approach is to include all of these costs so that the total is fully loaded.

Calculating the ROI

The return on investment is calculated using the meeting benefits and costs. The benefit/cost ratio is the meeting benefits divided by cost. In formula form it is:

$$\text{BCR} = \frac{\text{Meeting Benefits}}{\text{Meeting Costs}}$$

The return on investment uses the net benefits divided by meeting costs. The net benefits are the meeting benefits minus the costs. In formula form the ROI becomes:

$$\text{ROI\%} = \frac{\text{Net Meeting Benefits}}{\text{Meeting Costs}} \times 100$$

This is the same basic formula used in evaluating other investments where the ROI is traditionally reported as earnings divided by investment.

Identifying Intangible Benefits

In addition to tangible, monetary benefits, most meetings and events will have intangible, nonmonetary benefits. The ROI calculation is based on converting both hard and soft data to monetary values. When data items are not converted to monetary values, they are considered intangible benefits. These intangible benefits include items such as:

• Increased job satisfaction
• Increased organizational commitment
• Improved teamwork
• Improved customer service
• Reduced complaints
• Reduced conflicts

During data analysis, every attempt is made to convert all data to monetary values. All hard data such as output, quality, and time are converted to monetary values. The conversion of soft data is attempted for each data item. However, if the process used for conversion is too subjective or inaccurate and the resulting values lose credibility in the process, then the data are listed as an intangible benefit with the appropriate explanation. For some meetings, intangible, nonmonetary benefits are extremely valuable, often carrying as much influence as the hard data items.

The Approach

Data will be collected directly from a sample of 200 participants immediately following the conference as well as three months later. The sample size was selected based on what is economically feasible. A larger sample would have increased the cost of the study significantly. A sample of 50 exhibitors, representing a stratified random sample, will be selected for the vendors study. A larger number would have increased the cost significantly, and this number should be appropriate to determine the payoff for a typical exhibitor. Three months is considered an appropriate time frame for the follow-up, given the nature of the conference and the opportunity for individuals to utilize what they had learned.

The 200 participants are to be selected at random to prevent bias. Groups will be stratified according to two job levels: practitioners versus managers, and international versus domestic. It is important to see if specific job groups (practitioners versus managers) have a different impact. The conference is designed for both; there is some speculation that practitioners benefit more than managers. Grouping by international versus domestic will determine if there is a difference in their use of the conference. There is some speculation that international attendees benefit more than domestic attendees.

Individuals will be sent an e-mail prior to the conference requesting a commitment to participate in providing the data. In this memo, the process will be explained and the requirements for commitment outlined. Data input will require about one and a half to two hours beyond the conference. If individuals are unwilling to provide data or a response is not received, they are excluded from the group. Essentially, the sample of participants is attending the conference with a commitment to provide data.

A similar arrangement will be in place for exhibitors, except the selection will be by type of product and size of exhibitor in terms of revenue. Exhibitors will be contacted by e-mail explaining the project and requesting a commitment. If they are incapable or unwilling to provide data (or do not respond), they will be eliminated from the analysis and another exhibitor will be chosen. Thus, 50 exhibitors will come to the conference with a commitment to provide data. From an exhibitor's perspective, this is something they want to see: the actual ROI.

In addition to the selection process above and the preconference commitment to provide data, several strategies will be used to increase response rates:

- The correspondence with the participants and exhibitors will come from the CEO of NSPD and the chairman of the board, pushing it to the highest level in the organization. This high level of involvement should help obtain the additional data sets.
- During the conference, participants and exhibitors will attend a breakfast, lunch, or reception meeting, hosted by NSPD, to discuss the project and their role in it. The follow-up questionnaire will be reviewed in detail at the meeting.
- Participants will be provided with several incentive gifts at the meeting, including a copy of NSPD's new book, *ROI Basics.*
- Participants in the study are promised three documents: the tabulation of the data three weeks after submission, a copy of the study as it is completed, and the actions taken as a result of the study.
- An e-mail is sent to the participants prior to the conference to remind them of their commitment and to instruct them to contact the evaluator if they have any questions.
- Participants will receive both an e-mail questionnaire and a paper-based copy. Using their choice of submission, they are asked to respond in two weeks.
- A follow-up telephone call is made one week after they receive the questionnaire. A post card is sent one week later reminding those individuals to send the data.

Collectively, these measures should ensure an 80 percent return rate.

Exhibit 1, below, shows the initial draft of the Data Collection Plan for the participant ROI study. This will be adjusted during the evaluation planning meeting. Exhibit 2 shows the initial draft of the Data Collection Plan for the exhibitor ROI study.

Exhibit 3 shows the ROI Analysis Plan for the participant ROI study. Exhibit 4 shows the ROI Analysis Plan for the exhibitor ROI study. These are the planned approaches and may be adjusted during the project.

Data analysis involves analyzing and reporting the data. The ROI Analysis Plan begins with the specific measures anticipated from the project and lists the methodology of isolating the effects of the meeting and the methods to convert data to monetary value. This plan also includes the anticipated

Exhibit I

Data Collection Plan (Draft)

Evaluation Purpose: ROI Participant

Program: NSPD ACE Evaluation

Responsibility: Jack Phillips   **Date:** _____

Level	Broad Program Objective(s)	Measures	Data Sources	Data Collection Method/Instruments	Timing	Responsibilities
1	**REACTION/SATISFACTION** • Relevance to current job • Usefulness in my work • Important to job success • Intent to make changes as a result of the meeting • Recommendations to others	5-point scale	200 Randomly Selected Participants	Questionnaires	End of Conference	External Evaluator
2	**LEARNING** • Knowledge about the L&D field • Techniques to solve a problem • Information on resources • Skills to address an issue • Confidence to change practices • Ideas for presentations • Contacts for future follow-up • Insights into latest technology	5-point scale	Participants	Questionnaires	End of Conference	External Evaluator
3	**APPLICATION/IMPLEMENTATION** • Use of knowledge • Application of skills • Use of resources • Use of contacts • Completion of action plans • Barriers/Enablers	5-point scale	Participants	Questionnaires	3 Months After Conference	External Evaluator
4	**BUSINESS IMPACT** • Productivity • Efficiency • Time savings • Cost savings • Quality • Client satisfaction	Varies—Open-ended questions	Participants	Questionaires	3 Months After Conference	External Evaluator
5	**ROI** 20%	**Baseline Data:**				
		Comments:				

Approval

_____   _____
NSPD CEO   NSPD Conference Director
Exhibit I

_____
NSPD Education Director

Exhibit 2

Data Collection Plan (Draft)

Evaluation Purpose: ROI Exhibitor

Program: NSPD ACE Evaluation

Responsibility: Jack Phillips   **Date:** _____

Level	Broad Program Objective(s)	Measures	Data Sources	Data Collection Method/Instruments	Timing	Responsibilities
1	**REACTION/SATISFACTION** • Responsiveness of attendees • Value of meeting • Quality of attendees • Helpfulness of NSPD staff • Intent to follow up with prospects • Booth activity • Recommendations to others	5-point scale	50 Randomly Selected Exhibitors	Questionnaires	End of Conference	External Evaluator
2	**LEARNING** • Knowledge about the conference • Knowledge about the exhibiting process • Information about resolving issues • Information on resources • Ideas for future exhibits • Contacts for future follow-up • Insights into competition	5-point scale	Exhibitors	Questionnaires	End of Conference	External Evaluator
3	**APPLICATION/IMPLEMENTATION** • Follow through from NSPD • Improvements in the exhibiting process • Use of contacts • Requests for information • Completion of follow-up • Barriers/Enablers	5-point-scale	Exhibitors	Questionnaires	3 Months After Conference	External Evaluator
4	**BUSINESS IMPACT** • Closed sales • New accounts • Revenue • Quality brand awareness • Client satisfaction	Varies—Open-ended questions	Exhibitors	Questionnaires	3 Months After Conference	External Evaluator

5	ROI		**Baseline Data:**			
	20%		**Comments:**			

Approval

_____   _____   _____
NSPD CEO   NSPD Conference Director   NSPD Education Director

Exhibit 2

235

Exhibit 3

ROI Analysis Plan

Evaluation Purpose: <u>Participant ROI</u> Program: <u>NSPD ACE Evaluation</u> Responsibility: <u>Jack Phillips</u> Date: _____

Data Items (Usually Level 4)	Methods for Isolating the Effects of the Program	Methods of Converting Data to Money	Cost Categories	Intangible Benefits	Communication Targets for Final Report	Other Influences/Issues During Application	Comments
• Productivity/efficiency • Direct cost reduction • Time savings • Quality • Client satisfaction	• Estimates from participants (method is the same for all data items)	• Standard values • Expert input • Participant estimates (method is the same for all data items)	• Design and development • Travel costs • Participant time • Admin. support • Admin. overhead • Telecom expenses • Meeting expenses • Incentives • Facilities • Evaluation	• Increased commitment • Reduced stress • Increased job satisfaction • Improved customer service • Enhanced NSPD image • Improved teamwork • Improved communication • Enhanced professionalism	• NSPD leadership • NSPD staff • Participants • Prospective participants • Participant's manager	A variety of other initiatives may influence the impact measures such as Six Sigma process, service excellence, and efforts to become a great place to work.	It is extremely important to secure commitment from participants to provide accurate data in a timely manner.

Exhibit 4

ROI Analysis Plan

Evaluation Purpose: Exhibitor ROI   Program: NSPD ACE Evaluation   Responsibility: Jack Phillips   Date: _____

Data Items (Usually Level 4)	Methods for Isolating the Effects of the Program	Methods of Converting Data to Money	Cost Categories	Intangible Benefits	Communication Targets for Final Report	Other Influences/ Issues During Application	Comments
• Closed sales • New accounts • Revenue • Brand awareness • Client satisfaction	• Estimates from exhibitors (method is the same for all data items)	• Standard values • Expert input • Exhibitor estimates (method is the same for all data items)	• Fees • Travel costs • Time • Admin. support • Admin. overhead • Telecom expenses • Meeting expenses • Incentives • Facilities • Evaluation	• Increased commitment • Reduced stress • Increased job satisfaction • Improved customer service • Enhanced NSPD image • Improved teamwork • Improved communication	• NSPD leadership • NSPD staff • Exhibitors • Prospective exhibitors • Exhibitor's manager	A variety of other initiatives still influence the impact measures, including advertising, promotion, and environment.	It is extremely important to secure commitment from exhibitors to provide accurate data in a timely manner.

intangible measures that will probably not be converted to monetary value, based on their subjective nature. It also involves listing the costs for the meeting that would be captured during the project. Finally, the individual stakeholders who should receive the data will be listed. This is important to understand which groups will be receiving information as it may affect the data collection.

Project Schedule

With proposal delivery scheduled for February 2007, it is anticipated that the final communication will be completed in October 2006. Exhibit 5 shows a complete project plan, outlining the key steps in the project and the months in which they will occur. This project plan may be adjusted as needed by either party if additional time is needed for collection and analysis.

Project Team

This project will be conducted by a team of professionals, with Drs. Jack and Patti Phillips serving as co-leaders. Monica Myhill, senior consultant, will provide additional project leadership and coordination. Crystal Bedwell will be the project analyst for the study. Biographies of all these individuals are attached.

Responsibilities

The responsibilities are as follows:

1. The ROI Institute will be responsible for all the items listed in the cost breakout of the proposal. This includes planning the study, designing appropriate tools and instruments, assisting with data collection, providing analysis, writing reports, and communicating data.
2. NSPD will provide coordination for the meetings, assist in data collection, and provide logistical arrangements necessary to execute the project.
3. The contact person for the ROI Institute will be Crystal Langford; for NSPD it will be _____ _____.

Deliverables

There are several deliverables connected with this project:

1. An impact study for both of the ROI impact studies. At NSPD's request, we can keep the two studies separate or present them as one.
2. Briefings of the studies. At least two face-to-face briefings are conducted, one with NSPD staff leadership and the other with the NSPD board.
3. A 6- to 10-page executive summary for each study, which provides the overviews.
4. A one-page quick facts sheet about the study that could be used as the basis for communicating to other staff members, selected NSPD members, and other stakeholder groups.

Exhibit 5

Evaluation Project Plan

	F	M	A	M	J	J	A	S	O	N	D	J	F
Decision to conduct ROI study	▪												
Evaluation planning complete		▪											
Instruments designs		▪											
Instruments are pilot tested			▪										
Participants selected			▪										
Data collected at conference				▪									
Data collected in follow-up							▪						
Data tabulation preliminary summary							▪						
Analysis conducted								▪					
Report is written								▪					
Reported printed									▪				
Results communicated									▪				
Improvements initiated										▪			
Improvements complete											▪		

Costs

The projected costs of the study are listed as Exhibit 6. As indicated, costs are for conducting one or both studies, listed as stakeholder Option One and Option Two. This provides NSPD the flexibility of conducting only one of the studies or both of them.

Exhibit 6

Stages of Study	Option One ROI Impact Study for One Stakeholder Group	Option Two ROI Impact Study for Two Stakeholder Groups
Evaluation Planning • One-day planning meeting to be held at NSPD's offices in Washington, D.C. • Finalize ROI study objective. • Determine a data collection plan that will cover measures, data collection methods, source of data, and timing of data collection for each stakeholder group. • Develop an ROI analysis plan that will cover methods to isolate the impact of the program and convert data to monetary value for each stakeholder group. It will also list cost categories needed for the ROI calculation, anticipated intangible benefits, and possible influences or issues during application. • Develop an ROI project timeline that will outline key milestones as well as responsibilities. • Create promotional and invitation text regarding this ROI impact study for the purpose of securing sample group participants. • Recommend a communication plan for sharing results with key stakeholders.	$ 10,000	$ 12,000
Instrument Design and Testing • Design, pilot test, and finalize data collection.	$ 12,000	$ 15,000
Project Administration • Selection of stakeholder sample group participants according to demographic criteria. • Develop text and documents to be used for sample group invitations and on-site conference session for sample group participants. • Collect sample group acceptance and denial information. • Respond to sample group questions about ROI impact study and questionnaires. • Assist in securing sample group participants (as necessary). • Planning and on-site delivery of conference session for sample group participants.	$ 15,000	$ 20,000

Exhibit 6 *(Continued)*

Stages of Study	Option One ROI Impact Study for One Stakeholder Group	Option Two ROI Impact Study for Two Stakeholder Groups
Data Tabulation • Tabulation of data from questionnaires.	$ 10,000	$ 15,000
Data Analysis and Interpretation • Analyze reaction data. • Analyze learning data. • Analyze application data to determine extent to which knowledge, skills, professional contacts, and/or business leads were utilized and applied on the job. • Analyze data to determine extent to which business measures were impacted due to utilization of knowledge, skills, professional contacts, and/or business leads. • Determine ROI from stakeholder perspective(s).	$ 10,000	$ 15,000
Report Writing • Draft and finalize the ROI impact study report that will include background on study, ROI methodology, data collection plan, ROI analysis plan, data collection instruments, actual data, data interpretation, data trends, costs, ROI calculations, and recommendations.	$ 15,000	$ 20,000
Communicating the Results • Present findings to NSPD board of directors and staff leadership through face-to-face meeting(s) and conference call(s) as necessary	$ 10,000	$ 12,000
Total Direct Costs	$ 82,000	$ 109,000

Additional Charges: NSPD will reimburse ROI Institute for travel, shipping, printing, and/or telephone/fax line (usage beyond routine calls) expenses directly related to this project.

Unique Advantages

This study offered the by ROI Institute represents a unique advantage. This methodology has been adopted by the Meeting Professionals International (MPI) as the recommended approach to measure the financial impact on meetings for associations and organizations.

As the founder of the ROI Institute and the developer of this methodology, Dr. Jack Phillips will personally be involved in every phase of this project. Dr. Patti Phillips has written about this methodology in six books and regularly consults with organizations on the methodology. Monica Myhill has tremendous experience in the meetings and events industry. Together, the quality of the team and the proven methodology makes this a unique advantage for measuring the success of this important NSPD meeting.

Satisfaction Guarantee

The ROI Institute guarantees complete satisfaction with the study. If NSPD is not satisfied with the progress of the study, the methodology used, the professionalism provided by the team, the quality of the report, and the reporting of data, NSPD will be relieved of any financial obligation. If problems or concerns develop, NSPD should contact the institute for early resolution throughout the study. However, at the end of the study, if the client is not satisfied, there is no charge.

Biographies

Jack J. Phillips, Ph.D.

As a world-renowned expert on accountability, Dr. Phillips provides consulting services for Fortune 500 companies and conducts workshops for major conference providers throughout the world. Phillips is also the author or editor of more than 40 books—12 about measurement and evaluation—and more than 150 articles.

His expertise in measurement and evaluation is based on almost 30 years of corporate experience in five industries (aerospace, textiles, metals, construction materials, and banking). Phillips has served as training and development manager at two Fortune 500 firms, senior HR officer for two firms, president of a regional federal savings bank, and management professor at a major state university.

His background led Phillips to develop the ROI Methodology—a revolutionary process that provides bottom-line figures and accountability for all types of training, performance improvement, human resources meetings and events, and technology programs. Phillips has received numerous awards for his books and work.

Phillips regularly consults with clients in manufacturing, service, and government organizations in 38 countries in North and South America, Europe, Africa, Australia, and Asia.

Phillips has undergraduate degrees in electrical engineering, physics, and mathematics, a master's degree in decision sciences from Georgia State University, and a Ph.D. in human resource management from the University of Alabama. He can be reached at jack@roiinstitute.net.

Patti P. Phillips, Ph.D.

Dr. Patti Phillips is president and CEO of the ROI Institute, Inc., the leading source of ROI evaluation education, research, and networking. She is an internationally recognized author and consultant, supporting organizations and their efforts to build accountability into their training, human resources, and performance improvement programs.

Since 1997, she has embraced the ROI methodology by committing herself to ongoing research and practice. To that end, Patti has implemented ROI in private sector and public sector organizations. She has conducted ROI impact studies on programs such as leadership development, sales, new hire orientation, and human performance improvement programs, as well as K-12 educator development, educator National Board Certification mentoring program, and faculty fellowship programs.

Patti's academic accomplishments include a Ph.D. in International Development and a Master of Arts degree in Public and Private Management. She is certified in ROI evaluation and has been awarded the designation of Certified Performance Technologist. She can be reached a patti@roiinstitute.net.

Monica Myhill, CMP

Monica currently serves as president of Meeting Returns, an organization specializing in ROI impact and evaluation studies for the meetings industry through the use of the ROI methodology developed by Jack Phillips. Meeting Returns is a partner to Jack J. Phillips, Ph.D.; Patti P. Phillips, Ph.D.; and the ROI Institute, Inc. (www.roiinstitute.net) to provide ROI impact studies for meetings, incentives, conferences, and events.

Monica has over 12 years experience in developing, marketing, managing, and evaluating education programs, conferences, and special events in North America and Europe. She formerly served as Director of Professional Development for Meeting Professionals International (MPI), an international professional association for the meetings industry. During her tenure at MPI, she directed the overall planning, design, implementation, and evaluation of MPI's professional development offerings and created customized educational experiences through MPI's Certification in Meeting Management (CMM) designation, Professional Education Conference—Europe, Professional Education Conference—North America, World Education Congress, Chapter Leadership Conference, and Platinum Series programs.

Monica holds a Master of Arts degree in teaching from George Washington University, Washington, D.C.; and a Bachelor of Arts degree in museum studies from Baylor University, Waco, Texas.

Crystal Langford, Communications Manager

Crystal obtained her Bachelor of Arts degree in Communications Studies from Huntingdon College, Montgomery, Alabama in three years. She has won several awards for her academic work and leadership in volunteer organizations.She joined the ROI Institute in November 2005, specializing in marketing and communications. In addition, Crystal is involved in data collection, database management, data analysis, and data presentation. Before joining the ROI Institute, Crystal was involved in marketing in a large multimedia organization.

INDEX

Staffing and support:
  business management, 23, 27
  consulting practice launch, 24, 27, 84
  consulting ROI shortcuts, 191
  financial responsibility, 67–69, 81–82
  guarantee of satisfaction, 190
  independent contractors, use of, 64–65
  legal advice, 37
  as operating expense, 52, 54
  organizations vs. consulting practice, 24
  work life shift, 7, 24–25
Stakeholders:
  business plan, 36–37
  consultant attention to, 11
  consulting RI guiding principles, 182
  guarantee of satisfaction, 190
  project objectives, 150–151
  proposals, 130–133
  as results communication audience, 201, 203–205
Standards, consulting, 10
State government consulting, 140–141, 142
Strategy development as success factor, 24–26
Structure of firm, legal, 26, 27, 76–78, 81–82
Subchapter C or S Corporation, 77, 81
Subscriptions and dues, 52, 54
Success:
  business plan, 25–26
  documented results, 17
  guarantee of satisfaction, 188–190
  myth of, 10
  proposals, 28–29
  reasons for measurement, 167–169
  report development, 206
  stories of, 108, 109
  success factors, 30
  (*See also* Consulting ROI)
Supply chain partners, 113, 114

T
Tag lines, 100
Tangibles, 177, 178–180
Target audience (*see* Audience)
Target market, 28, 40–41, 94, 99

Tax issues, 52, 55, 64, 77
Team participation, 215, 238
Technology support, partnerships, 113–114
Telemarketing, 95
Telephone, 52, 81, 95, 96
Terms and conditions, proposal, 137–138
Thinking styles, proposal philosophy, 128–129
Three rules business plan test, 47
Time issues, 148–149, 184, 188, 189, 192
Tool development, 100–102
Top ten attacks on consulting, 5–6
Topics vs. logic, proposal philosophy, 128
Tracking, consulting ROI, 167–169
Trade publications, 99–100
Trade shows, 117
Training, organizations vs. consulting practice, 25
Transfer of knowledge and capability, delivery, 212
Transition management, 20, 82
Travel and entertainment, 52, 55
Trends related to consulting, 2, 11–12, xiii
Trust, 74, 214–216

U
Unresponsive client and proposals, 144
Utilities, 52, 55

V
Vagueness of proposals, 143
Value added, 10, 15–17, 213
Values statement, business plan, 24, 28, 40
Variable pay, 63
Video clips, 110
Vision in business plan, 24, 38, 39–40

W
Web sites, 71–74, 97, 208
Work-life shift, 7, 24–25
Workplace needs, 158–159, 164
Workshops, 101, 102–104, 113, 114
Worst-case scenarios business plan test, 47
Writing, for client development, 104–106
  (*See also* Proposals)

ABOUT THE AUTHOR

As a world-renowned expert on measurement and evaluation, Dr. Jack J. Phillips is chairman of the ROI Institute. Through the Institute, Phillips provides consulting services for Fortune 500 companies and workshops for major conference providers throughout the world. Phillips is also the author or editor of more than 30 books and more than 100 articles.

His expertise in measurement and evaluation is based on more than twenty-seven years of corporate experience in five industries (aerospace, textiles, metals, construction materials, and banking). Phillips has served as training and development manager at two Fortune 500 firms, senior HR officer at two firms, president of a regional federal savings bank, and management professor at a major state university.

His background in learning and HR led Phillips to develop the ROI Process—a revolutionary process that provides bottom-line figures and accountability for all types of learning, performance improvement, human resources, and technology programs.

Phillips has undergraduate degrees in electrical engineering, physics, and mathematics, a master's degree in decision sciences from Georgia State University, and a Ph.D. in human resource management from the University of Alabama. Jack can be reached at jack@roiinstitute.net.